Historical Justice and Memory

Critical Human Rights

Series Editors
Steve J. Stern & Scott Straus

Books in the series **Critical Human Rights** emphasize research that opens new ways to think about and understand human rights. The series values in particular empirically grounded and intellectually open research that eschews simplified accounts of human rights events and processes.

Demands for truth and justice, familiar in the contemporary age of human rights law and activism, often arise in response to recent atrocities and the ongoing suffering of victim-survivors and their relatives. What happens, however, when advocates for justice and repair invoke memory of injustices that took place longer ago and have become normalized as part of the enduring structure of society? Do human rights demands and attendant legal norms lose force as the direct survivor-victim community gives way to a descendant community? This book boldly explores the rise of a historical justice and memory movement—both its positive aspect as a moral and social imperative that inspires significant truth and reconciliation initiatives, and its troubling aspect as experiences that call into question the contemporary politics of human rights and historical victimization.

Historical Justice and Memory

Edited by
**Klaus Neumann and
Janna Thompson**

The University of Wisconsin Press

The University of Wisconsin Press
1930 Monroe Street, 3rd Floor
Madison, Wisconsin 53711-2059
uwpress.wisc.edu

3 Henrietta Street, Covent Garden
London WC2E 8LU, United Kingdom
eurospanbookstore.com

Printed in the United States of America

Library of Congress Cataloging-in-Publication Data

Historical justice and memory / edited by Klaus Neumann and Janna Thompson.
        pages   cm — (Critical human rights)
        Includes bibliographical references and index.
        ISBN 978-0-299-30464-5 (pbk.: alk. paper)
        ISBN 978-0-299-30463-8 (e-book)
1. Transitional justice.   2. Truth commissions.   3. Reparations for historical injustices.
    4. Collective memory.   I. Neumann, Klaus, 1958–, editor.   II. Thompson, Janna, 1942–,
    editor.   III. Series: Critical human rights.
JC578.H567   2015
320.01'1—dc23
2014038395

published with a grant by
Figure Foundation
to translate the anagram of time

Contents

Acknowledgments

The origins of this collection can be traced back to the establishment of the Historical Justice and Memory Research Network in late 2010 by researchers at the Swinburne Institute for Social Research at Swinburne University of Technology in Melbourne, and the associated Historical Justice and Memory conference held at that university in early 2012. Two of the chapters in this collection (by Barkan and Bakiner) are substantially revised versions of papers first presented at the 2012 conference, while the others were either commissioned by us (Blustein, Torpey, Thompson, Violi, Barkan and Bećirbašić, Pendleton) or are extensions or major revisions of previously published essays (Huyssen, Walker, Butt).

Over the past few years, the dialogue between memory studies, transitional justice studies, peace and conflict studies, and political and moral philosophy has continued to attract the interest of many scholars in the humanities and social sciences; the network has since morphed into the Dialogues on Historical Justice and Memory, hosted by the Institute for the Study of Human Rights at Columbia University, and the Melbourne conference has been followed by three further international conferences on historical justice and memory.

We are grateful to the Australian Research Council (Discovery Grants DP0771714 and DP0877630), Swinburne University of Technology, and La Trobe University for funding our research, the establishment of the research network, and the 2012 conference. We would also like to thank the University of Wisconsin Press for embracing this project and for providing guidance and support throughout the editorial process; our particular thanks go to the commissioning editor, Gwen Walker, and to the series editors, Steve J. Stern and Scott Straus. Finally, we thank the two anonymous reviewers engaged by the press for their constructive comments and suggestions.

Historical Justice and Memory

Introduction

Beyond the Legalist Paradigm

KLAUS NEUMANN and
JANNA THOMPSON

In May 2013 the media reported that Jorge Rafaél Videla had died in an Argentine prison at the age of eighty-seven. Videla led the military junta that engineered the coup d'état against the government of Isabel Perón and until his retirement in 1981 served as the president of a regime responsible for the murder, torture, and disappearance of thousands of people. The dictatorship collapsed following the Falklands War, and Videla was sentenced by an Argentinean court to life imprisonment. In 1990 he and other members of the junta were pardoned by the then president, Carlos Menem. In 2007 a court declared this pardon invalid. Videla was tried again, this time for the murder of thirty-one prisoners, and was sentenced to fifty years in jail.

Also in May 2013, the German government agreed to pay a total of €772 million over four years for the home care of approximately fifty-six thousand Holocaust survivors. In the words of the chief negotiator of the Jewish Claims Conference (JCC), this payment is "to help them live in dignity, after their early life was filled with indescribable tragedy and trauma" (quoted in Jewish Claims Conference 2013). The settlement with the JCC was, at that time, the latest in a long line of accords committing the government to make payments to the victims of Nazi Germany.[1] These recent agreements between the government and the JCC are the result of a commitment Germany made in 1990 when negotiating German reunification.

On 6 June 2013, the British foreign secretary William Hague told the House of Commons that his government recognized "that Kenyans were subject to torture and other forms of ill treatment at the hands of the [British] colonial government" during the eleven-year emergency triggered by the Mau Mau rebellion of the 1950s and that his government "sincerely regret[ted] that these abuses took place" (House of Commons 2013, 1692). Hague informed the House that Britain had agreed to make an out-of-court payment totaling £19.9 million to 5,228 survivors and to contribute funding for a memorial to be built in Nairobi to the victims of abuse during the colonial era.[2] He cautioned, however, that "we continue to deny liability on behalf of the Government and British taxpayers today for the actions of the colonial administration" and that the government did not "believe that this settlement establishes a precedent in relation to any other former British colonial administration" (House of Commons 2013, 1693).

These are just three examples, reported during the course of preparing this introduction in May and June 2013, of ways that governments in recent times have dealt with historical wrongs. There have been many more cases in recent months of a government making an official apology for a past injustice, an international court or national tribunal laying charges on account of gross human rights violations, a state offering to compensate victims of abuse, and a victims' organization successfully demanding that past suffering be commemorated.

Though each of our examples is about redress for a historical wrong, neither the injustices themselves nor the forms of redress have much in common. In the first a perpetrator was tried and punished for murders he authorized. In the second, a government representing the descendants of perpetrators and bystanders, which has repeatedly acknowledged its obligations, provided payments to surviving victims—not as a compensation for past injustices but as a means of improving the quality of their lives now. In the third case, a government agreed to modest financial and symbolic reparations for a wrong done under a colonial administration.

However, these cases have significant common features. In all of them the wrong was addressed decades after it had been perpetrated. The trial that would see Videla spend the final years of his life in prison took place twenty-seven years after the end of the dictatorship. The payment of €772 million to the JCC was negotiated sixty-eight years after the defeat of Nazi Germany. The British government offered to pay compensation to Kenyan victims fifty years after Kenya gained independence and more than fifty-five years after the end of the British military campaign against the Mau Mau rebels.

The jailing of Videla, the additional payments to Holocaust victims, and the British government's recognition of the atrocities committed in Kenya were not outcomes that could have been anticipated in the immediate aftermath of the injustices concerned. The pardoning of Videla and other members of the junta in 1990 seemed to preclude any further attempts to hold the principal perpetrators accountable for the human rights abuses between 1976 and 1983. The British government had repeatedly rejected calls from Mau Mau veterans for an apology; despite demands for compensation since at least 1999, no British court had found reason to hold the British government guilty of abuse to Kenyans or liable to compensation.[3] The West German government had once anticipated that all claims by Holocaust victims would be submitted by 1969, while the German Democratic Republic accepted claims only from its own citizens.

It was once assumed that historical wrongs could be addressed and then forgotten. Few would make this assumption now. In Argentina, efforts to prosecute military and police officers who perpetrated crimes during the dictatorship are ongoing, as are attempts to commemorate the suffering of victims. Neither non-Jewish Germans nor the descendants of Nazi Germany's victims can suppose that the passing of the last survivor will draw a line under efforts to come to terms with the Holocaust. Although Hague was anxious not to set a precedent, a few days after his announcement Kenyan television news reported that an additional eight thousand victims were seeking compensation (Capital News 2013). As one Nairobi-based journalist put it, the British government's compensation package "was likely to open a can of worms as more lawyers who had lined up victims, outside the officially compiled list, were bound to descend from the woods to claim part of the windfall" (Ngugi 2013). Eventually, Kenyans may demand a formal apology rather than an expression of regret. Not only is it now regularly assumed that any attempts to redress past wrongs—be they material or symbolic reparations, memorializations, or prosecutions—will be followed by claims for further redress; it is also often taken for granted that what Germans call *Vergangenheitsbewältigung*—the "mastering" of the past—is simply not possible.

Another notable fact about all three cases is that redressing the past is now regarded as a responsibility of the state—even when the injustice occurred in the distant past under a different regime. The acts of retributive or reparative justice that the cases involved were largely uncontroversial. Critics were more likely to point out that justice ought to have been served earlier rather than that it should not be provided at all. Following Hague's statement to the House of Commons, a Conservative member of Parliament demanded that another memorial be erected to the victims of the Mau Mau insurgents, but even he did not challenge the government's decision to recognize the suffering of Kenyans at the hands of the British colonizers (House of Commons 2013, 1696). In Germany the only sustained critical comments regarding the government's payments to the JCC tend to come from organizations purporting to speak for non-Jewish victims who claim that the people they represent have been neglected. Obituaries and other media reports of Vidal's death in prison did not question the propriety of his jail sentence.

There is no doubt that political motivations in these and other cases played a role in creating a willingness to make redress. In 1990, German leaders, recognizing the misgivings of European neighbors and the United States about the possible re-creation of a Greater Germany, were prompted to make concessions. In offering a settlement to Kenyan claimants, the British government was mindful of the strategic role that Kenya played in East Africa. "We do not want our current and future relations with Kenya to be overshadowed by the past," Hague told Parliament (House of Commons 2013, 1693). But political self-interest does not by itself explain why the German and British governments so willingly agreed to make redress for injustices that had been perpetrated more than half a century earlier. These governments were responding to a demand for justice that has become increasingly difficult to resist.

In the past twenty-five years, citizens and leaders all over the world have been forced to come to terms with the gross injustices of their nations' past. Historical acts of genocide, slavery, apartheid, systematic persecution of presumed enemies of the state, colonialism, and the oppression of or discrimination against ethnic or religious minorities have all become the focus of demands for apology or reparation by victims or their families. And the list of historical wrongs that governments are now expected to address is ever expanding. To deal with the misdeeds of past regimes, governments have embarked on truth and reconciliation projects. An international court now tries those held responsible for crimes against humanity. In response to demands for remembrance and restitution, governments have apologized for past injustices, offered compensation, promised to abide by the terms of long-ago treaties, erected memorials, revised history books, and redesigned educational programs.

In movements for historical justice, memory plays a key role. Even in cases where injustices have vanished from public memory or where governments have long discouraged reference to the past, memories of injustice often continue to fester among victims and their families and then resurface in the public realm. Sometimes such memories are given a boost through films or books. Outside Kenya, the suffering of Kenyans in detention camps run by the British colonial authorities had been largely forgotten until the publication of Caroline Elkins's *Imperial Reckoning* and David Anderson's *Histories of the Hanged*, both in 2005. The call of Kenyan government ministers for an apology from the British government was prompted by the publication of Elkins's book (BBC News 2005; Human Rights House 2005). In many instances, redress includes attempts to keep alive the memories that prompted or fueled campaigns for historical justice. The British government agreed to fund a memorial to the victims of colonial rule in Kenya, which is supposed to be a public acknowledgment that the injustice occurred and will not be forgotten.

A Brief History

Though the movement for historical justice has gathered momentum in recent decades, it has a much longer history. The trial before the International Military Tribunal in Nuremberg is often considered the foundational event of historical justice. For the first time, perpetrators of human rights violations were tried by an international court and successfully charged with "crimes against humanity." The tribunal brought to the attention of the world the Nazi genocide against Jews and other peoples and thus played a key role in motivating a widespread recognition of human rights. But Nuremberg was only the most visible instance of postwar historical justice. In 1946 the International Military Tribunal for the Far East tried the wartime leaders of Japan for war crimes. Other attempts were made to address Japanese war crimes (such as the Nanjing War Crimes Trial that was set up by the Nationalist Chinese government). In the second half of the 1940s numerous criminal proceedings for war crimes and other atrocities were conducted by domestic courts: from the Philippines to Poland and from Australian Papua and New Guinea to France. Survivors of the injustices investigated in these trials sometimes received compensation.

The memorialization of victims of war crimes and crimes against humanity also had its origin in the second half of the 1940s. While it had become common to remember the war dead, the public remembrance of the victims of injustice was new. Groups of survivors, the Allies, and local governments in all four zones of occupied Germany erected memorials and organized commemorations to publicly remember the victims of Nazi Germany. These commemorative activities were not isolated events; they were on a scale that—in Germany at least—was reached again only at the beginning of the "memory boom" some forty years later.

After the trials and memorialization of victims in the second half of the 1940s, the movement for historical justice stalled. The Federal Republic of Germany agreed to pay reparations for Nazi crimes, but only with respect to Jewish victims. In Europe, the memorialization of injustices committed by Nazi Germany was highly selective. In Japan, there was no public memorialization of the suffering inflicted on Koreans or Chinese. Amnesties were given to many of those convicted in war crime trials. In West Germany and Austria, attempts at lustration—so-called denazification—failed, and members of the Nazi elites were soon able to resume their careers in the judiciary, in the civil service, and in government. By the end of the 1950s it appeared that the movement for historical justice had been little more than the selective prosecution of collaborators in countries occupied by the Axis powers and a series of short-lived attempts by the Allies to hold Japan and Germany accountable for war crimes.

Although some Nazi perpetrators of crimes were put on trial—most notably Adolf Eichmann in Israel in 1961—there was no sizable movement for historical justice between the end of the 1940s and the mid-1970s, when members of the junta that had overthrown the Greek democratic government were prosecuted in Greece. In 1976, members of the Portuguese political police were tried in Portugal, two years after that country's return to democracy. The first truth commission was set up in Uganda in 1974—by one of the twentieth century's most notorious violators of human rights, Idi Amin. The Waitangi Tribunal was set up in 1975 in New Zealand to investigate and make recommendations with regard to violations of the Treaty of Waitangi between the Maori people and the Crown, and a highly symbolic and unreserved official apology was made by the West German chancellor Willy Brandt in 1970 in Warsaw.[4] But these events of the 1970s were still relatively unconnected, and it wasn't until the 1980s that the movement for historical justice spread rapidly throughout the world (Sikkink 2011).

From the 1980s, trials to prosecute human rights violations, apologies, truth commissions, reparations, and other transitional justice instruments proliferated in response to growing demands for historical justice. These developments were backed by organizations such as Amnesty International and Helsinki Watch (which later became Human Rights Watch) and by the International Criminal Court, set up in 2002. By 2013 there were few countries that had not experienced some attempts at historical justice. The recently published *Encyclopedia of Transitional Justice* (Stan and Nedelsky 2013) has entries on eighty-two countries.

In the late 1940s, the emphasis had been on retributive justice against perpetrators through courts and tribunals. The twelve death sentences imposed by the judges in the first Nuremberg trial were emblematic of the first phase of historical justice. By the 1990s the focus had shifted to mending the social fabric and to addressing the needs of victims through truth telling and material and symbolic reparations. The work of the South African Truth and Reconciliation Commission set the trend for the next phase. The South African Commission gave victims a chance to tell their own stories. It encouraged

Klaus Neumann and Janna Thompson

perpetrators to confess their crimes and offered victims a small amount of compensation for their suffering. Reparation of some kind has since become a standard way of coming to terms with historical injustices. In 2005 the United Nations General Assembly adopted the Basic Principles and Guidelines on the Right to a Remedy and Reparation for Victims of Gross Violations of International Human Rights Law and Serious Violations of International Humanitarian Law, according to which victims have the right to reparation and information about human rights violations (United Nations 2006b).

The South African Commission was also an example of another important trend: the attempt to combine truth telling and reparation to victims with reconciliation between victims and their families and perpetrators and their supporters. Reconciliation is supposed to be a means of overcoming the past sufficiently that both victims and perpetrators can work together in rebuilding the nation. While reparative and retributive justice can work hand in hand, restorative justice constrains the option of retribution. The South African Commission offered amnesty to perpetrators who cooperated.

Reparative justice has relied primarily on symbolic measures, such as apologies or commemorations, rather than on the payment of material compensation to victims. When reparations are paid, they are often token, more a symbol than full compensation for harms done. Apologies have become a particularly common device used by governments, churches, and other groups to acknowledge and take responsibility for past wrongdoing—including injustices of the more distant past. Memorials, museums, and annual commemorative events are also significant means of acknowledging and redressing past wrongs. Public memorialization not only teaches citizens about injustices of their history; it is also supposed to help survivors and the relatives of victims to live with their trauma by honoring those who suffered injustices and to prevent the recurrence of similar injustices.

The desire to right past wrongs has amplified the desire to remember such wrongs and vice versa. As a result there has been a proliferation of demands for historical justice and a broadening of the definition of what constitutes a historical wrong warranting redress. In the late 1940s, the striving for historical justice meant seeking redress for injustices that had occurred over the preceding decade. Today, there are increasingly calls for historical justice in relation to wrongs that did not take place within living memory, such as the Armenian genocide, transatlantic slavery, and the displacement and murder of native peoples.

Political scientists, historians, sociologists, legal scholars, anthropologists, human geographers, psychologists, and others have offered incisive analyses of processes of transitional justice, the dynamics of social and public memory, and the complexities of redress. Moral and political philosophers have put forward convincing arguments about why past wrongs ought to be redressed and remembered. The growing urge to redress historical wrongs and the "memory boom" spawned two vibrant fields of academic inquiry: transitional justice studies and memory studies. Lawyers and international relations scholars have prominently contributed to the former. The disciplines of history, anthropology, and sociology are primarily responsible for the existence of memory studies.

While the academic literature about issues of historical justice has grown exponentially, particularly in the past ten years, most of it has tended to remain compartmentalized: historians, for example, have largely focused on issues of social and public memory, while philosophers have been largely interested in explorations of ideas of justice and lawyers have focused on instruments of transitional justice. Only in the past ten years have *concerted* attempts been made to cross disciplinary boundaries and hold conversations between transitional justice experts and memory studies scholars, philosophers, and psychologists with a background in peace and conflict studies. Our book aims to make an important contribution to these interdisciplinary conversations.

Key Issues

To identify an action as an injustice is to mark it as something that demands an appropriate response. Ideas about what this response should be come from legal theory and practice and from common moral assumptions about what justice requires. The perpetrators ought to be put on trial and punished. They ought to be sorry for what they did. The victims ought to receive reparation for the harms they have suffered. They ought to be returned to the state they were in before the injustice was done—so far as this is possible. These assumptions about how a society should deal with injustice can be described as the "legalist paradigm." Memory plays a crucial role in this paradigm because legal processes depend on the memories of victims and other witnesses and because remembering the mistakes of the past is supposed to be an important factor in preventing future injustice.

Historical injustices are a challenge to the legalist paradigm. When injustices occurred in the more distant past, most or all of the perpetrators and victims are likely to be dead and are thus beyond retribution or reparation. Nevertheless, memories of the injustice linger, and harmful effects are often visited on descendants of the victims. What justice then requires, if anything at all, is a difficult and contentious issue. The problem of applying the legalist paradigm is often compounded by the fact that the most serious historical wrongs were not merely or primarily the acts of a few individuals. They were made possible by the laws and practices of a society; they were endorsed by the attitudes and prejudices of many citizens. These prejudices often passed for common sense at the time when the injustices were committed. Historical injustices raise questions about responsibility, harm, and duties in respect to the past. But they also require changes to the legalist conception of justice and a reevaluation of the role of memory.

The chapters in this collection provide an overview of how movements for historical justice have altered the way in which justice and the role of memory are perceived and how these changes have interacted with other social aims and values. They raise and discuss the problems associated with the rise of historical justice, the valorization of historical memory, and the social and political changes that are associated with these developments. Implicit in these discussions is a concern about the future development and fate of the movement for historical justice and the present emphasis on remembrance and memorialization.

The rise of historical justice has its critics, but there is now widespread agreement that historical injustices need to be redressed and remembered. Though some leaders and governments have resisted demands for apology and reparation or put barriers in the way of trying or punishing perpetrators, most have eventually capitulated to the demands of victims and their supporters. The movement for historical justice seems irresistible. But it is by no means self-evident that there will be yet more prosecutions, truth commissions, compensation packages, and memorial museums. Attempts to do justice to victims and to punish perpetrators have to contend with political and economic realities. Reawakening memories of past injustice does not always promote peace and reconciliation. Conflicting narratives about the past can exacerbate social divisions. Changes in political constellations or priorities or a public backlash could bring about the decline of historical justice as a force in social affairs. This volume is motivated by the belief that it is time to assess the movements for historical justice and memory and to consider their prospects for the future. It contributes to this project by its interdisciplinary approach to the issues raised by historical justice and memory, by its focus on the relation of the historical justice movement and memory discourses to other contemporary developments, and most of all by its emphasis on resolving conceptual difficulties that pose challenges to its future development.

The essays in the first part of this volume provide a critical overview of movements for historical justice, appeals to memory, and discourses about historical justice and memory. They attempt to identify the political and social factors that have made memory and historical justice into such predominant concerns. They inquire into the moral foundation of these discourses and their relation to each other. They relate them to moral and political developments of our times: the widespread acceptance of human rights as a moral touchstone, the rise of individualism and neoliberalism, and changes to the international order after the end of the Cold War.

The rise of historical justice has been accompanied by the rise of human rights as a moral and legal reference point. Crimes against humanity for which Nazi leaders were tried at Nuremberg are now conceived as serious human rights violations. Since Nuremberg, and especially in the past two decades, both human rights and historical justice have moved out of the shadow of Auschwitz and become a truly global concern. The setting up of the International Criminal Court to try those who commit gross violations of human rights is part of this development. But the cosmopolitan presumption of these developments is a sore point for those who value national or local autonomy and traditions. The very idea of human rights is criticized by those who see it as an imperialist imposition on peoples who have their own ideas of justice. Historical justice as a cosmopolitan affair can be seen as a threat to the autonomy of national legal processes and the traditions that lie behind them.

In his contribution, Andreas Huyssen argues that memory discourse is also implicated in the conflict between cosmopolitanism, as the idea that moral and legal standards are universal and apply everywhere in the world, and the "statist" assumption that ethical and legal standards have their home in national societies. Traditional conceptions of memory as a public phenomenon link it to national movements and to memorials and ceremonies that celebrate the history of a particular people or the lives and deaths of its notable members. The Holocaust by contrast is regarded as something that ought to be remembered not just by the Germans and the citizens of other countries involved in implementing the "final solution" but by the whole world. The very idea of crimes against humanity or human rights violations implies that they are everyone's concern and not merely the business of citizens of a particular state. But this universalization of memory can be seen as a threat to the particular meaning that a memory has for members of a nation or an oppressed group. Huyssen argues that there is a parallel between the problems for discourses about memory and human rights discourse. Both discourses have to avoid being co-opted by either cosmopolitanism or statism. Memory discourse cannot restrict its focus to the collective memories of members of nations, but neither should it abstract from the particularities of individuals and their situation.

Movements for historical justice are associated with the rise in the influence of human rights. They are also accompanied by a waning concern for social

Klaus Neumann and Janna Thompson

justice in liberal democratic societies. Social justice, as it is usually understood, requires citizens to ensure that everyone in their society has a fair share of social resources and equality of opportunity. Though liberal democracies continue to be welfare states, the ideal of equality that motivated the struggle for social justice has lost its appeal. Those who have been systematically disadvantaged by their social position are more likely to gain support by complaining about the historical injustices that have caused their suffering. In her chapter, Janna Thompson has two aims. One is to explain why this change has taken place. She argues that human rights and the individualism that they encourage play a role. But she also thinks that group identities and the desire of group members for proper recognition from those who have oppressed them have motivated struggles for historical justice. Thompson's second aim is to determine what the relationship ought to be between historical and social justice. She argues that neither can replace or subordinate the other but that there is no formula for determining how conflicts between claims for historical justice and the demands of social justice ought to be settled.

When philosophers and political and legal theorists discuss historical justice or memory, they emphasize the moral motivations behind demands for justice or memorialization. But, as an examination of particular cases makes plain, leaders and officials often have political reasons for acknowledging past wrongs. They and those who make justice claims are participating in a movement that political and social developments have made possible. The future of historical justice as a political force depends on the continued existence of favorable conditions. John Torpey thinks that the movement for historical justice, like the increasing popularity of human rights, is part of a broader tendency to transform political life into legal forms. He argues that this juridification of politics has to do with increasing individualism in contemporary societies, a greater sensitivity to the violence that can be inflicted on individuals, and the dominant position of the United States after World War II. He makes the provocative prediction that the decline of US power and the rise of China will mean the decline of the movement for historical justice.

Favorable conditions for historical justice movements also depend on the ability of oppressed people to successfully challenge the political status quo and the historical narratives that sustain and justify it. They depend not just on victims' ability to exercise political force but also on the willingness of other citizens to remember and acknowledge past wrongs. Jeffrey Blustein in his chapter aims to explain why individuals and collectives have moral obligations to remember. His contribution is a challenge to those who think of memory as having only a subordinate function in an account of historical justice. Memory is important in his view not merely because accurate testimony is needed to convict perpetrators or because memory of past wrongs might prevent injustice in the future. Remembering, he thinks, is itself a requirement of justice. Remembering wrongs is required by virtues that we ought to cultivate; it is a way of confirming the standing of victims and of expressing an attitude toward what was done.

Blustein's chapter moves away from a conception of historical justice and memory that subordinates it to legal concepts of retributive and reparative justice. The chapters in the second part of this volume show how these concepts have been challenged, revised, and sometimes replaced as the result of historical justice movements and the problems they have encountered in particular contexts or in respect to the needs or demands that they unleash.

Justice depends on finding the truth about wrongdoing: who was responsible, their culpability, and what harms they caused. In a trial or hearing, a just process is supposed to determine what narrative should be accepted as being a true account of wrongs done. But historical injustices often do not stand alone. In many cases they are part of a longer history of injustices committed by different groups of people. In a war or a civil conflict, wrongs are committed by both sides, and both are likely to construct narratives in which they appear as the victims and others as the aggressors. The difficulty of finding the truth of the matter and inducing antagonists to question their own narratives presents serious challenges to those who think that historical injustices require redress and that victims are entitled to demand justice for wrongs done to them. By describing how conflicting narratives exploited by nationalist leaders stand in the way of peace and reconciliation in Bosnia and Herzegovina, Elazar Barkan and Belma Bećirbašić demonstrate that remembrance does not always play a positive role in the ethical life of a society. In a sectarian context historical narratives can exacerbate conflict when warring ethnic groups advocate their own distinct historical truths and each regards itself as the victim of injustice. In this context, trials and demands for reparation are likely to make things worse. Barkan and Bećirbašić see some hope in the work of civil society organizations that are attempting to bridge gaps between opposing groups through empirical research and the production of a balanced historical narrative. However, they make it clear that these truth tellers face an uphill battle in their attempts to influence political discourse.

Conflict exacerbated by historical memory has motivated some governments to suppress it: to bury the past and discourage attempts to revive it and to concentrate on achieving a peaceful democratic society. Spain is an example of a country whose leaders for many years discouraged attempts to revive memories of past injustices. Only recently has a Spanish government initiated reparations for victims of the Civil War and the Franco dictatorship by passing a law that not only provides compensation to these victims but also attempts to change the national narrative. Patrizia Violi in her chapter provides an account of this law, its origins and consequences. She explains why the attempt to bring about cultural change through law is fraught with difficulties.

The failings of a legalist approach to historical injustice and memory have also become evident to citizens who have undergone a transition from an unjust regime to a democratic society. In this context, putting people on trial, as was done in Nuremberg, does not always serve the interests of victims, the nation, or justice in a wider sense. This recognition motivated one of the most important innovations of the historical justice movement: the establishment of truth and reconciliation commissions. One of the problems with conventional procedures of justice is that they are not an adequate answer to crimes in which many people have participated at all levels of government and society. But a more important issue is that they do not give victims what they need and want—a chance to tell the truth about what happened to them. In criminal trials such truths are of importance only insofar as they help to convict or exonerate the accused. In the operation of truth and reconciliation commissions, victims and the truths they tell are central. Margaret Urban Walker claims that truth telling can itself be a form of reparation. Injustices, she argues, damage moral relationships in a community by undermining trust and by destroying normative expectations and hopefulness in relations with others. Truth commissions not only bring the truth of the past to the attention of citizens; they also invest victims with a moral and epistemic standing that has the potential to effect a profound change in moral relations.

These commissions have another important function. The government that replaces an unjust regime has the task of rebuilding a society in which people are divided by the injustices of the old regime. Some truth and reconciliation commissions contribute to national reconciliation by encouraging perpetrators to acknowledge wrongdoing and victims to forgive. All are dedicated to uncovering the truth about injustices and enabling victims to speak. In his chapter Onur Bakiner focuses on these aspects of truth commissions. He takes issue with the claim that they provide a poor substitute for retributive and reparative justice. He argues that they make an important contribution to justice by opening up a space for the inclusion of silenced voices, by rejecting state denials of wrongdoing, and by inviting citizens to reflect on their nation's past. However, he aims to identify their limitations as well as their achievements. Their ability to reconstruct national narratives is often constrained by the limits imposed on their scope. Their reconciliatory effect can be undermined by political forces.

Neither Walker nor Bakiner thinks that giving a voice to victims is sufficient to achieve justice for historical wrongs. Reparations in the form of monetary payments, transfer of resources, and return of lost possessions may also be required. However, reparative justice in cases where injustices are historical raises serious difficulties. One of them is that there is no appropriate reparation for serious human rights violations. The victims are often dead or so severely harmed that no remedy can return them to their former state. Germany acknowledges this by admitting that its payments to Jewish victims cannot be regarded as reparation. Reparation for historical injustice is often conceived as payment not to individuals but to a family, group, or nation that is suffering from the consequences of injustice. But the problem of how to determine how much is owed remains. This is a particularly vexed issue when the effects of an injustice are widespread or when the injustice results in harm to both perpetrators and victims. Daniel Butt tackles these difficulties by providing an account of reparation appropriate for large-scale historical injustices. Imperialism, he argues, was a serious injustice that has continuing harmful effects on the people of former colonies and protectorates. Citizens of former imperialist nations have a reparative debt. Butt proposes that the amount of this debt should be determined by comparing the present situation of people in former colonies with how they would have fared if relations between communities had been characterized by a lack of domination and exploitation. This eliminates the need to compare actual harms and benefits or to return people to a situation that might have been unjust in the first place.

According to the standard legal and moral point of view, injustice requires redress, and anything that stands in the way of achieving it is also unjust. Perpetrators ought to be tried or compelled to participate in a process of reconciliation. The truth about what happened needs to be revealed; victims have a right to speak, and the public has a right to know. Some of the chapters in this volume question these assumptions. Attempts to revive the past and attribute responsibility can cause dissension and conflict. Those involved in peacekeeping or peacemaking operations often think that peace and reconciliation are more likely to be achieved if people put the past behind them and concentrate on building a future together. Elazar Barkan admits that peacekeepers may sometimes be right. Attempts to come to terms with historical injustices can interfere with prospects for peace and might be better postponed until relations have improved. However, this option is not available in conflicts where disagreements about history play a central role. He argues that historical dialogue aimed at constructing a balanced narrative could play a constructive role in peacekeeping processes.

Barkan and others in this book question legalist assumptions by pointing out that movements for historical justice can have negative consequences. Historical justice has its limits. In the final chapter, Mark Pendleton is concerned about the way in which historical memory is so often a motivation for demands for retribution or reparation. He takes to heart Paul Ricoeur's insistence that justice requires recognizing the victim in others and illustrates what this means by an account of the different ways in which victims respond to memories of injustice. The standard response is to condemn the perpetrator and to call for retribution. But there is an alternative option, and Pendleton illustrates it by the story of a man who was willing not only to forgive the person responsible for a terrorist attack that injured and eventually killed his wife but also to re-establish a sympathetic relationship with him. Pendleton makes it clear that this response is not only more humane but also more just.

Pendleton's appeal to Ricoeur's idea of justice represents a radical break from legalist assumptions. But it can also be regarded as a further step in the evolution of ideas of historical justice. Historical justice, as we have shown, had its origins in the legal processes that were initiated in the period after World War II, and the form it took was strongly influenced by traditional legal procedures and legal theory. It took over legalist assumptions: that justice requires identifying wrongdoers, finding out the truth about their crimes, punishing them appropriately, and providing appropriate reparation to victims. But these ideas about the requirements of justice do not fit many of the cases of historical injustice that societies were called upon to deal with. They do not do justice to the needs of victims and their ideas of repair. They ignore the large group of citizens who are not perpetrators in a legal sense but who are implicated in the injustices, if only because they failed to do anything to stop them. They do not address complex issues of responsibility in cases where injustice was systemic, where people adhere to conflicting versions of the truth, and where victims are also implicated in the wrongs of their society. They do not answer to a national need for reconciliation. Recognition of these failings led to the development of new processes for dealing with historical injustices and new conceptions of what justice requires. Pendleton's contribution points to a way of conceiving and responding to historical injustice that takes these complexities into account. The dialogue that Barkan recommends might be a way of bringing about the reflection and self-examination required by this more demanding and inclusive idea of justice.

Toward a Research Agenda

The chapters in this volume raise critical questions about the seemingly unstoppable movement for historical justice. They raise the possibility that historical justice may not always be possible or desirable. Here, we would like to extend some of these critical reflections and at the same time propose three avenues for further research to extend our understanding of the movements for historical justice and memory and the challenges they face.

First, we need to know more about the *drivers of historical justice*. Historians, in particular, have explored the genealogies of public memories and of attempts to right past wrongs. For example, in his monumental three-volume history of memories in Chile, Steve Stern (2004, 2006, 2010) analyzed the permutations of public and social memory over a thirty-three-year period. While national and local histories have added much to our understanding of how particular memories came to the fore and how demands to hold perpetrators account-able and make reparations to victims gathered momentum, comparatively little is known about the seemingly sudden eruptions of the desire to remember and do justice. Why do individuals—not only survivors or the descendants of victims but also the descendants of perpetrators—feel compelled to turn to the past and focus on episodes that are in many cases extremely traumatic? And why does that compulsion manifest itself at a particular point in time? In some cases memories of injustice may be extremely important to victims and their families and merely wait for a political opportunity to be made public. In her study of memories of Francoist repression in Aragon, Ángela Cenarro (2002) suggests that latent individual reminiscences that had lain dormant for decades could be articulated once revisionist historians helped to create an environment within which such memories could be meaningful. Cenarro seems to acknowledge, however, that there is more to the—often sudden— emergence of memories that have been suppressed or that are thought to have been erased; she refers to the work of Jo Labanyi (2000), who in her study of Spanish novels and films produced after the death of Franco makes use of a seemingly metaphysical concept: the ghosts of the dead who return to demand redress.

William Faulkner's dictum "The past is never dead. It's not even past," which has been quoted or paraphrased in numerous analyses of memories of injustice, draws attention to the permeability of the line between what is and what was. Trying to conceptualize this permeability, scholars such as Avery Gordon (2008) have in recent years productively analyzed the hauntedness of a present and the past's propensity to make an *unbidden* appearance. While Gordon's pioneering work has been informed by her critical reading of works of literature, other scholars have been inspired by the psychoanalysis of Nicolas Abraham and Maria Torok (1986) or by Jacques Derrida's engagement with Marx (Derrida 2006). These approaches are promising in that they can help us understand the presence of the past in the present, but to tap their full potential we need detailed ethnographic and biographical studies that can tell us about how precisely hauntedness manifests itself and what exactly animates the ghosts that make an unbidden appearance in the present.

Klaus Neumann and Janna Thompson

Second, we need to gain a better understanding of the *limits of historical justice*. Most of the injustices that have been made the subject of demands for redress occurred in the recent past. This is obviously so for those that become the subject of truth and reconciliation processes. But responses to injustices of the past are not confined to recent events. In 2001 and then again three years later, Pope John Paul II, a serial apologizer, formally expressed his sorrow for the sacking of Constantinople during the Fourth Crusade in 1204.

> Clearly there is a need for a liberating process of purification of memory. . . .
> Some memories are especially painful, and some events of the distant past have left deep wounds in the minds and hearts of people to this day. . . .
> [We are] imploring [God] to heal the wounds which still cause suffering to the spirit of the Greek people. Together we must work for this healing if the Europe now emerging is to be true to its identity, which is inseparable from the Christian humanism shared by East and West. (John Paul II 2001)

This is perhaps the most extreme example of a reaching back into a distant past—far beyond contemporary generations—to redress a historical wrong. There is no direct lineage that could link the perpetrators and victims of 1204 with John Paul II's contemporaries. For example, the "Greek people" of today, as Michael Herzfeld (1982), among others, has shown, are a product of the nineteenth century. This is not to deny that some of today's Greeks may be aggrieved by events that took place hundreds of years ago or that they strongly identify with people who lived in what is now Greece—or Istanbul, for that matter—in the distant past. But an apology, while responding to their grievances, only serves to ossify divisive myths that underwrite current identities.

In the past twenty years, there have been many other attempts to demand and provide redress for past injustices that happened beyond the living memory of all or most citizens. The British government's acknowledgment of atrocities committed under British colonial rule in Kenya in the 1950s is an example. American descendants of slaves brought from Africa more than two hundred years ago have demanded reparation from the US government, and Denmark, the first European country to ban the slave trade, is currently faced with demands for reparations by the descendants of slaves in the Virgin Islands, a former Danish colony that since 1917 has been a territory of the United States (Andersen 2013).

These and similar claims raise a host of difficult issues concerning responsibility, memory, and reparation. When do descendants have an entitlement to demand reparation? When their inherited memory of injustice continues to be relevant to their lives? When they are still suffering the consequences of the injustice? And who is responsible for reparation? Those who benefited? Those who committed the injustice? All of these answers raise further questions. One of the difficulties is that the truth about injustices that happened so long ago may be impossible to determine. And the people who committed them are long dead. Holding a state responsible for injustices of the distant past raises questions about identity and continuity of responsibility. The British state of today is not the same as the colonial administration that governed Kenya. These issues have been discussed by philosophers, but they are far from being resolved either in theory or in practice.

Demands that arise from the distant past raise the question of whether there should be temporal limits to claims for historical justice and how these should be determined. But demands for historical justice have not only expanded by delving into the more distant past. They have also expanded by including more and more categories of wrongdoing. Early claims focused on injustices relating to *foundational* aspects of the history of nations. For example, the symbolic and material reparation to Maori claimants by the New Zealand government was a response to breaches of the 1840 Treaty of Waitangi—which is regarded as that nation's foundational document. Similarly, the Australian apology to Indigenous people was about wrongs that are well known and central to Australia's history. But these acts of apology and redress were followed by many others. In 2002 the New Zealand government issued an apology to Chinese New Zealanders for imposing a poll tax on Chinese immigrants (Clark 2002) and to Samoa for a number of events that happened when Samoa was a New Zealand colony. The apology to Indigenous Australians was followed up by official apologies to Forgotten Australians and former child migrants (in 2009) and to families affected by forced adoption practices (in 2013). Not surprisingly, other groups have begun pushing for apologies from the government: victims of Australia's restrictive immigration policy (the so-called White Australia policy) and civilian wartime internees, among others. This expansion of the list of injustices for which redress is sought not only invites the question of whether and how a line can be drawn between legitimate and nonlegitimate claims. It also raises the question of whether these later apologies and the frequency of their occurrence devalue the ones that were originally given. Should a distinction be made between historical justice for foundational wrongs (such as the dispossession of Indigenous peoples in settler colonies) and other past injustices?

Finally, we need to know more about the *presumed and actual benefits of historical justice*—not only for victims and their families but also for others campaigning for it. Like other political acts, apologies by states and their willingness to pay reparations are motivated by political considerations and can

Klaus Neumann and Janna Thompson

serve governmental interests. Those who concentrate on the moral reasons for historical justice tend to ignore these underlying motivations and outcomes. They are also reluctant to interrogate claims about the value of achieving historical justice to victims and their community and to the rest of the nation. That there are immediate benefits to victims is undeniable. Even when the people who were victimized are dead, an apology can have value to members of their family or community. But the effects of movements for historical justice and memorialization, especially those that occur in the long term, have not been adequately studied. In recent years, there have been promising attempts to measure the efficacy of particular transitional justice mechanisms (for example, Olsen, Payne, and Reiter 2010; Sikkink 2011), but there is much more work to be done. For example, in his contribution to this volume, Onur Bakiner writes that truth commissions are able to reinvigorate debates about political and moral responsibility, irrespective of the intentions of those appointing them. We need to know more about the exact nature of those debates, of their reliance on the findings of truth commissions, and of their tangible outcomes.

Another assumption that needs scrutiny is that the health of a nation, as well as the well-being of victims of injustice, is served by remembering and dealing with past injustices. In their contribution to this book, Barkan and Bećirbašić point out that memory can exacerbate divisions. Far from being therapeutic, a focus on the injustices of the past can turn into a pathological competition in victimhood. Pendleton presents an idea of justice that transcends the accusatory stance that is often associated with memories of injustice and allows people to move forward. More attention is needed to processes and developments that could encourage this response.

More critical attention is also needed to the use of memory and historical justice as a nation-building exercise. Walker emphasizes that facing historical truths and letting victims have a voice encourages trust and overcomes alienation—thus making it possible for them to regard themselves as belonging to their nation. Bakiner thinks that one of the functions of truth and reconciliation commissions is to construct a national narrative that faces up to historical wrongs. However, the revision of a national narrative, even when its scope is not limited by powerful political forces, is never going to be uncontentious. And in the interest of national unity or national pride, people are likely to be selective in what they want to be officially remembered. The memorial in Nairobi to commemorate the suffering of Kenyans during the Mau Mau emergency will draw attention to particular colonial policies and practices, such as the detention of people suspected of being rebels. It is unlikely to draw attention to the collaboration of Kenyans with the colonial administration or to the use of the emergency by Kenyans to settle old scores. Selection in the "national interest" of what to remember and what to forget means that some voices will remain unheard and some truths unuttered. These are effects of the historical justice movement that need to be better understood and taken into account.

National governments are not the only ones who, in offering redress, are often acting in their own interests. Memorialization can serve the interests of those who pride themselves on remembering. We finish with a sobering reflection on an event that, like the cases with which we began, happened in the first half of 2013. According to a newspaper report, the mayor of Helmbrechts, a small German town near the Czech border, had announced that a second memorial would be built in his town to commemorate the suffering of concentration camp prisoners (Bußler 2013). In 1943, Helmbrechts became the site of a concentration camp for non-Jewish women, most of them from the Soviet Union, Poland, and Czechoslovakia, who manufactured cables and munitions in a former textile factory. The Helmbrechts camp was one of more than eighty satellites of the Flossenbürg concentration camp. Given its comparatively small size and the large number of such satellite camps all over Germany, the existence of the Helmbrechts camp would not have been remarkable. But, on 6 March 1945, 621 Jewish women prisoners from the Grünberg camp in Silesia were added to the Helmbrechts camp's population. And, one week after the arrival of the women from Grünberg, the SS evacuated the Helmbrechts camp and made its prisoners walk east, away from the approaching Americans. About two hundred of the women, nearly all of them recent arrivals from Grünberg, died or were murdered on what became known as the Helmbrechts *Todesmarsch* (death march).

The 2013 ceremony held in Helmbrechts concentrated on commemorating this event. The ceremony, which was led by the local Lutheran pastor, featured a poem by the German-Jewish poet and Nobel laureate Nelly Sachs and a hymn based on the poem "Das Zeichen" by Shalom Ben Chorin, a German-Jewish writer and founder of Israel's first reform synagogue. The participants then moved to an existing memorial in the cemetery: a rock from Volary, the end point of the *Todesmarsch*. There was a speech by a representative of the Verein gegen das Vergessen (Association against Forgetting), who drew attention to the activities of right-wing extremists in Germany. He also referred to the fact that the majority of Germans had supported the Nazi regime and commented: "We who were born much later note this with consternation." Announcing plans for the new memorial at the historical site of the camp, the Helmbrechts mayor proclaimed: "We have to confront the past and acknowledge human dignity, and we must not fail to remember and draw attention to atrocities" (Bußler 2013).

Nothing was said about the history of the local concentration camp, which would have been closely intertwined with the history of Helmbrechts and its residents.[5] The focus was on human suffering rather than on local responsibilities. Although the victims were identified as Jewish, they were remembered with the help of Christian symbols (crosses) and a song from the Lutheran hymn book. The newspaper article does not mention the presence of survivors or of their relatives. It seems that the commemoration was a decidedly non-Jewish German affair. The past was remembered as something bewildering that defies rational understanding. Although they occurred in the town's recent past, the wrongs commemorated had seemingly little to do with today's Helmbrechts residents. Only the local Germans benefit from such attempts to remember past injustices.

The events at Helmbrechts are an illustration of two common phenomena: the tendency to airbrush out of historical narratives facts that are inconvenient or that do not suit local sensibilities; and the use of these narratives to reinforce local or national ties and traditions while excluding outsiders, including those who were principal victims of injustice. This does not mean that historical justice is impossible or that attempts at memorialization always have an ulterior motivation. Despite its drawbacks and difficulties, the movement for historical justice and the refusal of people to forget injustices of the past are positive developments. It is important to critically evaluate them, not least because an evaluation of the search for redress helps us to gain a better understanding of justice in a broader sense. This volume tries to make a contribution to such a critical evaluation of what has become one of the defining global movements of our time.

Notes

1. In 2014, the JCC negotiated another settlement with the German Ministry of Finance. Pending agreement by the German parliament, a new fund will pay €2,500 each to all child survivors to subsidize psychological or medical treatment (Auswärtiges Amt 2014).

2. In May 2014, the Mau Mau War Veterans Association and other stakeholders agreed on a design for the memorial, which was under construction as this book went to press (Kihuria 2014; Turner 2014).

3. In 2011 and 2012, the High Court allowed the claims of initially five, later four Kenyans against the British Foreign and Colonial Office to proceed, but it made no findings with regard to the substance of their claims (Dowell 2013). Judgments: http://www.judiciary.gov.uk/Resources/JCO/Documents/Judgments/mutua-v-ors-judgment.pdf; http://www.judiciary.gov.uk/Resources/JCO/Documents/Judgments/mutua-fco-judgment-05102012.pdf.

4. In 1965 the Japanese foreign minister expressed "remorse" and "regret" for an "unfortunate period" in relations between Japan and Korea (Dudden 2008, 44; Nobles 2008, 155); arguably, his statement fell short of an apology.

5. The *Todesmarsch* has also been publicly remembered at other places between Helmbrechts and Volary. It is the subject of *Helmbrechts Walk, 1998–2003*, an art project by the American visual artist Susan Silas (Silas 2012; see also Apel 2002, 139–44; Kaplan 2011, 99–121).

Klaus Neumann and Janna Thompson

Part I

1

Memory Culture and Human Rights

A New Constellation

ANDREAS HUYSSEN

Human rights as a transnational social movement and the global spread of memory discourses first emerged in the 1970s, gained steam in the 1980s, and reached inflationary proportions by the 1990s. These discourses ran on parallel tracks separated by disciplinary specializations: debates about human rights played out in law, political science, anthropology, and sociology, while memory debates about trauma, experience, temporality, and the vicissitudes of representation were anchored in the humanities with foci as different as psychoanalysis, mass media, testimony, literature, and the arts. The discourses also had different orientations. The human rights movement, however much it was itself inspired by memories of past injustice, remained firmly oriented toward a future goal of establishing an international, perhaps even global rights regime. Memory discourse, despite its ritually incanted "never again," had its eye on the past. And yet there are fascinating points of contact in the emergence of rights and memory discourses that suggest closeness and connection rather than distance and separation. The emergence and development of both discourses were historically overdetermined, and both are now increasingly being questioned about their hidden assumptions, their effectiveness, and their prospects for the future.

Samuel Moyn (2010) has interpreted the human rights movement as a last utopia after the collapse of the earlier utopias of the twentieth century, which included communism and fascism, modernization and decolonization. In my book *Present Pasts* (2003), I argued in a similar vein that the collapse of an earlier utopian imagination was one condition that made it possible for the new memorial discourses to arise. I argued that the time consciousness of high modernity in the West tried to secure utopian futures, whereas the time consciousness of the late twentieth century involved the no-less-perilous task of taking responsibility for the past. The 1980s and 1990s thus saw a conjuncture of two significant political phenomena: the rise of human rights as a reference point for political and social struggles and the internationalization of appeals to memories of historical injustices.

This conjuncture of discourses raises a question that defies any quick or easy answers: what do human rights have to do with memory in the first place? At the simplest level, one could argue that only the memory of rights violations can nurture the future of human rights in the world, thus providing a substantive link between past and future. But all too often memory discourse and contemporary rights debates remain separated by more than just disciplinary specialization. Human rights advocates are likely to find the concern with memory politically deficient and self-indulgent, while the memorians lament the ingrained universalism of much human rights discourse. Suspicions on both sides abound. From my vantage point in the humanities, I would argue, however, that contemporary memory studies should be linked more robustly with human rights and justice both discursively and practically to prevent memory, especially traumatic memory, from becoming a vacuous exercise feeding parasitically on itself. I would also suggest that unless it is nurtured by memory and history, human rights discourse is in danger of losing historical grounding and risks venturing off into legalistic abstraction and political abuse. Recognizing the inherent strengths and limitations of human rights and memory discourse is important if we want to enable their interaction in the future. In fact, the individual strength of each field can supplement the other, thus mitigating their respective deficiencies, since both are fundamentally concerned with the violation and protection of basic human rights and draw on history to do so.

History of Human Rights and Memory Discourses

Both human rights and memory discourses grew out of legal, moral, and philosophical discourses about genocide and rights violations after

World War II. The Universal Declaration of Human Rights (UDHR) and the UN's Genocide Convention of 1948 were the political result of the memory of these violations, though in their phrasing both UN documents circumvented the ethnic and particularist dimension of the Holocaust. Memory, not only of the unspeakable genocides and forced population transfers in the interwar period after the collapse of the Russian, Habsburg, and Ottoman Empires but also of the legacies of the natural law tradition, was influential in the shaping of these UN documents. And yet it took several decades more before the international human rights movement took off and memory became an international discourse.

The development of these discourses in response to the interweaving of Holocaust memory with memory projects in South Africa and Latin America, the fall of the Berlin wall, the collapse of the Soviet Union, ethnic cleansing in the former Yugoslavia, and the genocidal massacre in Rwanda poses radically new dilemmas in the sphere of international human rights and confronts memory studies with an expanded set of political and ethical questions. The contemporary human rights movement in its historical evolution and politically changing complexion closely parallels the rise of memory discourse then and now, and the problems it raises are similar to those that arise from discussions of memory.[1]

The political theorist Jean Cohen has distinguished three phases of human rights discourse since the 1940s (Cohen 2008, 2012).[2] A first wave developed after World War II in recognition of the atrocities and massive human rights violations committed against civilians before and during the war; it was based not only on the American tradition of inalienable rights but also on the revival of much earlier religious theories of natural law and moral rights, which were deployed to counter a largely discredited legal positivism.[3] The focus shifted from the protection of the rights of minorities, which had been so ineffectual in the interwar period, to the rights of individuals, which were now framed within the context of international human rights. It resulted in the Genocide Convention and the Universal Declaration of Human Rights of 1948. As opposed to the declaration of rights from the American and French revolutions, which resulted from concrete political struggles, this new codification of rights was shaped by the politics of diplomats and state representatives, and it lacked any mechanism for enforcement, which would have been difficult, if not impossible, to create in the early years of the Cold War.

In a second wave, Cohen argues, human rights discourse played a central role in the internal weakening of the Soviet Union and the East European communist states in the 1970s, when the Soviet Union first accepted certain human rights claims by signing the Final Act of the Conference on Security and Co-operation in Europe (1975) and rights violations were front and center in the transitions from military dictatorship to democracy in Latin America in the 1970s and 1980s. Cohen (2008, 580) writes: "Despite being largely exhortatory, the human rights declarations and covenants were an important normative referent for domestic civil society and social movement activists." The collapse of the Soviet empire and the negotiated end of apartheid in South Africa shortly thereafter were further markers for the renewal and spread of civil society debates and rights implementations in many countries in Eastern Europe and Latin America. Rather than still operating exclusively within traditional national frameworks, rights struggles at this stage took on an international dimension. And what's more, Cohen argues that what distinguishes "this second wave of post-war international human rights politics from the first elite-dominated and UN-focused discourse of diplomats and state-executives is that it was adopted by grassroots movements and organizations whose transnational activism bypassed the UN machinery" (Cohen 2012, 171).[4]

The third wave differs dramatically from the two that preceded it. Since the end of the Cold War, Cohen continues, human rights violations have been selectively "invoked as justification for the imposition of debilitating sanctions, military invasions and authoritarian occupation administrations by multilateral organizations (NATO, UN Security Council) and/or states acting unilaterally under the rubric of 'humanitarian' or even 'democratic' intervention" (Cohen 2012, 172). Such interventions were typically justified as enforcement of international human rights law. Kosovo, Afghanistan, Iraq, and most recently Libya are pertinent though politically very different cases. However one evaluates the intervention in Kosovo and the invasion of Iraq, the political and conceptual problem is the same. At stake here is the conflict between an emerging institutionalization of transnational human rights and a formerly sacrosanct idea of national sovereignty.

The International Commission on Intervention and State Sovereignty (ICISS) has perhaps gone furthest in calling for limits on state sovereignty in its 2001 report, "The Responsibility to Protect," which was adopted by the UN in 2005. While this report clearly came out of the failures of the UN in the 1990s in Srebrenica and Rwanda, it is not clear to me whether the shift from humanitarian intervention ("military humanism," as some have called it) to R2P (Responsibility to Protect) is anything more than a semantic shift, given that the potential protectors will inevitably still be the major powers that also lead humanitarian interventions (minor exception: the UN's African Union troops in Darfur). But, for better or worse, human rights at this stage have become genuinely international and are tied, albeit problematically, to military intervention in sovereign states.

From these interventions come two opposing positions: the statists who

Andreas Huyssen

insist on national sovereignty in a traditional sense and the liberal cosmopolitans who celebrate the waning of state sovereignty and the emergence of an international human rights regime. Both these positions are problematic. Statists tend to ignore or downplay the serious human rights violations of national governments. Cosmopolitans ignore local traditions and understandings, often to the detriment of the aims and struggles of grassroots movements. Going beyond this opposition requires the articulation of a position that combines the advantages of universalization encouraged by human rights discourse with sensitivity to the particularities of local conditions and understandings.

Jean Cohen and Ruti Teitel have made important contributions to this project from the perspectives of political theory and legal studies. Cohen's worries about neo-imperial hierarchies of power and the hegemonic tendencies of international law make her want to hold onto the notion of sovereignty, which for her has important implications for the continuing rights struggle at the national level. On the other hand, she does not want to surrender all of the universalizing aspects of human rights law. She argues in favor of

> two political conceptions, one referring to those human security rights violations, specified by the international community, that can legitimately and legally suspend the sovereignty argument against forceful intervention and other forms of international enforcement, the other referring to international human rights that function as public standards of critique to which citizens and denizens, domestic rights activists, and social movement actors can refer in their political struggles against domestic oppression, injustice, and arbitrariness, and in order to make their own governments more democratic, more rights respecting, and more accountable to the citizenry. (Cohen 2012, 16)

Teitel, an international and comparative law scholar, seems closer to the liberal cosmopolitan position, even as she does not entirely deny the continuing importance of the nation state. What she calls "humanity's law" differs substantively from an unreflected universalism of human rights. Humanity's law[5] provides a "framework that spans the law of war, international human rights law, and international criminal justice" (Teitel 2011, 4) all of which reshape international relations in our globalizing world. She argues that the emerging international regime of global justice is characterized by "innovative hybrid judicial institutions [which] involve sui generis blends of the international and the national and apply a continuum of humanity law as a complement to the state's prosecutorial processes" (Teitel 2011, 65).

Both these thinkers provide fruitful examples of how the opposition between statism and cosmopolitanism can be transcended. Both acknowledge the shift in international relations from sovereign impunity to a responsibility of states to the international community. At the same time, both take great care to separate their positions from an unreflective universalism of human rights. Neither Cohen nor Teitel identifies any explicit connection between human rights discourse and memory studies, but they share an implicit interest in a point raised by Teitel (2011, 205): "The premise of humanity's law is the shared experiences of the memory of inhumanity." Today this "shared experience" of the past has certainly tempered the triumphalist promises of modernity of an earlier time.

In memory studies, just as in legal studies and in political theory, traditional statism and an uncritical cosmopolitanism have become obsolete. The statist position is represented by research that focuses exclusively on a memory constellation within one national culture, treating culture as a closed rather than always porous unit. This is the nationalist model that also underwrites the notion of state sovereignty. It was the dominant mode of early memory studies and continues unabated and often unchallenged. The cosmopolitan position in legal and political discourse, on the other hand, is found among those who interpret the Holocaust as a universal model for understanding any and all forms of state terror, ethnic cleansing, and genocide. Universalizing the Holocaust in this way, as many have pointed out, risks erasing history and the more local specificity of injustice and its memorialization.[6] Clearly, neither one of these two positions captures the current state of memory studies, and they should be rejected just as statism and cosmopolitanism are rejected by Cohen and Teitel.

Michael Rothberg (2009) acknowledges the complexity of memory structures in national contexts. Daniel Levy and Natan Sznaider (2006) speak of cosmopolitan memory and a global cultural memory imperative in ways that are similar to Teitel's positing of humanity's law. They argue, correctly I think, that the emergence of a new human rights regime was "driven largely by the continuous transposition of cosmopolitan memories of failures to prevent human rights abuses" (Levy and Sznaider 2006, 43). And they highlight one of the major contributions of memory discourse when they say that such mnemonic transpositions are not construed solely as universal demands or interdictions but are "articulated through memories of particular experiences" (Levy and Sznaider 2010, 43). This points to the central role of testimony, itself a legal concept, in memory studies. These more recent discussions show that the fields of memory studies and rights discourse, which are all too often kept separate, can be mined for substantive affinities that will continue to let us see how they are, paradoxically enough, parallel but connected.

Andreas Huyssen

What's the Difference?

Memory is necessary to human rights discourse and to laws that uphold human rights. Where would today's international human rights movement be without memory of the killing fields of the twentieth century? Memory and the law, including human rights law, interact in complex ways, but we also need to understand certain epistemological, moral, and practical differences that determine their affective range, their operations, and their long-term effects and sometimes bring them into opposition.

Even if we recognize that human rights law is as fragile, contested, and often ineffectual as memory, there remains a fundamental tension between memory and the law. Restrictive limitations of scale and social range exist on either side of this discursive divide. Memory discourse is usually concerned with collective pasts and their effects on the present, but it lacks a strong normative juridical dimension that would lead directly toward individual or group legal rights claims, let alone to prosecutions or potential redress. Not coincidentally, the field of legal redress and restitution based on memory remains highly controversial.[7] Some legal scholars and political theorists have even argued that memory of past injury can be only a weak substitute for justice. The debate about the South African TRC is a case in point, in that perpetrators were guaranteed amnesty if they gave public confessional testimony about their past actions (Mamdani 2002).[8] At the same time, however, all legal proceedings, especially in cases of retroactive or transitional justice, as after the end of dictatorships in Chile and Argentina, depend on individual memory to enable a court to arrive at convictions, just as they also depend on a functioning court system and an independent judiciary. More important for my view about the role of memory in relation to the law, I would argue that the active prosecution of human rights violations in the courts also depends on the strength of memory discourses in the public sphere: in journalism, film, media, literature, the arts, education, and even urban graffiti. Argentina today is perhaps the best example of how a new wave of trials of perpetrators from the years of state terror has arisen from a public politics of memory operating through various groups of memory activists deploying all available media of representation. It shows that cultural and artistic representations of historical trauma can play a significant role in relation to public trials and prosecutions.

Memory discourse also brings out into the open a moral imperative that can come into conflict with how we understand the purpose of legal processes. A claim to total closure often accompanies the conclusion of criminal trials. Once the legal judgment is made and the criminal is dealt with, the crime is supposed to be relegated to history. But an obligation to remember cannot so easily be put to rest. As Walter Benjamin suggested, the dead do have a claim on us, since we are, from their point of view, the coming generations (see also Booth 2011). Benjamin (1968, 254) argued that we have therefore been endowed with a weak messianic power. Max Horkheimer pointed out that the dead are dead and cannot be reawakened—no need for messianism, no use for redemption. But perhaps Benjamin meant no more than to say that the dead do have a right to remembrance. The dignity of the victims of genocide and other serious violations of human rights requires that their struggles and their fate be preserved in memory, all the more so since it was the express aim of the masters of genocide to obliterate all memory of their victims.

However, the biblical demand to remember, so strong in contemporary worldly culture of the West as a counterweight to rampant amnesia, is a moral demand that is not legally or socially enforceable. Reasonably so, since were it enforceable, it would violate the right to forget, which is always in conflict with the need to remember. Memory always remains fragile and difficult to verify, let alone legislate. Human rights, on the other hand, are themselves Janus faced: morality and the law. They share the moral and emotive dimension with memory discourse, which by itself lacks the juridical dimension, even though, paradoxically, there can be no justice without memory. Linked and yet separate: this is why there remains a fundamental tension between memory and rights discourse beyond disciplinary specializations.

Moreover, given contemporary media culture's often frivolous and exploitative obsessions with memory, one may legitimately ask whether memory helps or hinders justice. Defenders will legitimately point to the trials of war criminals and perpetrators of state terror or to successful restitution claims. Detractors of memory discourse will cite cases where memory and the mantle of victimhood are used to incite violence (as in Slobodan Milošević's Serbian propaganda campaign about the 1389 battle of Kosovo) or to prolong hostilities (as in the memory competitions between Israel and Palestine). In Serbia, memory of past injury was mobilized in the service of nationalist goals that triggered the ethnic cleansing in Bosnia and Kosovo. The Croatian writer Dubravka Ugrešić, in her book of essays *The Culture of Lies* (1998), has made the powerful argument that the disintegration of Yugoslavia was characterized by the simultaneity of a terror of forgetting and a terror of memory: forgetting the reality of multiethnic and multireligious Yugoslavia, remembering and reviving mostly forgotten enmities of the past. Strengths, limits, and abuses of memory need to be acknowledged in their interplay case by case.

The same is true of human rights discourse, which makes strong normative legal claims in the name of justice but often ends up in an idolatry of abstract

Andreas Huyssen

principles, ignoring the historical and political contexts that must be recognized and negotiated if a politics of human rights is to take hold in a specific country at a given time. Legitimate differences of opinion on what is human about human rights or which rights count as human rights in the first place are often overridden by an inflation of rights discourse that risks devaluing the whole enterprise. Today, the ubiquity of rights claims parallels the inflation of memory claims, and both rights and memory discourse are easily abused as a political veil for particular interests. Critics of human rights and of memory never cease to point this out in order to discredit one another.

Rights, Democracy, Modernity

Just as we need to rethink rather than abolish concepts such as universalism and sovereignty, we must also put pressure on the relationship between universal rights and liberal democracy, which is too often simply taken for granted. Idolatry and abuse are especially visible internationally in the facile equation of universal human rights with Western democracy, a point raised powerfully in Cohen's critique of humanitarian intervention. They are implicit in the notion that rights should spread from the United States to other parts of the world. This argument draws on a discredited post–World War II modernization theory resurrected in terms of human rights. While the genealogy of today's human rights debate goes back to European sources of natural law of the seventeenth and eighteenth centuries, Jürgen Habermas (2009) was right to suggest that international human rights standards should be neither legitimized nor delegitimized by their origins in European civilization and the Westphalian system of sovereign nation states. Opponents often cite this historical origin in order to discredit rights discourse as Eurocentric and imperialist; proponents themselves often remain oblivious to the fact that one cannot simply cite the genealogy of rights in order to describe or justify current universalizing practices.

If we go back to deep history at all, we must first acknowledge that the relationship between human rights and Western democracy is complex and fractured rather than seamless. Struggles for rights have been waged over centuries in European states with widely varying definitions and understandings of rights, and democracies have all too often violated the rights of minorities and sometimes still do. In addition, the propagation of human rights was always coupled with their denial in colonial situations and slaveholding societies. This history made it possible for some postcolonial states to denounce human rights as a Western imposition and to deny rights to their own populations.

The question of rights has always been a question of power and asymmetrical relations, and the same is true for what Michael Rothberg (2009) has criticized as the zero-sum competition among memory discourses today, where one social group's memory is elevated at the expense of another's.

While the colonial genealogy must be recognized, the idea and practice of human rights have undergone so many transformations that the concept's origins in divine natural law or even in the American and French revolutions have become largely secondary as a legitimizing device. International human rights today are rather legitimized by the need across the world to respond to the challenges of a social and economic modernity that, however locally fractured and transformed, has become global.[9] This inevitably involves a certain level of abstraction in the judgment of atrocities and human rights abuses. It is the abstraction of modernity itself without which memories of atrocities would not attain their transnational power of affect and mobilization beyond the communities of the victims themselves.

And yet, a human rights regime entirely beyond states and nations is not yet imaginable today, even if some political theorists have begun to conceptualize a *Weltbürgergesellschaft* (global civil society) as opposed to or without a world government (see Habermas 1999). Despite certain forms of denationalization of citizenship in some parts of the world (e.g., dual citizenship, EU passports, the granting of regional voting rights to noncitizens), states do remain important legislators and guarantors of expanded rights, especially via constitutions, new regulations of citizenship and cultural rights, and commitments to transnational organizations. Most of these rights struggles, which have no models in the past, still play out within such local or national contexts, even though there has been a growth of transnational rights organizations such as the European Court of Human Rights and the International Criminal Court. Despite such advances, new forms of de facto statelessness have developed in the context of "illegal" migrations, the sex trade, and other new forms of slavery and indentured labor. This is particularly pertinent in the case of "third-country immigrants" to the EU and of mainly Latin American and Chinese immigrants to the United States. Hannah Arendt's analysis remains pertinent as a warning: "The conception of human rights, based upon the presumed existence of a human being as such, broke down at the very moment when those who professed to believe in it were for the first time confronted with the people who had indeed lost all other qualities and specific relationships—except that they were still human" (Arendt 1958, 299). Analogously, the belief that memory of genocide as a crime against humanity might prevent further genocides from happening broke down at the moment that the world confronted new forms of genocide, state massacres, and ethnic cleansing in Bosnia, Rwanda, and Darfur.

Memory and the Nation

As debates rage today about the timeliness or untimeliness of the nation, another concept intimately tied to nation-ness needs to be rethought. Here, too, memory and rights are linked even if they don't map easily onto each other. Just as the sovereign nation once did and still does provide the framework for rights, it also served as the privileged space for collective memory as defined by sociologists and historians from Maurice Halbwachs to Pierre Nora and beyond. But, while human rights discourse since the Universal Declaration of Human Rights of 1948 aims at universality, discourses about collective memory have typically been limited to national or regional situations.[10] This tends to block insight into the ways a new transnational politics of memory has spread across the world since 1989 in conjunction with rights discourse and yet separate from it. The idea of collective memory mostly relied on an anthropological notion of culture as homogeneous and closed or self-contained.[11] A memorian like Carol Gluck (2007) has therefore argued for differentiating among official, vernacular, and individual memory rather than assuming one seamless collective memory, and I have argued elsewhere that we should abandon or at least bracket the notion of collective memory altogether (Huyssen 2009). This seems especially called for at a time when "collective memory," mostly understood today as national memory, is inevitably shot through with group memories at the subnational or regional level as well as with the diasporic memories of the increasing flows of immigrants that challenge notions of cultural homogeneity. In addition, the construction of memory via the mass media makes a sociological view of group memories ever more illusory. However you define it, collective memory as a guiding idea has become conceptually and sociologically problematic.

With the expansion of rights since World War II, notions of national cultures as distinct and coherent units not subject to cross-border international rights claims have slowly weakened but not become irrelevant, as national-language politics and conflicts about migrant cultures demonstrate. Tendencies toward the globalization of finance, economics, and migrations have created new networks that subvert traditional notions of national sovereignty. But, as Cohen has argued, this requires a redefinition of sovereignty rather than its abandonment. Nations once contained economies. Today the economy contains nations. Could one suggest analogously that once nations contained memory, whereas now a global memory culture contains nations? Indeed, Levy and Sznaider (2006) have suggested that the old notion of collective memory could be rethought as global or cosmopolitan memory. While I agree with their thesis that globalization, technological media, and the political events of the 1990s have changed the status of memory across the world, I remain somewhat skeptical of the language of cosmopolitanization. After all, discourses of lived memory will remain tied primarily to specific communities and territories, even if the concern with memory itself has become a transnational phenomenon across the world and Holocaust memory has migrated into other historically nonrelated cases (see Levy and Sznaider 2010). Two recent developments in literary and visual memory studies in particular seem promising. One trend increasingly links Holocaust memory to the memories of the colonial and postcolonial periods (see, for example, Huyssen 2009; Rothberg 2009). The other, more micrologically focused, discusses "postmemory" as generational transmission distinguishing between direct familial transmission on one hand and indirect affiliative transmission mediated by art works, documents, films, and other media as well as by increased generational distance on the other (Hirsch 2012). In both cases, historical specificity and context are claimed for discussions that clearly push beyond national confinement without going cosmopolitan.

But even at the national level, memories are always in conflict with each other, more so nowadays than at the highpoint of the Westphalian regime that first saw the invention of national traditions (Hobsbawm) and the construction of national memories. Memories clash just as rights claims confront each other. In any collectivity, there will inevitably be conflict and struggle over memories that rarely, even within small groups, amount to something one could call collective, let alone cosmopolitan. Such tensions and conflicts are a key constituent of the public sphere in open societies and must ideally be subject to political recognition, democratic deliberation, and negotiation. The fact that groups of people rather than individuals are usually singled out for persecution or oppression does not guarantee a homogeneous collective group memory. Conflicts concerning rights mirror conflicts over memory. The rights of indigenous peoples, language rights, gender rights, sexual rights, citizenship rights, and political rights for immigrants have become key areas of conflict. Hannah Arendt's fundamental claim that there is a right to have rights, a claim that goes back to the period between the two World Wars in which whole populations were denaturalized and deprived of individual and citizenship rights, has become a shaping political force in the contemporary world.

Debates in the humanities about memorials, monuments, films, literature, and the visual arts reveal the complexities of group memories. They have also contributed a great deal to our understanding of historical trauma in their focus on testimony and witnessing. Some have asked to what extent such a focus on subjectivities, legitimate as it is, risks losing sight of the political dimensions of rights discourse in the present and its implications for the future

Andreas Huyssen

(Sarlo 2005). While this objection does have some force in relation to an over-playing of trauma in a poststructuralist and psychoanalytic vein, I would argue that it is precisely the focus on the force of individual memories of rights viola-tions that can keep human rights discourse from slipping too quickly into ahistorical abstraction. Human and cultural rights discourse must be supported by concrete cases of rights violations read in the context of systemic conditions and deep histories, and it can be supported by works of art that train our imagination not only to recognize what Susan Sontag called the pain of others but to construct legal, political, and moral remedies against the unchecked proliferation of such pain. Classical Greek tragedy first articulated this constitu-tive link between memory and rights: *Antigone* is a play not only about obliga-tions to the dead but about the rights of the living.

Memory and Cultural Rights

The issue of collective memory leads directly to the vexed ques-tion of cultural rights. To Cohen's account of three phases of human rights discourse since World War II, which I mentioned earlier, one might add a fourth dimension that has emerged in recent years. It concerns the transforma-tion of human rights discourse to highlight cultural rights claims pertaining to indigenous populations or descendants of slaves in Latin America, Canada, or Australia. And it also arises around civil and social rights in the wake of new forms of immigration and diaspora. While Cohen's third phase challenges tradi-tional notions of state sovereignty by allowing for cross-border interventions, this fourth dimension asserts claims of cultural group rights within sovereign nations but enters into conflict with the traditional notion of human rights as the rights of individuals and with a homogeneous self-understanding of nation-hood. Thus it further destabilizes notions of national identity, especially when civil, social, and sometimes even limited political rights are reasonably granted to noncitizen immigrants or when cultural rights are granted to indigenous peoples as long as those rights don't conflict with the law of the land, as in the Colombian Constitution of 1991.

Since cultural group rights are invariably invested in tradition and memory, this of course raises another question: can there be a legally enforceable right to cultural memory just as there is a right to free speech? It does not seem to make much sense to speak of a legally enforceable right to memory except perhaps in a context in which human beings might be technologically or geneti-cally manipulated to forget. Sci-fi films like *Blade Runner* and *Total Recall* have addressed such issues. Only in such a situation would it make sense to speak of a legal right to one's own memory.[12] Of course, in a certain dark view of global historical developments, as articulated in Horkheimer and Adorno's *Dialectic of Enlightenment* (1972) on the threshold between total war and the Cold War and long before genetic engineering, this kind of manipulation and the resulting destruction of memory was compellingly though reductively analyzed as the project of the capitalist culture industry and its consumerist ideology. It was a first, though over-the-top, theory of ADD (Attention Deficit Disorder), amnesia, and the loss of subjectivity in mass-media societies. The threat to memory would indeed be a threat to human identity itself—an identity always shaped by our embeddedness in a given time and place. Even if media of memory and the very place of memory in a culture will differ greatly over time and space, Luis Buñuel was right when he said: "You have to begin to lose your memory, if only in bits and pieces, to realize that memory is what makes our lives. . . . Our memory is our coherence, our reason, our feeling, even our action. Without it we are nothing" (Buñuel 1983, 4–5).

The right to memory could be interpreted as a right to maintain the culture or a tradition that makes a group's historical narrative relevant to its present way of life. As such, group memory can therefore be related to what has come to be known as cultural rights, which pose their own kind of problems. Some cultural rights, it should be said, are already reflected in several provisions of international human rights law (freedom of thought, conscience, and religion, Article 18; and freedom of expression, Article 19 of the UDHR). Cultural group rights are also implicitly recognized in the Genocide Convention of 1948 in light of the fact that genocidal policies often are preceded by attacks on an out-group's culture.[13] The notion of cultural rights, however, as it is now often articulated, does pose serious problems. Following rights theorists like Seyla Benhabib, I reject the notion that cultural rights can be separated from individual rights. Cultural and individual rights cannot be separated because individual autonomy, contrary to certain liberal beliefs, is not given by nature but emerges in reciprocal recognition of citizens embedded in a culture and engaged in social and political relations. All individuality is inherently social. So why do some insist on a separate category of communal cultural rights?

The cultural rights movement has arisen recently around issues of minority and first nations' rights within nation-states such as Canada and Australia, as well as within Colombia, Brazil, and other Latin American countries. It can be seen as an expression of the growing emphasis on cultural diversity in an increasingly interconnected world, and it is itself a transformation of earlier struggles, especially struggles for land rights that were formerly often couched in Marxist terms. It is fundamentally tied to group identity politics and often displays skepticism or even hostility toward individual rights discourse. A

Andreas Huyssen

major problem here is that cultural rights discourse often resonates ominously with the tradition of what colonialists called customary law. Its claims thus go back to lineal descent rather than responding to current needs. It can of course be seen as a legitimate reaction formation against globalization and the fearful prospect of cultural homogenization by financial capital, developmentalism, rampant consumerism, and global English. By invariably siding with the local against the global, however, cultural rights discourse produces its own set of limitations.

There is indeed a tendency to romanticize so-called non-Western forms of cultural diversity and to freeze-dry them in terms of cultural rights and traditional values. The irony here is that the very claim to cultural group rights, often posited against the privileging of individual rights, is itself articulated on the terrain of that very European tradition of rights some want to reject. And indeed, cultural group rights were already asserted in the very early Catholic articulations of natural law (school of Salamanca) that reflected the colonial encounter more than, say, the rights tradition that came out of the French or American revolutions. At any rate, today's struggles for rights (group or individual) across the world represent an active response to a situation that does not permit any escape from mutant modernities.

The problematic nature of cultural rights claims becomes especially visible when cultural rights are mobilized to make claims not on behalf of marginalized groups (First Nations of Canada, indigenous peoples in the Amazon) but on behalf of states and state power. This happens in the international arena with attempts to counter alien influence, whether Western influence in Islamic societies or the effects of Islamic presence in Western societies. And it happens within nations when cultural rights are called on for conservative purposes on behalf of a national culture vis-à-vis its immigrant communities. The recent German example of the *Leitkultur* debate is a good example of the latter and the European cultural claims against Turkish membership in the EU an example of the former. In both cases recognition of cultural diversity is turned against diversity itself in order to favor the dominant culture. These politically very different claims of cultural rights operate on the basis of an obsolete unitary notion of culture. All cultures affected by modernity are invariably split, whether such splits operate in vertical ways (high versus low, indigenous versus diasporic) or in terms of privileging different media (print versus orality, literature versus music). Such stratifications will always be a site for struggle over meanings and cultural self-understanding. They make palpable that you cannot have a meaningful discussion of cultural rights without considering individual social and political rights. Culture is not to be separated from the rights of the person or the rights of citizenship. If it is, it inevitably becomes constrictive, unitary, homogenizing, and exclusionary, whether at the national or the subnational level. Rather than overcoming the power problems inherent in national-majority cultures, cultural rights claims as articulated by subnational groups may just reproduce these problems in another register. I would argue that only if such claims do not posit some homogeneous and enforced collective memory can they have legitimacy.

And yet, with Benhabib (2002), I recognize the claims of culture, especially of language and the expressive values embedded in it, and I think that cultural rights must be reconciled with the broader category of human rights as rights of individuals. Anything else may lead to cultural oppression and legal relativism or worse. To construct an irreconcilable binary between universal human rights as rights of individuals only and cultural rights as the rights of ethnic or racial groups risks overruling the individual rights of group members in the name of culture. It would be equally unacceptable, however, to ignore all cultural group claims by limiting rights to autonomous individuals only, as if autonomy could exist outside social relations. Positing such a binary also reproduces the unproductive rift between liberal and communitarian or republican political theory rather than seeing the two as interrelated and in need of mediation. Let me highlight the problem by a simple example. Just as human rights include the right of exit from a nation or state, cultural rights must preserve the prerogative of an individual born into a culture to leave it and to choose another. This dimension, not sufficiently addressed by the proponents of cultural group rights, is especially pertinent to women and other disenfranchised people in societies or in ethnic or religious groups that ascribe inferior legal status to them. Cultural rights can be made productive as a springboard for social and political demands, but they become stifled if they remain at the level of identity compensation within continuing poverty and misery.

Cultural rights discourse shares another problematic dimension with memory discourse. It often assumes a homogeneous collective memory as it pits the rights of one group against those of another, most interestingly today in the claims of indigenous peoples against the dominant culture of the nation within which they live; it can even lead to a bifurcation between civil law and customary law, as in some Latin American countries, such as Colombia. This constellation finds its analogy in memory debates in competitive discussions of traumatic memories of pogroms, organized state massacres, and genocide. Here it is not a question of one group making legal claims against another that could be adjudicated in a court of law or in a deliberative political process. Memory culture is rather characterized by often vicious and resentful memory competitions that claim priority for one kind of traumatic memory over

Andreas Huyssen

another, thus creating insidious hierarchies of suffering (see Rothberg 2009). The most difficult and contested of such memory competitions is the one between Holocaust memory and the memories of colonialism, which seem separated today by what W. E. B. Du Bois in another context once called the color line. In debates about the politics of memory, we should try to avoid such vertical hierarchies of past sufferings in which one kind of memory tries to supplant another. Here memory discourse can learn from legal developments. The negotiation of indigenous rights within the framework of nation and constitution, as it has slowly evolved in Canada and Colombia, may indeed provide a theoretical model for reconciliation as opposed to irreconcilability and fierce competition. The task is to recognize a universal dimension in systemic oppression and human suffering rather than pitting one kind of memory against another. Both memory and rights discourse need to nurture a universalizing dimension that recognizes particularity without reifying it. Just as there is reciprocity between memory and the law, cultural and individual rights, we must also soften the boundaries between competing memories of suffering and persecution.

Can we then persuasively say that in our time memory politics and human rights are already more intimately connected than ever before? Indeed, it seems to be a mark of human rights discourse today that it feeds on memory discourse while often disparaging it. At the same time, memory discourse in the humanities often indulges in a facile critique of a Eurocentric or even imperial universalism of human rights. More mutual recognition would be salutary. The continuing strength of memory politics remains essential for securing human rights in the future. As much as its presence is essential for establishing human rights regimes where they do not yet exist, we cannot forget that memory may also nurture human rights violations just as human rights discourse is open to political abuse. But even where memory does support human rights, we may want to probe further. With the fading of the social and political utopias of the twentieth century—the imagined futures of fascism, communism, and global capitalist modernization—and the mountains of corpses that the dictatorships of that dark century have bequeathed to our remembrance, the struggle for righting past wrongs via redress or restitution claims is of a different order from the work in interpretive memory fields. In both, however, the belief that we can secure the past via interpretive or restitutional means may be as perilous an undertaking as attempts to secure the future via utopian projections. If human rights activism were to become a prisoner of the past and of memory politics, it would mean only that it will always have come too late. But if it becomes prisoner of some vague and abstract notion of globalization, the outcome will be equally problematic. Perhaps we have to remain content with understanding cultural memory and human rights as two stars that shed light on each other in the same galaxy but remain different in their trajectories toward historical justice.

Notes

This essay is a revised and expanded version of Andreas Huyssen, "International Human Rights and the Politics of Memory: Limits and Challenges," *Criticism* 53, no. 4 (2011): 607–24. Copyright © 2011 Wayne State University Press, adapted with the permission of Wayne State University Press. I thank Klaus Neumann and Janna Thompson for urging me to rethink and clarify parts of my earlier argument.

1. Some recent work by sociologists and political scientists has begun to explore the constitutive link between law and memory. See Booth (2001); Savelsberg and King (2007); Levy and Sznaider (2010). For an attempt to map a genealogy of memory discourses since the 1980s, see my book *Present Pasts* (Huyssen 2003), especially the title essay.

2. See also the superb account by Dieter Grimm (2009).

3. Here the work of René Cassin was crucial; see the magisterial biography by Antoine Prost and Jay Winter (2011).

4. Cohen (2012) then focuses on the proliferation since the 1970s of transnational human rights organizations and NGOs, such as Amnesty International and Human Rights Watch, which supplemented such domestic struggles within sovereign nations.

5. Teitel (2011) uses both "humanity's law" and "humanity law" without recognizable distinction.

6. I described and criticized this view in my work on Argentina (Huyssen 2003, 94–109).

7. On issues of restitution, see the influential work of Elazar Barkan (2000).

8. See also the powerful literary account by Antjie Krog (1999).

9. On the importance of economic justice, see Sen (2009).

10. Exceptions to this trend include Huyssen (2003); Levy and Sznaider (2006); and Rothberg (2009).

11. This usage does not quite agree with the definition of the term in Maurice Halbwachs's work. Halbwachs acknowledged different groups as carriers of different collective memories, but his framework remained the French nation. Projects to map *lieux de mémoire* (Nora 1984–92; François and Schulze 2001) are marked by the same national focus.

12. See Violi in this volume. I am not completely persuaded of the conceptual purchase of Spain's 2007 *Ley de memoria histórica*, even if I recognize that it may fulfill an important tactical role in Spain's coming to terms with the Civil War and the Franco dictatorship.

13. I cannot address here the problem of "cultural genocide," an ambiguous formulation in the early debates about genocide in Lemkin's (1944) work. See Clavero (2008); Rabinbach (2009, 43–73).

2

Reparative Claims and Theories of Justice

JANNA THOMPSON

The publication of John Rawls's *A Theory of Justice* more than forty years ago marked a high point in philosophical reflection on the nature of justice. Rawls offered what is commonly referred to as a theory of social justice. He provided principles for determining how basic goods of a society ought to be distributed among its members. These principles were meant to serve as a standard for making judgments about whether a society is just and for indicating what would have to be changed in order for it to become more just.

Rawls's theory belongs to a long tradition of liberal thought. In its approach to justice this tradition is forward looking. It tells us what we ought to aim to achieve. It gives us an ideal to strive for. Justice in this tradition is also what Robert Nozick (1974, 160–62) describes as "patterned." It provides a template for how things ought to be distributed. A deviation from this template counts as an injustice. According to Rawls's theory, inequality in the distribution of resources is justified only to the extent that it has the effect of improving the well-being of everyone, especially those groups that are least well off. If inequalities of wealth cannot be justified in this way, then they are unjust (Rawls 1971, 14–15).[1]

Liberals in the social justice tradition are not much concerned with history. How resources came to be distributed in an unjust way is not relevant to their theories. They may allow that it is sometimes necessary to pay attention to the history of an injustice in order to understand how their society can be made more just. But they deny that historical events should have an effect on the way that resources are distributed. What happened in the past cannot, for them, be a justification for disrupting the pattern dictated by requirements of social justice.

Since Rawls wrote *A Theory of Justice*, the intellectual climate has shifted. Social justice has lost much of its appeal, especially in the form of the egalitarian ideal of resources distribution favored by Rawls. On the other hand, demands for justice for historical wrongs have proliferated. Native peoples who demand the return of land that was unjustly taken from them, American blacks who want reparations for slavery, and victims of institutional childhood abuse who demand compensation payments are appealing not to requirements of social justice but to what they believe they are owed in rectification for a past injustice. Since many of the individuals and groups that make these demands suffer from disadvantages, obtaining what they demand would also serve the ends of social justice. But there is no necessity that this be so. Historical claims could also be made by people who are relatively advantaged. As Nozick points out, claims based on history have the potential to disrupt any pattern of distribution prescribed by social justice. But even when such claims do not come in conflict with requirements of social justice (at least as most people understand them), they are motivated by a different conception of what justice is and, behind that, different ideas about the needs of individuals and their social relationships.

This chapter is about the relation between justice as restitution for historical wrongs and social justice. It aims, first of all, to uncover reasons for the shift away from social justice and toward demands for repairing historical wrongs. In doing so it explains why historical justice has such a strong appeal. Second, it aims to show that both social justice and justice for historical wrongs must play a role in a wider conception of what justice is, and it considers how conflicts between them ought to be resolved.

Restitution for historical wrongs belongs to the general subject of reparative justice. All injustices require repair. A failure to distribute resources according to the requirements of social justice, whatever the reason, is an injustice that ought to be rectified, and if a group persistently fails to get its due this could count as a historical injustice. However, the injustices that I will be concerned with are injustices constituted by the deliberate causing of harm or disadvantage to particular individuals or groups—harm that almost everyone now recognizes as unjust: for example, stealing land and other resources, unjust discrimination, slavery, abuse, and exploitation. I concentrate on historical injustices because demands for restitution for historical wrongs are those that can challenge present distributions of resources—including those regarded as equitable.

The Rise of Historical Justice

The shift away from social justice means that demands that in earlier times were advanced as a means to achieve a fairer distribution of social resources are now frequently put forward as demands for repair of historical wrongs. For example, Gladys Ladson-Billings (2007) argues that more educational resources should be given to black students in American schools—not in order to make results between black and white students more equal but because black students are owed these resources as descendants of victims of historical injustice. The question raised by this development is why appeals to reparative justice have become more prevalent and attractive. Why do those who in earlier times might have rested their case on forward-looking appeals to requirements of social justice now favor an appeal to rectification of past wrongs?

The reasons for the decline of social justice as a motivating ideal are undoubtedly complex. Global pressures make it increasingly difficult for governments to fulfill requirements of social justice while exercising "fiscal responsibility" and preventing the flight of capital. Moreover, programs aimed at achieving social justice in the past few decades have not been as successful as many people had hoped. Despite affirmative action policies, black Americans continue to be underrepresented in universities, governments, and businesses and overrepresented in prison populations. Despite government programs, Aboriginal Australians continue to have a shorter life expectancy and much poorer educational outcomes than non-Aborigines. Jeff Spinner-Halev (2012) argues that the existence of enduring injustice—injustices that have proved resistant to attempts to achieve social justice—encourages a turn to history and demands for reparative justice.

Changes in social attitudes are also a source of this development. The ideal of social justice depends, as Rawls emphasized, on citizens valuing the relationships that enable them to maintain their political institutions and to produce economic wealth. Valuing their relationships with their fellow citizens and the good things that they achieve together is supposed to motivate individuals to accept a conception of social justice and to make sacrifices to achieve it. However, this source of motivation has been undermined—by global developments that loosen economic ties and interdependencies among citizens of nation states and by the philosophy of neoliberalism. Neoliberalism emphasizes the right of individuals to liberty, especially from the interference of governments. It encourages them to take responsibility for themselves and to believe that they deserve whatever they can acquire by exercising their talents. It predisposes them to regard political institutions and government-sponsored programs with suspicion. Neoliberalism has not done away with the belief that citizens have some kind of responsibility for one another's welfare. Social justice is not dead. But it has lost much of its force as a motivation for social action.

Along with neoliberalism has come the rise of human rights as the primary reference point for moral demands. The increased popularity of human rights discourse since the 1980s parallels the increasing emphasis on historical injustice and reparative demands. The rise of human rights is also implicated in the declining fortunes of social justice. Human rights are supposed to belong to individuals simply because they are human—and not because of their political affiliation. Human rights discourse emphasizes the value of individuals and their independence from others and from the bonds of their society, thus encouraging a move away from theories of justice that, like that of Rawls, are predicated on social bonds.

Human rights as a moral reference point also encourage and validate reparative demands. The violation of a human right is a serious injustice—one that calls for punishment of the violator and acts of repair. Moreover, reparative claims for violation of human rights do not require the acceptance of abstract, impersonal principles of justice. They focus on the particular history of an individual or a group: on what was done to victims and what is owed to them or their descendants as a consequence. Reparative claims are demands that individuals or groups are entitled to make because of a relationship that results from an injustice. The existence of this relationship puts pressing moral demands on perpetrators to take responsibility for what they have done. It gives victims firm grounds for demanding repair. The concreteness of this relationship—as opposed to abstract appeals to social justice—is one reason why appeals to reparative justice can be so powerful. It is why they are generally assumed to take precedence over other moral requirements—including requirements of social justice.

Historical Justice and Recognition

The current focus on reparative justice can also be understood as a manifestation of the demand for recognition that Axel Honneth (1995) and Charles Taylor (1994) identify as an important strand in contemporary politics and social life. A failure to treat other individuals with respect is, according to their accounts, a serious injustice. We can be disrespectful of others by denigrating them as persons—by treating them as inferiors. Indeed, all injustices involve a failure to be properly respectful of others as persons. Wrongdoers treat other people as mere means to achieve their own ends; they disregard others' welfare or regard it as less important than their own. Sometimes they

Janna Thompson

fail to regard the humanity of their victims altogether. Human rights are supposed to tell us what is required to respect human individuals and, by extension, the groups that they value. But Honneth and Taylor stress that agents can also fail to give others proper respect by not acknowledging and appreciating their differences: by failing to treat them as individuals who have values and characteristics that distinguish them from others, a history of their own, and an identity that depends on their relationship to particular others.

It is recognition in the second sense that plays a large role in many accounts of historical injustice. Japanese Americans who demanded and received reparation for their internment during World War II from the US government did not merely want compensation for their material losses. They wanted the injustice done to them to be officially acknowledged. Australian Aborigines who demand the return of their land or the bones of their ancestors are not merely claiming what they believe belongs to them. They also want recognition of their cultural traditions, their attachment to their land, and their relation to their ancestors. They want to be acknowledged as a people. Victims of childhood clerical abuse do not merely want a payment for what they suffered. They want their suffering to be recognized. They want the people or institutions responsible for the abuse to face up to the wrong that they did to them. To take recognition into account, reparative justice must be conceived not merely as restoration of rights and property or compensation for injury. It must be expanded to include acknowledgment of suffering caused by the injustice, apology from institutions or persons who did the wrong, and acts designed to restore relationships that were damaged by the injustice.

The identity of an individual—what kind of person she becomes and what she values and identifies with—is crucially affected both by her own history and the history of her community. Her own history consists not only of her own past decisions and actions but also of the relationships that have formed her. Annette Baier (1985, 85) makes this point by saying that individuals are "second persons." They are, she says, "essentially successors, heirs to other persons who formed and cared for them, and their personality is revealed both in their relations to others and in their response to their own recognized genesis."

Relationships of dependence affect psychological development and one's sense of self. They make it possible for individuals to learn how to function as capable, confident, and responsible persons. So if someone's development as a second person is marred by injustice—if she is abused or neglected by someone who is supposed to care for her, if those who are supposed to guide her development as a person abuse their trust, if she is denied a proper relationship with her parents and community—then the resulting harms are likely to have lasting effects on her development and her ability to function as a person. Even if she is not psychologically crippled, she is likely to have continuing feelings of resentment, insecurity, even shame about what she suffered. The past affects her present in a way that seems to demand a role for reparative justice. It is this perception that has led to widespread support for the reparative demands of individuals who suffered institutional abuse in childhood or who were forcibly removed from their parents and communities as the result of government policies.[2]

Individuals belong to communities: to families, clans, tribes, nations, religious and ethnic groups, and in many cases these relationships are central to their values and their identity as persons. Communal solidarity, as Honneth and Taylor stress, plays a central role in the lives of individuals and in their demands for recognition. It matters to them that they are Americans or Australians, that they are Aborigines belonging to a particular community, or that they are Catholics or people with a Greek ancestry. They understand who they are in terms of their group membership. Their ideals are shaped by their community. Though neither Honneth nor Taylor discuss the effect of a group's history on identity and individual development, the transgenerational nature of communities means that their triumphs and defeats, the sacrifices that past members have made for their sake and the injustices that have been done to them are bound to play a role in how present members understand themselves and their place in the world.

If the history of a community affects the sense of self of those who identify with it, then a failure to appreciate what a historical injustice means to them is a failure of proper recognition. But historical injustices done to a group can adversely affect the lives of members in other ways—even those who don't identify with their group. They can warp mainstream culture so that the descendants of victims continue to be looked down on and disadvantaged. They can undermine self-respect, stifle ambition, and make people feel that they are not accepted as full members of their society.[3]

The demand for recognition thus motivates people to be concerned about the past and how it has affected their development and the development of their communities. When the past contains injustices, then the demand for recognition becomes a demand that others acknowledge the injustice and the harm that it has done and that the perpetrators make appropriate recompense for it.

Social versus Reparative Justice

This analysis identifies two sources for the prevalence of reparative justice claims. The first is neoliberalism and the discourse of human rights, particularly the emphasis on the responsibility of agents not to violate rights and to repair the harm caused by violations. The second is the demand of individuals and communities for recognition of their particular identity and history. These two sources come from opposing philosophical perspectives. The appeal to what is owed to people as the result of a violation of their rights depends on entitlements that belong to individuals simply because they are human. It does not depend on who they are or on their relationship to others. This is why such appeals are congenial to those who accept a neoliberal conception of individuals as independent rights bearers whose activities should generally not be interfered with by governments or other agents. If unjust violations occur, then the victims ought to be restored to the full enjoyment of their rights—for example, by a return of possessions that were illegitimately taken.

The appeal to recognition of differences, on the other hand, stresses the dependence of individuals on others—on those who nurtured them and on those who share their communal identity. It stresses the ways in which individual identity depends on relationships with others. It emphasizes the social identity of individuals and how they acquire their values in association with others. Injustice, according to this perspective, is, above all, a failure of proper respect for these relationships and communities and the history that has produced them, and rectification must involve acts that acknowledge this wrong and repair the distrust, alienation, and enmity that are an inevitable effect.[4] Rectification, according to this perspective, places an emphasis on reconciliation— the achievement or restoration of respectful relationships. It presents a view of reparative justice that is congenial to communitarians and others who stress the central importance of communal bonds and relationships of trust.

Though these two perspectives are at philosophical odds with each other, the appeal of both can be traced to an outlook that rejects or has become pessimistic about the grand projects of liberal or socialist reformers—projects that put an emphasis on making progress toward a future in which resources and powers will be distributed according to a universally held conception of what is just. In the place of these projects and the ideas of justice that sustained them are individuals and groups that struggle for recognition and pursue their own interests and values. In this social environment, justice becomes a matter of respecting the right of individuals and groups to define and pursue their own ends in a world where there is no agreement on what ideals of social justice a society ought to achieve or no immediate prospect of achieving them.

This analysis raises a number of questions. Is the present emphasis on reparative justice sustainable? Is it likely to lead to an unmanageable plethora of reparative claims as more individuals and groups and subgroups see it to their advantage to identify injustices in their history for which they can demand rectification? Are these demands likely to become too onerous or impossible to fulfill? Is there any limit that can be put on who can make a claim or what kind of claim can be made?[5] I think that there are reasonable answers to all of these questions. However, behind these questions is a more fundamental issue: the role that rectification for historical injustices should play in a wider conception of justice. Is there a need for both social justice and reparative justice in an account of how societies should respond to historical injustice? And if so, how can their potentially opposing claims be reconciled? I will argue that any viable theory of how to respond to historical injustice must take both into account. But I will also explain why we are not going to be able to construct an overarching theory of justice that tells us how the claims of reparative and social justice should be brought together and adjudicated.

Reparation and Theories of Justice

There are theories of justice in which rectification plays a dominant role and social justice makes no appearance. There are also theories in which social justice is dominant and rectification has no role at all in cases where injustices are historical. A critical examination of these theories—and an appreciation of their inadequacies—will help us to understand why both kinds of justice must feature in any account of remedies for historical injustice.

According to Nozick's libertarian theory, individuals possess inalienable moral rights over their own person that give them an entitlement to reap the benefits of their actions and to use or transfer resources that they legitimately acquire (Nozick 1974, 171). No government or person is entitled to interfere with the exercise of these rights (except in dire emergencies). His conception of these rights of ownership means that governments are not permitted to transfer resources from wealthy to disadvantaged individuals in order to realize some conception of social justice. So justice depends entirely on whether possessions are in the right hands, and this depends on their history: on how they were originally acquired and how they were transferred from one agent to another. If somewhere in its history a possession was stolen or taken without consent, then justice requires that it be returned to the rightful owners or their heirs—or that they get a compensation of equivalent value if return is impossible. In principle there are no historical limits on the scope of rectification, though Nozick admits that his theory may be inapplicable when a multitude of historical injustices, one piled on top of the other, makes it difficult or impossible to determine who are the rightful owners (if anyone).

Those who put forward theories of social justice do not accept the conception of rights propounded by Nozick and other libertarians, and most do not accept his view that the right to property is a human right. They insist that

Janna Thompson

governments are entitled and obligated to distribute collectively produced goods of a society according to the requirements of social justice. People count as disadvantaged and thus as deserving of a greater share if what they have is less than what they should have according to standards of equity as defined by principles of justice such as those of Rawls.

Suppose, says David Lyons (1977), a group of outlaws invades an island and forcibly takes over the land and other possessions of the native people. Morality requires that the invaders give back what they have taken. Theft is an injustice in anyone's book, and it calls for rectification. But the passing of time and changes of conditions supersede requirements of rectification. Once an unrectified injustice has become a matter of history, what counts, in Lyons's view, is the situation of those who now inhabit the island. If changes wrought by time have brought about a just distribution of resources between the descendants of the outlaws and the descendants of the islanders, then the requirements of justice are satisfied. If they have not, then the descendants of the islanders can justifiably demand a remedy for the disadvantages they continue to suffer. But their demands ought to be understood as an appeal to social justice. According to Lyons's account they are owed a greater share of social resources because, and only because, they have less than they ought to have according to its requirements. Lyons intends the conclusion he draws from his imagined history to be applied to claims of Native Americans for the lands of their ancestors. Indians should get the land, he says, because this is a way of overcoming their disadvantages—not because they have a historical claim.

Nozick and Lyons have different and opposing views about justice. Nozick's theory is resolutely backward looking, and there is no statute of limitations on the demands of reparative justice. Lyons takes as his reference point objectives of justice that he thinks a society ought to achieve, and he insists that historical injustices are superseded by the demands created by these objectives. But there is one notable respect in which these theories are alike. They have nothing to say about injustice that is intrinsic to the failure to respect or the failure to appropriately recognize the individuality of a person or the identity of a group. This failure is not an accidental omission that can be easily rectified by an appropriate change to the theories. It points to serious problems in both of these approaches to justice.

Respect and Injustice

History plays the leading role in Nozick's theory, but it is history of a particular kind: the history of property, its acquisition and transfer. This means that the theory has nothing to say about rectification for injustices that do not involve violations of property rights or injustices for which there is no adequate compensation—injustices like genocide or torture. Compensation can be given for enforced enslavement—since this is a violation of the rights that a person has over her own body—but not for the disrespect, the violation of human dignity that is intrinsic to slavery. Land that was taken from native people can be restored and/or compensated for, but there is no room in Nozick's theory for repair of the harm done by a failure to recognize and respect the integrity and culture of an indigenous community.

The history of communal relationships, the way that victims and perpetrators understand a historical injustice and their relationship to each other, has no place in Nozick's theory. Reconciliation plays no role. Nor is it possible to amend the theory so that these things do have a place. To require, for example, that perpetrators show victims respect by acknowledging the wrong or apologizing for it has no point in a theory that insists that unjustly taken property ought to be returned to its rightful possessors, regardless of whether those who illegitimately possess it had anything to do with the injustice or even knew about it. The theory is about returning possessions, not about coming to terms with the past, paying respect to victims, or reconciling victims and perpetrators.

The narrowness of Nozick's theory has to do with his conception of rights-bearing individuals. Individuals appear in his theory as fully rational, self-interested, independent agents who pursue their own interests and have relations with others that depend on mutual consent. The ways in which individuals are shaped by their relationship with others and obtain their values as members of communities play no role in his account. Material things have histories that are essential to an understanding of them as possessions and to the rights and obligations of individuals. But individuals seem to have no history that is essential to the identity and value of the self that is the basis of his theory of rights. This seems a curious omission for someone who insists on the fundamental right of individuals to control their own persons. The identity of an individual and the value to him of his self can be marred or impaired by injustices in his history or in the history of his community. If the consequences of this history injure him, undermine his ability to make use of his talents, or destroy his confidence in himself, then this is surely a violation of his rights as a possessor—something that a theory of rights and rectification ought to take into account.

However, taking it into account would bring into the picture what Nozick and other libertarians want to leave out: the dependence of individuals on others, communal bonds, and the importance to people of their relationships. Once the social aspects of individual existence are featured, it becomes difficult to resist the inclusion of considerations of social justice. Interdependence, communal solidarity, and common concerns are reasons that people can be persuaded to accept requirements of social justice. Having a communal identity predisposes members to accept sacrifices for the sake of others in their group. Cooperation encourages an idea of fair shares. Communal bonds make people responsive to the needs of their fellows. Dependence encourages the construction of institutions and relationships that ensure that people can have their needs met.

Moreover, if reconciliation is allowed to play a role in an account of reparative responses to historical injustices, then it will be difficult to stick to a view of justice that leaves out considerations of welfare. The very idea of reconciliation is predicated on the assumption that former victims and perpetrators ought to aim to create a social world in which both can peacefully coexist. But this means that demands for rectification will have to be tempered by a consideration of the needs and interests of those who now possess what was unjustly expropriated. Recognizing that reparative claims have to take into account present needs does not require an abandonment of Nozick's central claim: that individuals have rights of property that ought to be respected. But it would require a different account of these rights, one that allows that property rights have to be modified and adjusted in cases where the welfare of others is at stake. It would require attention to the demands of social justice.

Like Nozick's theory, Lyons's account of what justice requires has nothing to say about rectification for failures of recognition. He assumes that justice depends only on the present situation of people on the island in his example: whether standards of social justice are now satisfied. But this is also a mistake. Even when the descendants of victims have nothing to complain of as far as social justice is concerned, it does not follow that they can make no legitimate claims. If they continue to care about their communal identity, their culture, and what happened to their ancestors, then they are likely to demand an acknowledgment from the government or the descendants of the perpetrators of the wrong that was done to their community. If social justice was accomplished without returning to the native people patrimony of importance to their community—their sacred sites, the burial grounds of their ancestors, or land that is particularly important to their history—then they are likely to regard the return of these things as a matter of justice. And they might also reason that the fact that their ancestors legitimately possessed the whole of the island gives them a claim that goes beyond the share given to them by the requirements of social justice. It is not obvious that this demand would be unjust.

If the worse scenario is realized—if the native people in Lyons's imagined example do not have their fair share—then the requirements of social justice are not satisfied. But what is likely to be uppermost in people's minds is that they continue to be denigrated and disadvantaged because of what happened in the past. They will see the injustice done to them in the present as a continuation of the injustice done in the past, and any attempt to deal with it will have to take this into account. Being just will involve confronting a history of injustice.

Repairing Accounts of Social Justice

A theory of social justice that discounts history—that ignores demands that people make because of historical wrongs or because of the continuing harms that result from these injustices—is inadequate. But some defenders of social justice think that they can repair this inadequacy without surrendering what is essential to their position: that reparative justice is superseded by the requirements of social justice when injustices are historical.

Jeremy Waldron (1992) allows that history plays an important role in forming a communal identity and recognizes that failure to acknowledge a historical injustice shows a lack of respect to members who care about their history and the wrongs done to their forebears. Showing appropriate respect requires acknowledging these wrongs and perhaps making a token form of restitution. But he does not think that victims of a historical injustice or their descendants are entitled to make reparative claims for lost resources. Injustices, he thinks, are superseded in the course of time and change and in the face of our lack of knowledge about what would have happened if an injustice had not been done.

His main argument for the supersession of historical injustice has to do with the value that a possession has for its owner. It not only gives him security; it also plays a role in his projects. It may be central to his way of life. So if it is stolen, this is a serious injustice, and the possession ought to be returned to him. But if the injustice is not undone and time passes, then it can no longer be central to his life. He or his descendants will have had to find another way of living. "If something was taken from me decades ago, the claim that it now forms the center of my life and that it is still indispensable to the exercise of my autonomy is much less credible" (Waldron 1992, 18–19). Meanwhile, the possession will have become central to the lives of people who might have had nothing to do with the injustice. To take it away from them would be a wrong.

Waldron deals with the damage to self-respect and communal identity that can be caused by injustice by recommending gestures of acknowledgment and reconciliation. Otherwise his position is the same as that of Lyons. What counts is social justice—the welfare of individuals of a society relative to one another. Demands of reparative justice cannot and should not be allowed to upset a state of affairs that counts as just according to these standards.

The assumption that people can and should be able to live a good life without long-lost possessions discounts what is of central importance to members of communities who treasure their sacred sites or want the bones of their ancestors to be returned. But the main problem with Waldron's account is that he regards injuries to respect and identity caused by historic injustice as a psychological problem that can be dealt with by token gestures. By doing so he underestimates the seriousness and extent of these injuries. People in groups that were done an injustice often suffer from what Spinner-Halev (2012) calls "enduring injustice." What happened in the past to members of a group continues to injure its members as the harm is passed down from one generation to the next. The disadvantages these inheritors of injustice suffer are not merely measured by theories of social justice. People who suffer from continuing injustice are likely to be alienated from mainstream society and distrustful of its institutions. Their ability to take advantage of what their society offers is often undermined by prejudice and a history of reduced expectations and discouragement. This means that attempts to overcome disadvantage by providing more resources are generally not an adequate solution. Finding a solution depends on taking the past into account; it requires a form of rectification that addresses a long-term failure of recognition as well as material disadvantages.

Spinner-Halev argues that much more drastic remedies are often needed to overcome historical injustices than Waldron allows. It might be necessary to give special privileges to members of groups suffering enduring injustices, to allow them more control over their own affairs, or to give them land or possessions that are particularly important to their cultural life. Some of these measures, he admits, are likely to go against ideas of social justice, but they can be justified as a way of overcoming disadvantages that liberal reforms have not succeeded in removing. The end goal is to remove disadvantage and thus finally to achieve social justice—so far as this is possible. Spinner-Halev's position is similar to that of those who advocate affirmative action on the ground that a temporary departure from liberal ideas of fairness—giving special advantages to members of a disadvantaged group—serves the purpose of making society more just in the future. But he insists that more drastic remedies may be required and is not so optimistic about the possibility of ever achieving social justice. Liberal justice, he says, "will not fully unfold in a clear and obvious fashion" (Spinner-Halev 2012, 17). Nevertheless, he is in the company of Lyons and Waldron in his rejection of reparative justice for historical wrongs. In his view, individuals or groups are not owed reparation for wrongs of the past, and no one has a responsibility for making reparation for these wrongs.

Historical Injustice and Intergenerational Relationships

Those who reject historical obligations and entitlements can allow that people care about their communal history and that they can be severely damaged by it. They can insist that these bad effects of history give others in a liberal society the duty to acknowledge wrongs done and to alleviate the harm, as do Waldron and Spinner-Halev. But they do not think that people have obligations or entitlements that come from history—at least not from history beyond their lifetimes. Underlying this view are some questionable assumptions about individuals, their relations to others, and how they acquire moral obligations.

Those who reject historical entitlements and obligations seem to accept the liberal idea of the individual as someone who ought to be able to determine the goals for her life and to effectively pursue them. Having a damaged self or belonging to a damaged group is a bad thing because it prevents an individual from being self-determining and from developing and pursuing worthwhile goals. But the view plays down or regards as problematic the way that communal life can form people's values or become central to what they regard as a good life. These liberals deny the reasons why the need for recognition plays such a central role in the claims of individuals and groups. Those who deny historical obligations also seem to assume that obligations and entitlements arise only from relationships that people have with their contemporaries: from the projects they engage in with their fellows, from their commitments, and from the way they treat one another. This view ignores the possibility that they might acquire obligations and entitlements in respect to past people or their deeds.

What these assumptions leave out is the moral importance to many people of intergenerational relationships. The assumption that individuals are or should be concerned with formulating and fulfilling goals for their own lives not only plays down the importance of their communal bonds; it also tends to ignore objectives that transcend their lives. People can and often do have concerns that span generations. They value some of the things they received from their predecessors and want to pass them on to their descendants. The heritage that they value and want to preserve can take many forms, depending on their interests and the nature of their community. It may be the institutions of their

Janna Thompson

society that they value or a tradition, a religion, artifacts of certain kinds, land that has a meaning to their community, an ideal that their ancestors fought and died for, or simply memories about people and events in the past. That people have such desires is not surprising. If members of an intergenerational community value its existence or at least some of the things that it has achieved, then they are likely to want to maintain these values for their successors. And along with this desire goes a sense of obligation—not merely an obligation to provide things of value to future generations but also an obligation to past generations: to remember their deeds, to honor their sacrifices, to carry on their work of maintaining a heritage. When people think of themselves as participants in the intergenerational project of maintaining a valued heritage, they are predisposed to believe that they have obligations in respect to other participants, past and future.

To people who are embedded in intergenerational relationships, historical injustices to their family or community are not merely a cause of psychological harm or continuing disadvantage; they also give rise to a belief in the existence of moral entitlements and obligations. Members are predisposed to believe that they have a duty to remember the injustice and the harm done to their ancestors, to remember and continue the struggle to have the injustice repaired. They believe that they have an entitlement to reparation from those who did the wrong. These beliefs about obligations and entitlements and resulting ideas about self-respect and honor are manifested in many struggles for reparation. "We are lesser Aborigines if we don't get these remains back," said Michael Mansell, the leader of the campaign for the repatriation of ancestral bones of Tasmanian Aborigines (quoted in Cove 1995, 161).

If historical injustices give rise to obligations and entitlements in the present, then they are not superseded by time or change. They continue to motivate demands of justice. Those who support supersession must either deny that these obligations and entitlements really exist or argue that reparative demands, however well motivated, cannot be fulfilled because no individual or group has a responsibility for fulfilling them. A denial of their existence goes against what many people strongly believe and for that reason alone is hard to accept. Moreover, these ideas of obligation and entitlement come from participation in an intergenerational project or ideas about what each generation ought to do for its predecessors and successors. To deny that these duties exist is to deny what is fundamental to most theories of social justice: the assumption that cooperation gives rise to duties of justice. We can allow that not every belief in the existence of moral obligations is a true belief. Communities can have intergenerational projects that are morally questionable. In these cases, intergenerational cooperation does not give rise to moral obligations, whatever members might think. But given that there is nothing morally wrong with the project or the heritage that members regard themselves as duty bound to pass on to their successors, there is no reason to deny the existence of the intergenerational obligation.

The denial that present people have reparative responsibilities for historical injustice is motivated by the belief that it is wrong to make innocent individuals pay for injustices done by their forebears. But even if this is true, it does not follow that they cannot acquire reparative debts as members of an intergenerational community. If members can gain responsibilities by being participants in an intergenerational project, then there is nothing implausible or morally questionable in supposing that they should take responsibility for past wrongs committed in pursuit of that project. If, for example, the project is to maintain institutions of justice (as Rawls and many liberal philosophers suppose), then it seems reasonable to suppose that present members of a society have a duty not only to pass on these institutions to their successors and to honor their forebears for the sacrifices they made for the sake of creating and maintaining them but also to acknowledge and repair the historical failures of these institutions to be just.

Reconciling Reparative and Social Justice

I have argued that both social justice and reparative justice should figure in attempts to deal with the consequences of historical injustice. Reparative demands are based upon defensible and often compelling ideas about intergenerational obligations and entitlements. On the other hand, attempts to remedy historical injustice have to attend to the needs and interests of present people, including those who are the beneficiaries of past wrongs. Reparative and social justice must find a way of coexisting in cases where injustices are historical.

How can forms of justice that have such different justifications and that make different and sometimes incompatible demands be brought together? Appeals to justice based on history, as we have seen, have the potential to upset any pattern established by the requirements of social justice. Returning resources that were taken away in past generations can upset the reasonable expectations of those who now possess them. Giving to members of a group the privileged treatment required to overcome a history of failure of recognition may violate deeply held ideas of fairness. Can such conflicts be resolved?

Most philosophers who construct theories of justice aim to produce an account that can, in principle, resolve all disputes about justice. Rawls's

Janna Thompson

influential theory set the standard by providing an order of priority for his principles of justice so that conflicts between them could always be resolved. Those who adhere to this standard resist the idea that there could be a conflict between different demands of justice that cannot be adjudicated by an overarching theory. One possible solution is to subordinate one conception to the other without denying the existence of either. We could lay it down that the requirements of social justice apply only when there are no justifiable reparative claims that have to be met. Or we could insist that reparative claims should never be allowed to disrupt the pattern dictated by requirements of social justice but that a liberal society ought to give those who suffer from historical injustice priority over others in any program for removing social disadvantages.[6] The main problem with these attempted solutions is that they are arbitrary. Why should requirements of social justice dominate over reparative claims or vice versa when both conceptions of justice have strong moral justifications? But if there is no reason why one should be systematically favored over the other, then the prospect of conflict remains.

It is worthwhile to point out that conflicts of this kind arise in other, closely related areas of social and political life. Laws and customs that allow individuals to make bequests to particular members of the succeeding generation are also a problem for those who advocate social justice. Inheritance tends to concentrate wealth. In the worst case, it can lead to most of the resources of a society being controlled by a few families. Those who advocate social justice have good reasons to object to inheritance. On the other hand, recognizing a right to bequest and inheritance answers to the moral concerns of individuals as participants in intergenerational relationships. It acknowledges that people have interests that transcend their own lifetimes. It recognizes that many people labor not just for themselves but also for their families and are predisposed to think that they have a duty to pass on something of value to those they love. It allows that people can have projects central to the meaning of their lives that they want their successors to inherit.

In practice, the conflict between demands of social justice and rights of bequest and inheritance is settled by a compromise that depends on the traditions of a society, the balance of political forces, and existing conditions and problems. People can make judgments about what compromises are better or worse in particular social and political circumstances, but there is no overarching theory of justice to tell us how to strike a balance between social justice and the justifiable desire of individuals to benefit their heirs.

The same is true of the conflict between social justice and rectification for historical wrongs. Theories of justice tell us why each is morally important. Reflection tells us that one cannot be sacrificed or subordinated to the other.

We are unlikely to find a general principle of justice that tells us how to resolve any conflicts that might occur. But this simply means that we have to shift our attention from efforts to put forward general principles to an attempt to work out what counts as a satisfactory compromise in particular circumstances and how it should be reached. Reaching a compromise that all or most people can regard as fair requires dialogue between the affected parties; it requires an appreciation of each other's interests and an understanding of why history can be the basis for reparative claims.

Notes

1. Rawls (1971) also says that liberty and opportunity ought to be equal for all citizens.

2. These were harms described by survivors of the child removal policy practiced by Australian states up to the mid-twentieth century. See Commonwealth of Australia (1997). Not every victim of a serious injustice is subject to continuing harm, but the government inquiries in recent years into child abuse in institutions, forced child migration, and other wrongs indicate that these effects are common.

3. Randall Robinson (2000) argues that these lingering effects of historical injustice are the main cause of the disadvantages suffered by the black population of the United States.

4. For an important discussion of this approach to injustice, see Walker (2006b).

5. Opponents of reparative justice usually emphasize the difficulties of interpreting and applying it, particularly in cases of historical injustice (see, for example, Vernon 2012). These criticisms must, of course, be answered, but in this chapter I deal with what is often the underlying motivation for opposition to reparative appeals: a preference for social justice.

6. I argued for this solution in chapter 6 of *Taking Responsibility for the Past* (Thompson 2002).

3

The Political Field of Reparations

JOHN TORPEY

As a result not least of the reparations paid and the enormous amount of memory work done in connection with the destruction of the European Jews during World War II, the idea of "coming to terms with the past" has in recent years come to be regarded as a crucial element of progress toward more satisfactory and more democratic political and social relationships. In connection with this broader trend toward "coming to terms with the past," there has also emerged a widespread expectation that what are called "reparations" are due to those who have been wronged by states and other entities in the past.

To anyone familiar with twentieth-century European history or with foreign affairs generally, it will immediately be clear that the use of the term "reparations" here involves a novel departure. Before the past couple of decades at most, in international affairs the term "reparations" referred to obligations incurred by a party to war that were to be paid to another country as compensation for the damages caused during the conflict. The contemporary usage of the term to designate efforts to repair gross violations of people's human rights is thus quite new and reflects important changes in the way in which we think about human social life.

In what follows, I want to consider the prevalence today of the demand for reparations for human rights violations and what that demand has come to entail. I then want to explore several causes of this development. My main claim here is that the emergence of the expectation of reparations for violations of human rights results from the post–World War II *juridification* of international affairs—the spreading transformation of international political questions into legal ones. The notion of juridification must be understood broadly—not merely as the use of legal venues strictly speaking but involving as well all sorts of quasi-judicial institutions, such as truth and reconciliation commissions, historical tribunals charged with establishing contentious facts, international criminal tribunals, and the like. In analyzing the juridification of international affairs, I examine developments in the four realms of "social power" identified by Michael Mann (1986, 1993): the ideological, the economic, the military, and the political. I conclude by asking where we may be heading with regard to reparations claims making and the achievement of human rights claims more broadly.

The Institutionalization of the Idea of Reparations for Gross Violations of Human Rights

The contemporary prevalence of the idea of "reparations" is reflected, among many other places, in the Chinese "Charter 08," a document propagated in 2008 by China's liberal community that advances many demands for a more democratic political order governed by the rule of law. In language that will sound familiar from other contexts, Charter 08 calls for "Truth in Reconciliation": "We should restore the reputations of all people, including their family members, who suffered political stigma in the political campaigns of the past or who have been labeled as criminals because of their thought, speech, or faith. The state should pay reparations to these people. . . . There should be a Truth Investigation Commission charged with finding the facts about past injustices and atrocities, determining responsibility for them, upholding justice, and, on these bases, seeking social reconciliation" (Link 2009).

Clearly, these are all very radical demands in contemporary China, as they imply a reckoning with perhaps the greatest famine in world history during the so-called Great Leap Forward, with the atrocities associated with the Cultural Revolution, and with the killings and arrests arising from the 1989 protests at Tiananmen Square. And although demands for coming to terms with the past are by no means always successful in democracies, it is only in democracies that one can reasonably expect them to be realized. In short, these demands are not likely to be fulfilled in China anytime soon.

The varied elements of the demand for coming to terms with the past in the Chinese Charter 08 remind us that the UN definition of "reparation"—

not *reparations*—has a number of different dimensions. The Basic Principles and Guidelines on the Right to a Remedy and Reparation for Victims of Gross Violations of International Human Rights Law and Serious Violations of International Humanitarian Law (to which I will henceforth refer as the "Guidelines"),[1] adopted after years of discussion in December 2005, envision that victims of these wrongs should have a right to "reparation," which can take the following forms:

- restitution
- compensation
- rehabilitation
- satisfaction
- guarantees of non-repetition

Note that only two of these have anything to do with economic considerations; even "restitution," as the UN defines it, has relatively little to do with money. That term is defined in the Guidelines as "restoration of liberty, enjoyment of human rights, identity, family life and citizenship, return to one's place of residence, *restoration of employment* and *return of property*." "Rehabilitation" mainly refers to the provision of necessary medical, legal, and social services; "guarantees of non-repetition" refers to institutional changes that would militate against repeat offenses. The more elusive notion of "satisfaction" involves a range of measures including establishment and publicization of the facts behind the injustices; the clearing of the names of those unjustly victimized; apologies; and the commemoration of victims. Truth commissions—those much-heralded vehicles for coming to terms with the past—would thus generally fall under the rubric of "satisfaction." Such bodies have assumed an iconic status in efforts to come to terms with the past and to make reparation for past injustices and have spread to many parts of the world (see Hayner 2011). There has even been an attempt by religious leaders to create a truth commission in the United States to call attention to the economic harms done by the recent (and ongoing) financial crisis.

In short, the terms "reparation" and "reparations" have a variety of meanings in international law and human rights parlance, only a relatively small proportion of which have to do with monetary compensation. This fact is consistent with the claim that is frequently made by those seeking reparations that "it's not about the money." For many such claimants, the noneconomic forms of reparation would suffice. Nonetheless, the term "reparations" has come to be widely associated with monetary compensation for some past wrongdoing. This is certainly true in the United States, where "reparations for slavery" are generally assumed to involve some sort of monetary reparations. Indeed, the advocates of reparations for black Americans have been chiefly focused on the economic consequences of slavery and segregation and hence on the way in which reparations might improve the situation of the most economically disadvantaged blacks in America today. The campaign has little to do with any of the noneconomic aspects of "reparation." This is an anomaly from the standpoint of the broader field of reparations claims making, which tends to involve persons still alive today who have suffered injury at the hands of states or other entities and who are seeking amends from the state or other parties. The "reparation" to which the Guidelines refer is meant primarily for *living victims* of maltreatment, not the descendants of those who suffered injustices and who seek compensation for the wrongs done to their relatively long-dead ancestors. Yet this case of reparations claims making reflects the ways in which the iniquitous past may be said to persist into the present. Such cases pose difficult dilemmas in a context in which individuals may ultimately have to be compensated, often on the basis of varying criteria, even if their claim arises from group membership of some sort.

The Juridification of International Affairs and Its Sources

Where did all this reparations talk come from? Notwithstanding the variety of contexts that have given rise to demands for reparations, they all reflect a broader tendency to transform political life into legal forms. This tendency was perhaps first identified by Alexis de Tocqueville in his famous travelogue about life in America. In the first volume of his classic study *Democracy in America*, Tocqueville (2000, 257) wrote that "there is almost no political question in the United States that is not resolved sooner or later into a judicial question." While this may have been true in the United States when Tocqueville wrote it, the trend did not take serious hold in the rest of the world until the post–World War II period, in connection with the creation of the United Nations and its quasi-governmental apparatuses and especially since the end of the Cold War. But since then it has done so with great rapidity. The legal scholar Karen Alter (2012) has observed that in 1989 there were six permanent international courts, whereas there are now more than twenty-five that have collectively issued more than twenty-seven thousand binding legal rulings. For example, a special international court recently convicted Charles Taylor, the former president of Liberia, for war crimes and crimes against humanity during his brutal campaign in Sierra Leone in the 1990s. There have been many indictments of leading war criminals, such as those responsible for the atrocities in Bosnia in the 1990s and the Sudanese leader Omar Bashir for atrocities in Darfur, but Taylor was the first head of state convicted of such crimes. These are among the diverse phenomena that constitute the juridification of international affairs; clearly, the list could be multiplied many times over by invoking the names of international courts, criminal tribunals, international administrative courts, and the like.

How did this process of juridification happen? I want to consider several factors: ideological, economic, military, and political.

Ideological Factors

In 1898 the sociologist Émile Durkheim argued in the context of the Dreyfus affair that a "cult of the individual" had emerged in modern society. Yet he was not referring to the "individualism" that his compatriot Tocqueville feared might undermine the common good in America; instead, the cult of the individual referred to the exaltation of the human person qua person. "Whoever makes an attempt on a man's life, on a man's liberty, on a man's honor," Durkheim (1973, 46) wrote, "inspires in us a feeling of horror analogous in every way to that which the believer experiences when he sees his idol profaned." Indeed, despite Tocqueville's concerns about the problem of individualism in America, he, too, had seen that the breakthrough of a more autonomous individual as a move away from traditional forms of social organization would lead to new forms of human solidarity. That is, there would be less loyalty to individual persons, as in feudalism, and more to humanity as a whole (Tocqueville 2000, 535–39). One might see this vision of a new, more general kind of solidarity among humans as the secularization of the Christian idea of universal human salvation; there is surely some of that involved. In all events, that idea entailed the notion of the sanctity of the person and the right to be secure in one's person. In other words, it entailed the idea of human rights.

The idea of human rights was at the heart of the French Revolution and its Declaration of the Rights of Man and Citizen, which suggested that the rights of French people and the rights of human beings as such could be enunciated in the same document. On the basis of Europe's experience during World War II, however, Hannah Arendt (1958) insisted that human rights were nothing unless enforced by a state (even if it is also true that human rights violations and crimes against humanity frequently occur with impunity as long as they remain within the borders of a given state). Some states do endorse those values within their own borders and promote them at least rhetorically outside those borders. But states always have their own parochial interests.

What came into existence to transcend the particular interests of states was an intergovernmental quasi state—the United Nations—and, in due course, a panoply of quasi-judicial institutions that promoted what is typically known as "soft law." Soft law involves largely unenforceable statements and principles concerning desired states of affairs with regard to individual treatment and well-being in the world. The Guidelines on Reparation for Gross Violations of Human Rights is such a statement. Such documents can do relatively little to bring about these desired states of affairs, but they constitute a standard for shaming those reprobates that fail to live up to them. But these statements and principles constitute an important part of the climate of international opinion today. As leader of a country with a seat at the United Nations, one normally wishes to be seen as a member in good standing of the international community, which presupposes adherence to the norms of democracy, the rule of law, and respect for human rights. And while some may regard the present and the future as the only relevant time periods for achieving human rights, many have looked to the past as the source of contemporary inequalities and injustices and have sought to fix the present by way of the wrongs of the more or less distant past. The fact, of course, is that these apparently distinct periods meld into one another in ways that make them and their consequences difficult to disentangle, opening the door to claims making about what may seem to some to be long-forgotten events.

Economic Factors

The major economic shift that has promoted the ideas of human rights and reparations has been the transition from a predominantly industrial to a postindustrial society. Industrial society, particularly in its Fordist variant, involved the creation of large factories into which substantial numbers of more or less interchangeable personnel were inserted. Industrial conflict thus typically took the form of unions grouping together massive numbers of workers who were arrayed against the employers of their labor power contesting wages, working conditions, and the like. Notwithstanding their elimination of labor markets, Soviet-type societies largely followed this basic framework of organization and indeed were typified by huge industrial combines that also served a variety of their workers' needs, from child care to burial arrangements. By 1989 this Fordist model was buried as it came under challenge from a service economy in which tiny bits of gadgetry would soon transform the way people lived their everyday lives.

The electronic/microchip revolution overwhelmed the mass-production economy, at least mentally speaking, and turned everyone into his or her own center of communications. Computerization strengthened the drive toward individualization that was widely observed to have accompanied the decline of factory employment. The shift to computers and the Internet thus facilitated a significant hollowing out of earlier ideas about working-class solidarity and economic justice. Now, it seemed, everyone was (or was expected to be) a consultant, a freelancer, or an entrepreneur. The middle-class "golden age" (Hobsbawm 1994) that had attended postwar Fordist and Keynesian socioeconomic arrangements came under assault by employer organizations and conservative think tanks in the United States and elsewhere, leading to the global predominance of the so-called Washington Consensus concerning the desirability of free-market principles and practices. Instead of enjoying the well-being once made possible by collective-bargaining agreements, workers were increasingly thrown back on themselves. Increasingly it was the new idea, the new device, the new app that generated wealth. Having intellectual capital and making it pay became the order of the day. All of this rendered individuals more exposed to markets and more dependent on their services, even for some of their most intimate needs (Hochschild 2012).

Against this background, human rights and the idea of reparations as compensation for past wrongs resonated with a broader neoliberal and individualistic mindset that has dominated the sensibilities of educated elites for the past three decades and more. Insofar as monetary reparations are the aim, the idea of reparations for historical injustices fits in with a broader legalistic outlook that assigns values on the basis of individual "desserts" rather than on the basis of membership in a community as such. It also harmonizes with the general trend in policing toward "victim's rights," which reflect a broader shift away from public notions of justice and toward more private ones (see Garland 2001, 11–12). This is emphatically not to say that the idea of reparations for past injustices is a bad thing but simply to assert that it is part of a wider trend toward a thinner conception of national citizenship.

Many reparations claims makers are of course defined as members of groups—indigenous peoples, victims of overseas colonialism, the descendants of slaves—and may seek nonmonetary objectives from their former tormentors rather than money. Yet money is often the medium through which amends are made, simply because there may not be any other way to set things right if lands have been taken, people killed, or cultures disrupted. The interned (incarcerated) Japanese Americans wanted (and got) an apology from the US government for their mistreatment during World War II, but they also got $20,000 per person as a way of demonstrating that the United States was serious about righting this wrong.

Military Factors

With regard to military developments, the decisive transition has been that from mass conscription to a combination of rarely used nuclear weapons and highly professionalized commandos combined with unmanned or abstract forms of conflict (e.g., drones and cyberwarfare). The French Revolution introduced the *levée en masse*, the idea that it was the obligation of every French *citoyen* to defend the revolution against its antagonists. The idea of a militia recruited from the citizenry thus came to be the norm for modern nation-states. Yet World War II, the last military conflict involving huge numbers of soldiers fighting interstate wars of conquest, ended in one theater in a defeat of conventional forces and in the other with the use of atomic weapons of unprecedented exterminatory power. Ever since, the world has been preoccupied with the problem of "nuclear proliferation" on one hand and with civil and "guerrilla" wars on the other. From Vietnam to Yugoslavia, Rwanda, and the larger Middle East, *inter*state warfare has declined notably in favor of the spread of various kinds of "internal" wars.

In the more developed parts of the world, therefore, conscription has increasingly been abandoned, with the result that the more comfortable members of these societies can scarcely imagine participation in military life. Meanwhile, the inhabitants of the world's poorer precincts are often exposed to the depredations of warlords and forced impressment into military service or are rented out as policemen for the international community. The general result is that war as we have traditionally known it has become an activity conducted by the world's poor and less educated, fighting it out over better grazing lands, profitable minerals, control of smuggling routes, or the old-fashioned spoils of government. War and the atrocities that frequently accompany them increasingly appear bizarre and incomprehensible to those located in the world's more prosperous and democratic countries. In this context, the notion that one ought to be compensated for pointless suffering may seem to go without saying to those who think such things far off and barbaric. The fact that reparations for victims of human rights violations are often hard to come by in those places where war and atrocities are endemic doesn't necessarily enter the discussion. One hopes that they might be made more accessible to victims, but it is not always clear how this is going to happen if the wherewithal is lacking to fund the various programs associated with reparations claims.

Political Factors

One major political factor overwhelms all others with regard to the spread of the idea of human rights norms and reparations as compensation for past wrongdoing—namely the geopolitical dominance of the United States in post–World War II global affairs. Unlike the British and the French, the postwar United States was not burdened with an extensive colonial empire with many grievances against its soon-to-be former colonial master. The United States could thus support decolonization, not least on the basis of its own heritage as a revolutionary, postcolonial state. The United States was also crucial to the creation of the United Nations and, in a reflection of the emerging Cold War rivalry, helped persuade the United Nations to reject Soviet efforts to tie the definition of genocide more closely to Nazi atrocities (Novick 1999, 100). The idea of genocide as outlined by Raphael Lemkin (1944) thus received much greater attention than it might have had the Soviet Union had greater influence in world affairs. Still, the Soviet challenge led the United States to behave better with regard to racial inequality than it would otherwise have done, although the granting of civil and political rights was not accompanied by reparations in the sense usually intended (i.e., leaving aside "affirmative action" measures) (Dudziak 2002). The post-Soviet era of even more untrammeled American dominance led to the opening of archives that made possible further inquiry into World War II and other pasts, which in turn stimulated a variety of demands for coming to terms with unsavory pasts, especially in the former Communist world.

Another aspect of the importance of American dominance to the spread of human rights and reparations claims making has been that international campaigners for reparations have taken advantage of the receptivity of American courts to lawsuits arising from actions that took place elsewhere. For example, the Alien Tort Statute, which allows US courts to hear suits for heinous crimes that may have taken place anywhere in the world, has been a crucial tool in this regard. Nigerian activists persecuted for their opposition to Shell Oil's activities took advantage of the statute to promote a settlement when their leader, Ken Saro-Wiwa, was killed in the 1990s (see Mouawad 2009; Weiss 2012). None of this is to say that the United States has been by any means perfect in terms of its record on human rights, and it has often had to be forced to live up to commitments it expected rhetorically of other countries but failed to meet itself.

American influence in the world is waning, however, and the United States now confronts a world with many different regional centers of power and attraction (Kupchan 2012). With growing pressure for a rebalancing of the Security Council to reflect this changing reality, there is every reason to think that there will in coming years be greater parity in international decision making, with countries such as the BRICs (Brazil, Russia, India, and China) acquiring increasing sway in global councils. But, as we have seen in the case of the Syrian rebellion, a possible global order dominated by Russia or China is not likely to be one in which human rights or reparations for past injustices receive much attention. The widespread support for human rights among European countries certainly helps sustain the human rights revolution and, with it, the pressure for reparations in particular cases. But Europe's influence remains limited compared to America's and is likely to do so for the foreseeable future—with the exception of human rights standouts such as Norway and Denmark.

The Future of Reparations

The foregoing discussion demonstrates that there are some very deep sources of the new expectation of reparations for victims of gross violations of human rights. The notion is now institutionalized, at least at the level of UN soft law. The term has become widely familiar—if not always a matter of enthusiasm—among scholars, NGO activists, and politicians. Yet the juridification of politics is not necessarily solidly entrenched or irreversible. There is little doubt, for example, that the campaign for reparations for slavery in the United States suffered a grievous blow with the attacks of 11 September 2001. While that campaign had begun to garner significant national attention, Americans' concerns quickly shifted to Al Qaeda and the greater Middle East and away from matters of domestic historical injustices. Little has been heard from the movement since. Yet that is a matter of American domestic politics; 9/11 hardly derailed the spread of reparations claims making globally, as reflected in the 2005 adoption of the UN Guidelines on Reparation for Gross Violations of Human Rights.

Still, this example suggests the problem with the juridification of politics: it has the vice of its virtues. That is, juridification shifts political questions to courts or court-like venues, and, while courts may help pacify otherwise violent conflict, courtrooms and UN hearing rooms are intrinsically the province of elites who may or may not represent a broader constituency. The point is often made with regard to reparations for black Americans that the courts have been a crucial venue in which blacks' interests have been promoted; activists seeking monetary reparations have argued that a court decision in their favor could help spark a broader legislative push. Yet so far there has been relatively little popular political support for the idea of reparations for blacks, no doubt in part because of the complexities inevitably associated with the distribution of compensation. One may doubt that the new National Museum of African American History and Culture on the Mall in Washington, DC, will mollify those concerned primarily with fixing racial inequality.

In cases of mass atrocities, the problem is often one of establishing mechanisms for reparation in places that are rebuilding war-torn economies or attempting to create a functioning political or judicial system of their own. Some have argued in the aftermath of the Charles Taylor decision that it would have been better to try Taylor in Africa than far off in the Hague. They also point to the enormous sum spent on the trial—$250 million over many years—that might better have been spent on rebuilding Sierra Leone. Most problematic, the decision has prompted renewed criticism of the "international community" for selective prosecution of miscreants. Critics noted that prosecutions of other leaders involved in the conflict that might be antagonistic to American interests would have resulted in the cutoff of US funding for the special court, notwithstanding America's historical role in helping to establish some of these mechanisms.

While elections are sometimes stolen, to be sure, there is always the danger that justice, too, may be tainted by the preferences of the powerful. The juridification of international politics has helped establish the notion that victims of gross violations of human rights deserve reparations of various kinds. But it cannot necessarily enforce that notion very effectively, and claims for reparations that may appear to be straightforwardly deserved are in fact always a matter of political contestation. The spread of legal mechanisms for handling international conflict and past wrongdoing constitutes an advance in human affairs. But we shouldn't imagine that these mechanisms are something other than a continuation of politics by other means.

Note

1. It should be borne in mind that, as is often the case in the contemporary human rights paradigm, the principal drafters of such documents have been lawyers, and this is very much reflected in the language and outlook of the relevant documents and institutions. Although long advanced by the Dutch human rights lawyer Theo van Boven, what came to be the Guidelines were long known as "the Bassiouni principles," after their proponent, law professor Cherif Bassiouni.

4

How the Past Matters

On the Foundations
of an Ethics of Remembrance

JEFFREY BLUSTEIN

In July 1942 the French police, acting under orders from France's Nazi occupiers, carried out a mass roundup of more than thirteen thousand non-French Jews from the streets of Paris and detained them in a bicycle-racing stadium, the so-called Vel' d'Hiv, for several days in deplorable conditions. From there they were deported to death camps in the East, from which all but about one hundred would never return. For decades after the war, the so-called Rafle du Vel' d'Hiv (the Vel' d'Hiv roundup) was denied, distorted, willfully ignored, or forgotten in France. This failure to acknowledge France's involvement in the Holocaust was facilitated by the postwar French government's decision, in the name of national unity, to order all documents relating to the treatment of Jews during the Nazi occupation destroyed. The French police were happy to comply, since they were the ones who had rounded up the Jews. When French collaboration with the Nazis was mentioned at all in the years after the war, French citizens usually dealt with it by differentiating between an ideal, guiltless France and the traitorous Vichy government: it was not "France" that committed these crimes, it was said, but the government that was forcibly imposed on the nation.

This silence about the Vel' d'Hiv roundup and the complicity of the French people was broken only in the 1990s with official ceremonies, museum exhibits, news-media coverage, and an official acknowledgment by President Jacques Chirac. France's current president, François Hollande, has again focused public attention on this long-neglected dark episode in France's history. He spoke forcefully about the need to acknowledge broad French responsibility for the operation: "To the Jewish martyrs of the Velodrome d'Hiver, we owe the truth about what happened 70 years ago. The truth is that the crime was committed in France, by France." Even the Paris police, long reticent about their involvement, have cooperated in this new openness, allowing access to the few remaining records of the time. As Bernard Boucault, the Paris police prefect, expressed it: the police administration is "conscious of the duty of memory that is incumbent on it" (Sayare 2012).[1]

Memorial practices solemnly commemorating events in the historical or recent past, especially those involving large-scale wrongdoing of some sort, have in recent years become a commonplace of public life in many societies around the world. The commemoration of the Vel' d'Hiv operation is but one of many examples. "We"—sometimes meaning the citizens of particular countries and sometimes meaning humankind in general—are enjoined as a matter of duty to remember these events and to honor the victims by memorializing them and their plight. Truthful remembrance, as in Hollande's remarks, is said to be owed to the victims, not or not only to present and future generations that may be in danger of suffering the same fate. Sometimes, as in the French example, the truth is not widely known or publicly acknowledged, and the duty of remembrance seeks to remedy this omission by bringing it to light. But this is not always the case. The truth may be known but may have become so familiar and formulaic that there is a danger it will cease to have any meaningful impact on how people orient themselves to the past. Here the duty of remembrance seeks not only to keep the memory alive but to ensure that it is or remains a vital presence in the life of the community. Either way, this duty of remembrance, I will suggest further, is also a duty of *justice*, justice of a particular kind. Modes of remembrance, officially and publicly implemented and supported, are instances of a type of historical redress or reparation for the harms caused by the wrongs of the past.

In this chapter, I aim to make the case for a duty of remembrance, which is part of a larger inquiry into what I call an *ethics of remembrance*. I begin by arguing that remembrance is a duty or obligation that enables the performance of other moral duties belonging to individuals and collectives. (I use the terms "duty" and "obligation" interchangeably.) Remembrance itself, however, can be a moral obligation in its own right, and the heart of this chapter examines a number of grounds of an ethics of remembrance and provides an account of the duty to remember in particular. I start with familiar consequentialist arguments but spend the most time on less familiar and commonly neglected nonconsequentialist justifications. During the course of this investigation, I hope to make clear why remembrance might be not only obligatory but also obligatory as a matter of justice for the victims who are remembered and, additionally, their communities. Finally, I show how an ethics of remembrance can be applied to collectives.

Remembrance and Moral Obligation

It seems intuitively obvious that there are certain things that individuals, groups, communities, and entire societies ought to remember. Boucault, the Paris police prefect, regarded it as a duty to remember the victims of serious wrongdoing: what happened to them and how they suffered. But remembrance is also thought to be imperative in cases involving less serious forms of wrongdoing or to commemorate acts of heroism and self-sacrifice or contributions to the advancement of human welfare. Imperative uses of moral language in connection with remembrance are, in fact, a common part of everyday life. If you promise to do something and then forget, you are liable to receive moral censure for your failure to remember. "You should have remembered" is not just an expression of disappointment but a moral accusation.

It also seems reasonable to suppose that collective entities, such as families, religious communities, and nations, can have duties of memory as well as other moral responsibilities. Collectives can act as agents; they can make promises and commitments. They can be given credit or blame for what they do. Remembrance plays an essential role in relation to all of these collective obligations, as it does in relation to the obligations of individuals.

The intelligibility of obligations of promise keeping and commitment depends on the intelligibility of individuals being morally responsible for remembering that they made a promise or commitment and what that promise or commitment requires of them. Memory is the conduit through which the normative force of obligation is transmitted to the present and future, and the latter entails obligations with respect to the former. This is also true in cases in which obligations do not depend on our prior choices. Duties can arise out of special relationships, for example, even though we did not choose to incur them. Whatever the source of the duty or obligation, it can be recognized as such only by, and be motivating only for, a self that can appropriate the past as *its* past and meaningfully relate its current actions to something—be it a choice, a relationship, or an event—in which it was involved in the past. This is why it is important that one have at least some relevant present memories of this past occurrence. The past is not merely what used to be the present; it has normative implications for the present (and future) that are transmitted to it by memory.

Likewise, if collectives have moral obligations, their existence and force are transmitted to them by memory. Indeed, without the capacity for memories of the relevant sort it would be pointless to hold them to obligations of any kind, and even if there is a sense in which they could still have obligations, they could not be action guiding.

I have been explaining obligations of memory as *auxiliary* obligations, that is, as individual or collective obligations without which claims about any obligation whatsoever would not be intelligible. The duty of remembrance, so understood, is an enabling condition of the fulfillment of other obligations, in the sense that these other obligations could not be binding on the individual or collective if they lacked the capacity to remember from whence the obligations arose and why they have them. But commonly in discussions of collective obligations to remember victims of historical injustice or human rights violations, for example the victims of the Vel' d'Hiv roundup, we have something else in mind. Remembrance in these cases is not just an enabling condition of other obligations, and obligations of remembrance are not just ancillary to obligations of any sort. Specifically, remembrance does not just enable a collective to fulfill the obligation of justice to the victims of past wrongdoing; as I said earlier, it is the form that doing justice can take.

But what is it for a collective to have obligations? A collective practice of remembrance is not the same as the aggregate of members' individual memorial activities. Avishai Margalit addresses the issue in the following observation: "Now the responsibility over a shared memory is on each and every one in a community of memory to see to it that the memory will be kept. But it is not an obligation of each one to remember all. The responsibility to see to it that the memory is kept alive may require some minimal measure of memory by each in the community, but not more than that" (2002, 58).

Some individuals will have greater impact on practices of public memorialization than others, and their contributions to these practices will be more publicly visible. But the obligation of memory is a collective one, Margalit claims, in the sense that all the members of the community must do something, must make some contribution even if small and indirect, to maintain it. He calls this a "division of mnemonic labor" (2002, 58): not everyone can or should remember everything, but everyone (or, perhaps better, most people) can and should contribute something to keep remembrance alive.

Margalit's notion of a mnemonic division of labor is quite abstract, but it is not difficult to make it more concrete in order to get a better handle on how obligations of remembrance can be collective. To illustrate, consider public remembrance in a political community. There are many ways that a division of labor for public remembrance can take place. First, this may occur with respect to what Richard Vernon calls "the memorial apparatus of a political society": "the socially and politically provided apparatus that promotes the formation of some beliefs while obstructing the formation of others" (2012, 66–67). Civil society actors and survivor communities might take the lead in proposing, designing, and implementing memorials and commemorations, with governments acting as "strategic facilitators" (Brett et al. 2007) of projects by initiating them and coordinating their activities. Or the state might initiate and take charge of the process of memorialization, with civil society actors and communities of survivors acting as consultants and applying pressure when the state's efforts fall short or its resolve weakens. Second, once memorials and commemorations are established, there can be a further division of labor: state and local partnerships for ensuring that memorials retain their memorial significance, citizen involvement in organizing memorial activities and providing support for memorialization in other ways, material, moral, political, and so forth. In short, there are all sorts of collaborative arrangements, between and among government, civil society actors, and individual citizens, that can constitute a social program of public memorialization. They do not all have the same tasks with respect to it, but there is a collective obligation in the sense that the community's various constituents must work together to promote and sustain the work of remembrance. I return to this later in the chapter.

Collective remembrance, understood in this way, is related to justice, which in my account of the foundations of an ethics of remembrance is chiefly a non-consequentialist principle of redress. Remembrance, with its social embodiment in practices of memorialization, has a number of moral dimensions, and securing a kind of justice for the victims of wrongdoing, both those who are living as well as those who are dead, is one of its purposes.

An Ethics of Remembrance (i): Consequentialism

Why should nations remember the wrongs that they or others have committed? Why should Rwandans remember the genocide of 1994, for example, and why should Americans remember the failure of their government to intervene quickly enough to stop the slaughter there and in Bosnia? Why should artifacts, photographs, documents, and personal testimonies be collected to document past atrocities? The most frequent answer given to these and other questions about the value and imperativeness of remembrance is this: *to prevent the wrongs from happening again.* The hope is that as a result of documenting past abuses and educating young people and the public at large about them, citizens will be more attentive to early warning signs of renewed violence and repression and will take the necessary steps to prevent a recurrence. It is a hope that is remarkably tenacious, despite the existence of frustratingly little evidence to support it. Brazilian president Dilma Rousseff expressed the view this way: "The duty of memory should not be mistaken for the passiveness of ordinary remembrance. Memory is the human weapon to prevent the repetition of barbarism" ("Brazil Approves Jewish Studies Agreement" 2012).

There are other ways of justifying a duty of remembrance in terms of the consequences that are projected to flow from it. Obligations to survivors and descendants because of past wrongdoing, including compensation for injury and restitution of property, would not be fulfilled, let alone acknowledged, if the wrongs were forgotten or only falsely remembered as justifiable or excusable. Without proper memory of the wrongs done, the historical character of the deprivations and injustices suffered by descendants would not be recognized as such; these descendants would have no chance of obtaining benefits that are due to them by virtue of their familial and communal connections to victims of wrongdoing.

Consequentialist moral philosophers claim that our sole ultimate moral obligation is to bring about intrinsically desirable states of affairs and that other sorts of things, such as motives and practices, are to be judged by how effectively they do this. They justify moral duties in these terms. Since obtaining compensation, mitigating suffering, and preventing a recurrence of wrongdoing are desirable states of affairs, consequentialists would, other things being equal, advocate remembrance if remembrance is necessary to achieve these good results. However, judgments about future consequences are often complex and always to some extent conjectural. For example, it may not be clear what the consequences of memorialization are for securing peace and justice in postconflict societies. There may be some evidence that it will lead to a resumption of conflict and violence, but from a consequentialist standpoint it may be worth taking this risk if there is a sufficiently weighty counterbalancing good that is likely to be achieved.

An Ethics of Remembrance (ii): Nonconsequentialist Sources

Reflections on and pronouncements about remembrance, in scholarly writings as well as in popular and political discourse, do not always adopt the consequentialist approach to the ethics of remembrance. They often display a different orientation. From this other standpoint, acts and practices of remembrance are not valued because of their consequences, and their imperativeness is not explained by the fact that they produce the best consequences that can be brought about in the circumstances. Though consequentialists will continue to insist that all moral norms and precepts ultimately derive from consequentialist principles, I share the belief of many philosophers that this oversimplifies the richness of our moral experience. "Understanding the value of something is not just a matter of knowing *how valuable* it is, but rather a matter of knowing how to value it," Tim Scanlon (1998, 99) says, and the promotion of good consequences is not always what determines the appropriateness of our valuing or our moral obligations.

The example of friendship helps to illustrate this point. Friends owe each other certain forms of care, consideration, and attention, and they can be criticized for not properly attending to one another's particular needs, interests, and desires. These special forms of care, consideration, and the like define the duties of friendship, and their repeated nonfulfillment entails that the so-called friends are not really friends after all. Fulfilling the duties of friendship is part of what is involved in being a good friend. Although fulfilling these duties can have good consequences, the duties that are most central to friendship are not *justified* by their propensity to bring about good consequences. The primary reason to be loyal to one's friend, to be concerned about his interests, and so on is not that it will be good for the friendship or that it will benefit one's friend. These duties are primarily justified as constitutive of the intrinsic good of a relationship that makes these benefits especially meaningful for those who are friends.

Some reasons for obligations of remembrance are similar: for example, reasons for the duty to remember one's friends and family members after they have died. This duty seems to have the same basis as other duties of friendship and family life, since remembering a deceased friend or family member is one of the ways that friends and loved ones show special concern for one another. Other reasons for obligations of remembrance will be different in important ways because there is no relationship between those who remember and those who are remembered that is like the relationship between friends and loved ones. This does not mean, however, that we must fall back on consequentialist justifications. There are a number of ways of arguing for the moral value of remembrance, and there are arguments for obligations of remembrance that resemble the argument about friendship in the respect described, even if the particular bonds of friendship are missing. These arguments have two features in common: they reject the idea that remembrance and its obligations can or must be fitted into a consequentialist mold, and they show instead how noninstrumental moral considerations can explain the moral value of remembrance and justify its associated obligations.

In the following, I discuss three viable nonconsequentialist alternatives for articulating an ethics of remembrance: virtue theory, deontology, and moral expressivism. Each makes a distinctive contribution to our understanding of the moral value of remembrance and helps to explain why remembrance is morally valuable and possibly imperative, apart from whether it brings about desirable consequences. In presenting these approaches I do not intend to take sides or to argue that one of them has an advantage over the others in being able to account for the widest range of moral phenomena. Nor do I attempt to synthesize them in a fully unified account of an ethics of remembrance. My intention is to probe each of these theories to see what insights they might be able to provide for developing a credible alternative to consequentialism for grounding such an ethics.

Virtue ethics, in a tradition going back to Plato and Aristotle, makes the character of the agent rather than the nature of action central to moral assessment. Virtues have multiple dimensions—rational, emotive, and volitional. To possess an excellent character is not just to reason well about what should and shouldn't be done. It is also to have the right emotional reactions and motivations with respect to morally relevant features of situations and to have the reasons, emotions, and motivations in harmony with each other. In addition, to have a virtue is to appreciate that its complex requirements are not reducible to simple rules and that its demands cannot be confined to one narrow area of life. An honest person, for example, is not honest just in business dealings but with friends, colleagues, acquaintances, and strangers. It is also the nature of the virtues that they are not exhausted in the performance of an individual act but are exhibited in patterns of action, feeling, and willing that provide a connecting thread between different moments of an agent's life.

Virtue ethics regards acts of remembrance as virtuous when they embody and flow from some virtue or combination of virtues. For example, a person who risks punishment for refusing to allow wrongdoers to bury the wrongs that they have done is exercising the virtue of courage. As an illustration, consider the activities of the Mothers of the Plaza de Mayo, who for more than a decade protested in the center of Buenos Aires to keep alive the memory of the abduction of their children by the military junta that ruled Argentina. Their weekly activities were not without significant personal risk. Three of the founders of the association were themselves disappeared. The courage displayed by these women in their defiant act of remembrance was, as they saw it, what justice for the disappeared demanded, and it was also evident in other ways, for example by their pushing for legislation to help in the recovery of human remains and the prosecution of ex-government officials.

Not to give in to despair about the possibility of justice, to be hopeful about the future, is another virtue closely associated with remembrance. Consider, as an illustration of the sustaining power of hope, the work of Emanuel Ringelblum, who, in the midst of the horrors of the Warsaw ghetto, organized the secret Oyneg Shabes archive to document the daily suffering endured by the Jews in the ghetto (see Kassow 2008). He and his collaborators were afraid that Polish Jews would be remembered only as their killers depicted them or as apologists in the future might prefer to see them, and they wanted them remembered as they were, in truth. They had no assurance that the archives would survive and accomplish their purpose, but they did not demand certainty or anything approaching it. They were hopeful that the archive would be found, and hopeful people focus on possibilities, not on the weight of evidence or probabilities. Indeed, sometimes those who engage in activities to preserve the memory of wrongdoing realize that the chance that the memories will actually survive is remote.

An ethics of remembrance can recruit virtue theory for its contributions to our understanding of the virtues without having to accept the theory in its entirety. It does not have to claim that only agents, not actions, are to be assessed directly or that virtues are the primary locus of moral value, and that ethical philosophy should therefore be structured around them. As a contributor to a nonconsequentialist alternative to consequentialism, it would not preclude explanations of moral value that draw on other nonconsequentialist moral theories. However, a virtue-based approach to practices and activities of remembrance is useful in shining the spotlight on character and bringing out a variety of morally relevant considerations that might otherwise be neglected or marginalized. Those who engage in activities of remembrance can sometimes exhibit moral virtues of different sorts for which individuals and collectives are morally praiseworthy, and virtue ethics is a rich source of reflection on the nature and interaction of the virtues.

Another nonconsequentialist approach that an ethics of remembrance can draw on is deontology, a group of theories that hold that what makes actions right is their conformity to a moral norm or principle that the agent is duty bound to obey, independent of the good it brings about. There are three deontological principles that relate to justice and that are typically invoked in discussions about securing justice for the victims of wrongdoing. These are: (i) principles of punitive justice that specify the conditions under which punishment is warranted and the standards for its appropriate application, (ii) principles of compensatory justice that seek to render a situation as it was before injury or to return the injured party to a situation of well-being equivalent to the original situation, and (iii) principles of reparative or reparatory justice whose aim is to repair the harm caused by wrongdoing by restoring and affirming the dignity and moral and political status of those who were wronged. This is something that principles of compensatory justice alone cannot accomplish, perhaps because the injuries are not truly compensable. These principles tell us that what is important is not to produce the maximum amount of good but to ensure that individuals and groups get what is due to them. I focus here on the third sort of principles because it is reparative justice that explains how the duty of remembrance can be a duty of justice.

Remembrance itself cannot make the victim whole or restore the status quo ante, and, while it is compatible with punishment of wrongdoers, its intent is not punitive. But remembrance can nevertheless be in partial fulfillment of a duty of justice. The sorts of wrongs with which both punitive and reparative justice deal typically communicate a degrading and demeaning message to the victims. The commission of these wrongs conveys to them that their interests impose little if any constraint on how it is permissible to treat them. As Jeffrie Murphy (1988, 25) puts it, "[moral] injuries . . . are ways a wrongdoer has of saying to us, 'I count but you do not,' 'I can use you for my purposes,' or 'I am up here on high and you are down there below.'" But reparative justice seeks redress by focusing on the needs and dignity of victims in addition to sanctioning offenders. It conveys a refuting countermessage, one that is powerful because, as publicly administered by an authoritative body, the political community speaks through it, and that is in large measure its justificatory purpose. Through this message, repair of the harm caused by wrongdoing is declared to be the primary objective of justice, and the victim's expectation to be treated as a respect-worthy person is validated. And much the same is true when the victim is an entire community, as in cases of genocide.

Memorialization, as a practice of reparative justice, has the same moral purpose, and its value as such is not dependent on whether it prevents or helps prevent future wrongs. Of course, officially sanctioned practices of memorializing the victims of wrongdoing, as individuals or as communities, restore their dignity and moral and civic standing symbolically, if they restore them at all. This fact, however, does not detract from their moral value. After all, even material means of reparation are reparative only in virtue of the message they symbolically convey to the victims and others. When the Mothers of the Plaza de Mayo refused to accept monetary damages offered by the Argentine government for the losses they suffered, it was not because the money, as such, was useless but because they believed it was "blood money" and felt it to be an insult (Borneman 2002).

But what about the subcategory of victims that is made up of nonsurvivors? While it is obviously too late for them to have the harm caused by wrongdoing repaired and their moral standing restored, obligations regarding others are not always coextensive with the duration of their lives and may be dischargeable after their deaths. There are such things as posthumous obligations, and underlying them is what Joel Feinberg (1980, 174) calls "an important fact about the human condition: we have an interest while alive that other interests of ours will continue to be recognized and served after we are dead." Like having wills and testaments honored, being remembered after one dies is normally something that is important to the living, indeed so important that practices are established that make it imperative for the living to remember the dead. While this may not be important to everyone, the presumption should be that forgetting victims and their suffering is an additional wrong on top of the initial one. Further, the dead can be given a kind of reparation by means of respectful treatment of those persons with whom they were connected, by way of community membership, family relationship, or acts of authorization. These persons can serve as surrogates for those who did not survive, and through them the dead are once again (symbolically) included in the moral community (see Blustein 2014).

The final nonconsequentialist source for an ethics of remembrance that I will discuss is moral expressivism. It evaluates actions in terms of their expressive meanings and proposes expressive norms to govern the expression of attitudes. In the version formulated by Elizabeth Anderson, which I follow here, "The basic form of an expressive norm is: act so as to adequately express attitude B toward Z" (1993, 33). This has an imperative form and resembles Kant's deontological principle that individuals ought to be respected as ends in themselves. But respect is only one of the attitudes with which expressive norms concern themselves. Moreover, there are two components to any expressive norm. The attitudes required by these norms must be *appropriate* to the object to which they are directed. It would not be appropriate to express an attitude of honor toward a moral scoundrel, for example. In addition, the act must *adequately* express the attitude, and adequacy is dependent on context and object. It might be an adequate expression of respect for one's teacher, for example, to listen attentively to his lectures, not to engage in disruptive activities in class or spread rumors about him outside class, and so on. Adequate expression of respect for one's parents, on the other hand, would require much more and something else.

The notions of appropriateness and adequacy that moral expressivism makes use of are often contentious in the context of redress for large-scale and historical injustices. Perpetrators, victims, and bystanders, especially in the aftermath of violence and conflict when peace has been newly restored, usually

Jeffrey Blustein

construct very different and conflicting narratives about the events in which they were involved, and these shape their views about how and even whether these events should be memorialized. There may be no single, agreed-upon, authoritative account of what happened, whether it was wrong, and who was responsible for it if it was. As long as these matters are unsettled, agreement among the different parties on the attitudes that are appropriately and adequately expressed in the establishment of public memorials will be lacking, although the distance between them might be narrowed through the disclosure of new information about the past or, failing this, through negotiation and compromise.

As a lens through which to view an ethics of remembrance, moral expressivism's emphasis on the expressive meanings of action and the standards that govern them orients that ethics in a distinctive way. Though reparative justice does take seriously the contempt that is conveyed toward the victim by the wrongdoer, justice is not itself one of the attitudes that remembrance conveys. This might be clearer with the following example. Consider persons who are stigmatized because they belong to a certain group and who, as a consequence, are denied rights and opportunities that others have. This harm, while significant, is not the only harm associated with stigmatization, nor is it uniquely associated with it. What is *distinctively* harmful about stigmatization is the negativity expressed by it, the derogatory and belittling attitude that is thereby communicated to the other person. "We might say," as Simon Blackburn (2001, 470) puts it, "that the harm occurs at the time and place of the expressive act, not in virtue of anything that happens at later times or places." The expressive meanings of actions are carried by the messages they convey, and the messages are harmful or beneficial because of what they reveal about how the agent "regards" the target. For this reason, moral expressivism is fundamentally nonconsequentialist. Moral expressivism also differs from virtue theory and deontology because it gives the expression of attitudes a basic justificatory role that it does not have in either of the other theories and because it thinks about value differently from how it is viewed in them. But since I have helped myself to these theories only for the particular insights they offer about moral value and have deliberately refrained from commenting on the overall merits of each as a distinctive theory, I need not say more about this.

From an expressivist standpoint, acts of remembrance are judged by whether they conform to expressivist norms for the appropriate and adequate expression of attitudes toward what happened in the past and those involved in it. Different events in the past and people affected by or involved in them as well as the ways in which they were affected or involved will call for different attitudes, and remembrance can be regarded as fitting or not for moral as well as nonmoral reasons. The attitudes that are important for understanding memorialization are those that we have toward or concerning persons, and they include respect, honor, love, reverence, and gratitude, among others. For moral expressivists, the primary considerations are the appropriateness of the attitude to the object of value and the adequacy of its expression, not just how people are treated, where this is characterized solely in behavioral terms. Consequences are still morally relevant, however, as they should be. After all, the adequacy of the expression of an attitude is determined in part by the action tendencies to which it gives rise and by their reasonably expected impact on the recipient. Moreover, uptake matters. To express an attitude is to bring it into the open, and generally one aims to communicate the attitude to others, to bring it into the open so that others can see it for what it is intended to be. An agent should therefore consider how the attitude he is trying to express is interpreted by others, although obviously one cannot have complete control over this. There can be value in the attitude expressed and in the agent's expressing it, however, even if it is not or cannot be fully appreciated by those who fall within its ambit and even if it fails to alter their condition. This is especially important in the present context, where many or most or all of the victims who are remembered are long dead or recently deceased and, as such, incapable of appreciating anything or being affected for better or for worse. It can be a reasonable injunction for people to act so as to adequately express respect toward the dead, even though obviously the reason for this cannot be that the dead themselves can benefit in some way from such expressions.

Though expressivist norms are intentional, persons are not only responsible for those attitudes they intentionally express. Actions can reveal attitudes that the agent knowingly holds but also ones she doesn't realize she holds, and in some circumstances she can be blamed for the attitudes her actions express, even if she is unaware that her actions express them and she doesn't intend to express them. For example, a person may not be a racist, but she may thoughtlessly make remarks that express racist attitudes and are hurtful to others. She cannot be absolved of responsibility for this simply by pleading ignorance, since her ignorance itself is blameworthy.

Can collectives engage in expressive actions? Acts of collective remembrance can be symbolic. Consider the recent French draft law that would criminalize the denial of the Armenian genocide by the Ottoman Turks (see Sayare and Arsu 2012). Passage of the law was a symbolic gesture. It symbolized France's support for a principle, the principle that genocide must be acknowledged wherever it occurs and must never be denied, and the Turkish government, realizing the gesture's powerful symbolic rebuke, threatened to penalize France if it went ahead with the law. This seems to be a clear case of a symbolic act with memorial significance performed by a collective. But how can an entity that is not a person, such as a nation, ethnic or religious community, or other association be the sort of entity that can express attitudes through its symbolic acts, except symbolically? Can a collective literally express respect or honor or fidelity or any of the other attitudes associated with remembering the dead and living victims of wrongdoing? Can a collective have emotions that are constitutive of affective attitudes? I have already argued that collectives can have intentions and be morally responsible for their actions. But perhaps those attitudes are fundamentally different in some way. I want to resist this suggestion, and I will take it up in the next section.

Remembrance, from the Individual to the Collective

Individuals perform their own private ceremonies of remembrance as well as engage in public rituals commemorating the dead. They remember loved ones who died—sons, brothers, and fathers who went off to war and never returned, family or community members who were disappeared and never heard from again or who were brutally tortured and murdered. They remember others for the good they did, for their bravery and compassion and the selfless love they showed others. Sometimes those who remain behind remember in the company of a small circle of friends and family; sometimes they are joined in their grief by the community at large. The previous discussion of an ethics of remembrance has assumed that its grounds apply both to individuals and to collectives. But it may seem a misuse of language or at best a metaphorical expression to say that collectives can exhibit virtues or express attitudes in their public commemorative activities. Such talk, we are asked to believe, can't really be taken literally (in other words, seriously). I think this is mistaken, and an ethics of remembrance for collectives needs to say something about what licenses us to think otherwise.

We might start by returning to Margalit's notion of a division of mnemonic labor, which he introduces to explain how collectives can remember and how the responsibility to remember can be shared by a community. I find this idea extremely suggestive and earlier tried to make it somewhat less abstract by giving examples of how this division can be realized in practice. Besides this, however, there are at least two other respects in which his account needs further elaboration. One problem is that requiring "each and every one in a community of memory to see to it that the memory will be kept" seems too strong, since there may be some in the community who do not participate in remembrance or have any obligation related to it. Of course, one might respond that then they do not belong to a "community of memory," since by definition this just is a community composed of all and only individuals who have obligations to support memory. But why can't those who, like children, are not full moral agents be included in a community of memory? More important for my purposes, Margalit only gestures in the direction of explaining the difference between a group of people collectively engaged in remembering and a mere assemblage of individuals, each doing something that, combined with what others are doing, keeps the memory alive. He says of a true collective memory that it "integrates and calibrates the different perspectives of those who remember the episode" (Margalit 2002, 51), but he gives no account of exactly what this "integration" consists of or how it takes place.

Here is where Margaret Gilbert's plural subject theory, one of the leading theories in the analytic philosophy of social phenomena, can be useful. Central to her theory is the notion of a joint commitment. Persons initiating a joint commitment, according to her account, "do not each create a part of it by making a personal decision. Rather, they participate in creating the whole of it along with the other parties. A joint commitment does not have parts, though it certainly has implications for the individual parties. That is, each is committed through the joint commitment" (Gilbert 2002, 126). Plural subject theory explains group phenomena as the product of a joint commitment on the part of individuals to do or experience certain things as a body, a single unified agent or subject of the phenomena. When they are jointly committed to this, they constitute themselves a plural subject.

Plural subject theory can explain both how collectives can have obligations and how they can collectively have attitudes and emotions and conform to moral norms. A plural subject account of collective obligations of remembrance would be this: for us to *collectively have an obligation* to remember X is for us to be jointly committed to remember X as a body. Similarly, a plural subject account of an attitude runs as follows: for us to *collectively have an attitude* A is for us to be jointly committed to having and expressing A as a body. And a plural subject account of an emotion is this: for us to *collectively feel an emotion* E is for us to be jointly committed to feeling E as a body. In each case, individuals are committed to others to experience something or to act to achieve some common goal, conditioned on others being openly willing to do the same. Joint commitments result when the commitments are no longer conditional because each has bound himself to the others and made this known to all. Moreover, Gilbert argues, the creation of a plural subject entitles members to make claims upon one another to follow through on what they have jointly committed themselves to.

An account of group phenomena along these lines is faced with the task of explaining their implications for the group's individual members, and Gilbert takes this up in her discussion of collective guilt:

For one thing, when talking among themselves they will characterize the action in question as morally wrong. They will do and say only what accords with that judgment. For example, they will refrain from proposing that it is morally acceptable for the group to engage in an obviously similar action . . . and will feel free to remonstrate with the person [who proposes such a thing]. In addition, they feel free to ascribe guilt feelings to the group, and to remonstrate with a group member who denies that the group feels guilty. (2002, 139)

The members of a plural subject of remembrance would presumably do similar things. For example, remonstrating with a group member who denies that the group has any obligation to remember could count as one way of seeing to it that that memory is kept safe within the group and of participating in a division of labor with respect to the work of remembrance. Perhaps little more than refraining from disparaging the obligation and not tolerating those who do or not obstructing those who are engaged in legitimate commemorative activities is all that is required of some who belong to a plural subject of memory. Parties to the joint commitment do not have to remember everything of importance about some event or be able to provide an ethical justification for committing themselves with others to remember some event as a body. But the joint commitment does obligate them to act in ways appropriate to it, so they are required to help preserve or at least not to interfere with remembrance.

Gilbert's plural subject theory is one response to the worry that groups, in contrast to their individual members, cannot have attitudes or emotions or be obligated to remember, and it can be used to explain how an ethics of remembrance for groups is possible. An account of collective emotions in particular is important for an ethics of remembrance as I have characterized it, since virtues partly consist in dispositions not only to act but also to feel emotions rightly, and the attitudes are partly constituted by emotional involvement in what concerns their objects. Plural subject theory captures the idea of a subject that is in an important sense singular, even though it is composed of a plurality of participants, and other accounts are available as well (see Bratman 2014).

Here is one difficulty for the theory: there seems to be something wrong with the claim that a collective emotion is *just* a joint commitment to feel emotion as a body. Gilbert recognizes that there may be some initial resistance to this, since being committed to feel something is not the same as feeling it, and this holds whether the agent is an individual or a collective. She doesn't think this causes a problem for her account because she assumes that there need be no "phenomenological conditions for specific emotion types" (Gilbert 2002, 120). However, if, as many philosophers have argued, emotions do not just consist of cognitions or judgments but have an affective component, then her account is missing something critically important.[2] It would therefore be of considerable interest to consider how affectivity might be accommodated in an account of collective emotion. It would also be interesting to see if affectivity can be compatible with the plural subject account of collective emotions.

One suggestion is that the central idea in the concept of a collective emotion is that of a person's having some emotion qua member of a community. Using this idea, a collective emotion would be defined as the aggregate of emotions that individual members of the group feel qua members, for example guilt, shame, or pride. An advantage of this aggregative account is that it would allow us to explain how collective emotions can have the full-blooded quality typically associated with emotion. However, this will not do for an account of collective emotion. A more promising tack is to explore the notion of *shared emotion*. Shared emotions are not just the emotions of different individuals combined, not just *his* emotion E_1 plus *my* emotion E_2 plus *her* emotion E_3, and so on. Rather, they are *our* emotions, the emotions that all of us share insofar as we belong to the same group, that we feel in concert, and where the common knowledge that these are our emotions provides sufficient cognitive linkage between us to secure collective and not just parallel emotions. Emotions that are shared, it should be noted, are not felt by some mysterious entity over and above the individuals constituting the collective. They are felt by individuals, but individuals who feel as one.

Thus we can say that groups experience shame, for example, not or not only when their members jointly commit themselves to feeling shame as a body—a rather bloodless and only partial explanation of collective shame, it seems—but when the feeling of shame is widely shared among them. It need not be shared by everyone in the group to count as collective, only by a designated large enough portion of the population. Those who do not share in the collective *feeling* of shame would still have certain things true of them, according to plural subject theory. They would still be bound by their participation in the joint commitment to feel shame as a body to act in ways appropriate to and required by that commitment, and they would be subject to censure by other parties to the joint commitment for failing to do so. Though the group would have the emotion, they would not participate in it.

Conclusion

Most philosophers would agree that we can intelligibly speak about an ethics (in contrast to a psychology or sociology) of remembrance for individuals and groups only if individuals and groups can be morally responsible for their memories. To be morally responsible for an action or mental state such as an attitude or belief is to be properly subject to credit, praise, blame, or censure for doing the act or having the mental state, and an ethics of remembrance, like any ethics, presumes that these attributions are sometimes appropriate. Our crediting and blaming practices suggest that memories are no different from other mental states in this respect: individual persons as well as groups are sometimes liable to moral praise and censure for remembering or forgetting.

Among the things for which we can sometimes be appropriately blamed is the failure to fulfill our moral obligations, and the importance of remembrance for this is clear. Obligations, of whatever sort, transmit their binding force through time and are acted upon because the agent can appreciate that the reasons for discharging them that arose in the past persist into the present. Memory is vital because obligations extend over time, and memory makes it possible to discharge them. This yields an ethics of remembrance in an indirect or derivative sense: it makes remembrance obligatory only because it enables the fulfillment of other obligations that individuals or groups may have. However, we commonly assume that there are also obligations whose focus and primary point is remembrance, and an ethics of remembrance should give an account of whether and why such obligations exist, having established that they do.

Providing such an ethics was one of the main tasks of this chapter. I have argued that an ethics of remembrance constructed on consequentialist foundations is only one approach, and that other nonconsequentialist theories, such as virtue theory, deontology, and moral expressivism, can make valuable contributions to an alternative nonconsequentialist view. It is not surprising that an ethics of remembrance should draw on insights from various theoretical sources, since focusing on one theoretical perspective only is likely to oversimplify its complexity as a moral phenomenon.

Another important task of the chapter was to explain how an ethics of remembrance for collectives, including collective obligations, is possible. I began with a historical case, the Vel' d'Hiv roundup of Jews during World War II, and the declaration by the French president that truthful remembrance is morally incumbent on the French people because they share responsibility for this crime. Whether this is in fact the case depends on a careful examination of the historical record—on the roles played by officials and ordinary citizens, what they could reasonably have been expected to know, opportunities for resistance, and so on. All of this is beyond the scope of this chapter. Still, it and numerous other examples of recent vintage compel us to think more abstractly about whether collectives as well as individuals can have memorial obligations and what the grounds of such obligations might be. The first step would be to show that collectives can be agents capable of intentional action and so are candidates for moral responsibility. We could not even get off the ground if there were no such thing as collective agency and if there were no actions for which collective agents could be morally responsible. But, having established this, the meaning, grounds, and implications of attributing obligations of remembrance to collective agents remain to be explored. How do we cash out the idea that collective entities have obligations to remember? What about the obligations of individual members? And, more broadly, how can the foundations of an ethics of remembrance also undergird an ethics of collective remembrance?

Each of the philosophers I have looked at, Avishai Margalit and Margaret Gilbert, helps us to better understand how obligations can belong to collectives, in other words, how they can flow from the shared-ness or collectivity of a collective. Notions of a mnemonic division of labor and joint commitments are likely to be important ingredients of an adequate account of this phenomenon. But even when all of these are included, there is something about remembrance that the account leaves out—that collective remembrance, like its individual analogue, is often an occasion for the experience and expression of a range of powerful past-directed emotions. We might in fact say that collective obligations of remembrance are, in part, obligations to create opportunities for individuals jointly to have emotional connections of the right sort to people and events from the past.

Notes

1. The exact extent of collaboration of the French people with Vichy is difficult to determine, of course (see Paxton 2014). The issue is complicated, but I use the example only to illustrate a certain attitude toward historical memory.

2. Burleigh Wilkins argues something similar in his criticism of Gilbert. As he says, "it is not clear what joint commitments to collective feelings . . . would amount to in the absence of a phenomenological component" (2002, 153).

Jeffrey Blustein

Part II

5

The Politics of Memory, Victimization, and Activism in Postconflict Bosnia and Herzegovina

ELAZAR BARKAN and
BELMA BEĆIRBAŠIĆ

Victims never fare well in the aftermath of conflict. Redress is, in the best of cases, symbolic. It is therefore not surprising that victims receive a great deal of outsiders' empathy, including acknowledgment of their own truth of their victimization. Empathy with the victims of injustice has driven the process of transitional justice; advocacy in the name of victims, the centrality of the victim in the national narrative, and support for victims' organizations are at the heart of the politics of transition and posttransition activism. Out of context, empathy for suffering is mostly viewed by the public as ethical and nonproblematic. Within a sectarian context, however, the validation of separate victims' truths may exacerbate or reignite the conflict. By focusing on the suffering of survivors and attempting to bring to justice the main perpetrators, the various stakeholders—whether the state, civil society groups, international organizations, or donors—have disproportionally validated victims' sectarian perspectives, while paying little or no attention to the impact these activities have on peace building. This explains why, over the past twenty years, transitional justice mechanisms have often been unable to bridge the conflicting narratives that foment sectarian animosity.

We do not mean to validate the desire of dictators and other perpetrators to escape accountability but intend rather to underscore the predicaments caused by the assumption that the claims of victims should not be contested (see Snyder and Vijamuri 2003; Sikkink 2011).

Our chapter comes out of a larger research project that seeks to uncover the dominant narratives shaping postconflict Bosnia and Herzegovina (BiH). While we discuss only one particular case, we believe that our observations are applicable elsewhere, such as in Northern Ireland and in Rwanda, where sectarian identities dominate domestic or international conflicts. In the following we highlight the way memories of the conflict in the former Yugoslavia, more specifically in BiH, are used to aggravate ethnic tensions. We show how nationalists cynically exploit discourses of victimization to pursue power and also pay close attention to how victims' organizations participate in and contribute to ethnic animosity by building on the capital of the ethics of victimization. In discussing the politics of victimization across identity lines, the chapter does not suggest parity of culpability or responsibility for the conflict or for particular crimes. Instead, we are concerned to analyze the conflict's traumatic legacy: a rhetoric of victimization that drives the politics of Bosnian Serbs, Bosniaks, and Bosnian Croats alike.

We also briefly discuss civil society projects that promote nonsectarian memory as a tool to further conflict resolution. The knowledge produced by organizations working to break through sectarian lines shows the potential of challenges to a nationalist discourse. They aim to emphasize respect for all victims—without, however, using such respect for political gains—and to closely involve victims' organizations, without, however, endorsing their distinct political goals.

Competing Ethnic Truths and Memories

In 2012 Bosnia and Herzegovina commemorated the twentieth anniversary of the longest siege in the history of modern warfare, the siege of Sarajevo, which began on 6 April 1992 and lasted until 29 February 1996. Throughout 2012, ceremonies were held all over the country as numerous cities marked their own distinctive and yet related sufferings. The commemorations in 2012 were not exceptional; remembering the war has been a leitmotiv of postwar Bosnia. Each year, new mass graves are discovered, and recovered bodies of killed victims are buried following the long and painful process of DNA identification. The war crimes trials have been going on for years, and only recently have the main suspected war criminals been arrested. The Dayton

Peace Agreement solidified the ethnic divisions in a divided country that has a weak central government and is composed of two semiautonomous entities—the Federation of Bosnia and Herzegovina (Federation BiH), with a majority population of Bosniaks and Croats; and Republika Srpska, which is largely composed of ethnic Serbs—as well as a self-governing administrative unit, Brčko District. As Kip Bastedo (2009) has noted, the structure of the country is a constant reminder of the ethnic conflict. The end of the war in Bosnia meant the beginning of another: the conflict of identities expressed through memories.

The history of the 1992–96 conflict still represents a major source of political turbulence in Bosnia and Herzegovina in particular and the Western Balkans in general and has been subject to historical manipulations, claims, counterclaims, and denials. The sectarian conflict of identities is informed by knowledge about the war that has been produced by multiple stakeholders, including international and national judiciaries, governmental and nongovernmental organizations, politicians, historians, and victims' associations. These multiple sources have led to discord that undermines any agreed or shared narrative. They have fostered three divergent ethnohistorical interpretations, which play a crucial role in the reconfiguration of collective identities and are all designed to inflame ethnonational memories with emotional capital to sustain the conflict. Memories and history are intertwined, with victims' memories claiming priority.

The parallel commemorations of the so-called Sarajevo column case are a good example. On 3 May 1992, in Dobrovoljačka Street in the center of the city, members of the Army of the Republic of Bosnia and Herzegovina (ARBiH) attacked a convoy of Yugoslav People's Army (JNA) troops that were exiting Sarajevo according to the withdrawal agreement. For a long time the "incident" was not the object of any controversy. In 2003 the International Criminal Tribunal for the Former Yugoslavia (ICTY) dismissed the case on the grounds that the actions of the ARBiH did not constitute a breach of law. However, the case was later investigated in two parallel inquiries by prosecutors in Serbia and Bosnia, which inflamed the ethnic memories surrounding the event. In 2009 a Belgrade court issued nineteen arrest warrants in relation to presumed war crimes committed in Dobrovoljačka Street against JNA troops, thereby aggravating the political tensions between two countries. The warrants led to extradition requests for, and the subsequent international arrest of, Ejup Ganić, a former member of the Bosnian wartime presidency, and Jovan Divjak, a former Bosnian Serb general in the ARBiH. Following legal hearings in London and Vienna, both requests for extradition were rejected. In the Ganić case, the City of Westminster Magistrates' Court ruled that the warrant was "politically motivated" (Workman 2010). Divjak was released because the court was concerned he would not "receive a fair trial in Serbia" (Reuters 2011). The Bosnian Prosecutor's Office has discontinued its investigation due to lack of evidence; this in turn has prompted criticism in Republika Srpska, whose political representatives have stated that the discontinuation has directly contributed to a year-long stalemate in forming a government. The memory conflict led to two parallel commemorations on 3 May on Dobrovoljačka Street. Since 2010 Zelene Beretke (Green Berets), the association of ARBiH veterans, honors the civilian victims of the siege of Sarajevo, since it considers the attack on the JNA convoy to have been the "first line of the city's defense," while, on the opposite side of the street, the Council for Nurturing the Traditions of Liberation Wars of Republika Srpska commemorates the JNA fatalities.

Each ethnic group in Bosnia and Herzegovina advocates its own particular "ethnic truth"—an interpretation of the past that is enslaved to dominant interests—and thereby has perpetuated the conflict. The fierce political battle between competing truths, memories, and ethnic identities has intensified in the past decade, especially because of the rise of a new generation of ethnonationalist parties. A report by the Bertelsmann Stiftung (2012, 4) noted that "the period between the 2006 and 2010 general elections witnessed more undemocratic rhetoric than the period immediately following the conflict" and that "the international community has not shown itself willing to stand up to such challenges, and appears unlikely to do so in the near future" (2012, 32).

Between the Pursuit of Justice and Historical Narratives

By indicting more than 160 persons responsible for war crimes, the ICTY has provided an unprecedented and most valuable forensic historical record on war crimes. It has also developed a new international criminal jurisprudence, led to the establishment of the International Criminal Court, and played a major role in the Bosnian transition to democracy by strengthening the local justice system as well as the formation of civil society organizations (Caine 2008). It defined the massacres by the Army of Republika Srpska (VRS) in Srebrenica as genocide and rape as a war crime and helped locate mass graves. Concerning the character of the war in BiH, the ICTY has concluded in several cases that an international armed conflict occurred between Bosnia and Herzegovina on one side and Serbia and Montenegro (that is, the Federal Republic of Yugoslavia) on the other, since the VRS was acting on behalf of

Elazar Barkan and Belma Bećirbašić

the latter. Although most of its cases have dealt with war crimes committed by Serb forces, the ICTY has shown that members of the ARBiH too were responsible for war crimes against the non-Bosniak population, such as the torture of Bosnian Serb detainees in the Čelebići camp. Six leaders of the self-proclaimed Croatian Republic of Herzeg-Bosnia have been convicted for participating in a joint criminal enterprise "with the objective of removing the Muslim population" and creating "a Croat entity, mostly within the borders of the Croatian Banovina as it existed in 1939, to enable a unification of the Croatian people" (ICTY 2013). By introducing the concept of a "joint criminal enterprise," the ICTY has demonstrated that in some cases war crimes were part of organized, planned, and instigated actions, as in the case of Slobodan Milošević, who, although he died during the trial, was still found to have been part of a joint criminal enterprise.

Notwithstanding its attempts to be impartial, the ICTY is often perceived to be biased, because both sides insist on having their claims validated by judicial verdicts. In general, many Serbs consider the tribunal anti-Serb, while a majority of Croats and Bosniaks believe it is ineffective and has failed to secure justice for the victims and to establish a conclusive narrative about the conflict in the 1990s. Lenient sentences and plea bargains privileged limited convictions over historical or even forensic truth and undermined trust in the process. Drawn-out procedures and the lack of a significant and effective outreach program have left many frustrated. These sentiments were aggravated by the dismissal of the indictment against former Bosnian Serb leader Radovan Karadžić for genocidal intent in the mass killings, persecutions, and expulsions of non-Serbs in BiH. While the Appeals Chamber reversed the decision, wide distrust in the ICTY's political impartiality remains among Bosniaks and Croats.

The decision by the International Court of Justice (ICJ) to clear Serbia of complicity in the genocide in Srebrenica amplified the criticism of international justice in BiH (Shaw 2007). Reduced sentences have been particularly criticized; some former VRS guards at the Omarska and Keraterm death camps have already served their sentences and returned to Bosnia, which hinders the repatriation of internally displaced persons and thwarts individual grieving and closure. On the other hand, many Bosnian Serbs in Republika Srpska are cynical about the ICTY's delivery of justice. They cite, for example, the case of Naser Orić, the former ARBiH military commander acquitted by the ICTY's appeal chamber of failing to prevent the killing of fifteen Serbs in villages surrounding Srebrenica after he had initially been sentenced to two years of imprisonment.

Given this pervasive skepticism, it is tempting to invoke Hannah Arendt ([1963] 2006) and hope that the Court would limit its jurisdiction to narrow and procedurally accurate decisions concerning the cases it dealt with and that it would not engage in wider issues such as the creation of artificial ethnic balances for the sake of reconciliation (Hoare 2008). However, the decision to focus on procedural and specific issues would also be a political decision, even if done under the pretext of legalism. The ICTY's verdicts shape not only the trials but also the history and the narrative of the conflict.

Because of the frustration stemming from the justice and the historical narratives produced in courtrooms, the struggle over truth has been transferred from the judicial space to that of ethnopolitics. The activism of victims should be understood within this context, as a result of the slow and controversial process of limited justice and widespread denial by the other side of the conflict. The sense that justice has not been served informs the activism of victimhood and produces angry politics; it compels survivors to constantly reassert their victim status.

The failure of any institution to provide a historical synthesis of the conflict and to offer alternatives to the nationalists' histories engenders the production of nationalist myths. The culture of denial and mythological constructions of the past are so prevalent in the region that, unless official institutions embrace the judgment of the war crimes trials and turn these into historical facts and narratives, the history of the breakup of Yugoslavia will continue to fan nationalist animosities. Indeed, the problem is less the lack of a concluding narrative than the widespread marginalization and highly selective reading of Tribunal verdicts and of the related historical record by ethnonational historians. Meanwhile, conflicting historical interpretations about the conflict prevail and are particularly visible in textbooks, memorials, and various alternative methods of knowledge production.

This institutional aversion to a substantive engagement with difficult historical issues has a long tradition in Bosnia and Herzegovina and is particularly evident in the education system. Despite good intentions, it was aggravated by the international community's recommendation for a moratorium on teaching the history of the recent war in schools, which provided for an uncontested space where shared histories became redundant and national myths flourished. The latter included, for example, representations of the iconic events of World War II through narratives of "century-long" sufferings and reciprocal ethnic blaming. The message thereby conveyed to young people is that wars are justified because of the long history of oppression. Reimagining history often reinforces current versions of the past that validate a cycle of revenge.

Dominant Interpretations of the Conflict

Despite the variations of the political landscape in the postwar era, the broad interpretations of the conflict have remained relatively stable, tracking closely Bosnia and Herzegovina's political divisions. The ideological core of the political parties is anchored in their connection to the war, a strong bond that ensures the continuity of conflict and political turbulence. Those positions are faithful reflections of the post-Dayton geo-ethnic divisions (or rather, its interpretations) and are manifested through several conflicting historical interpretations that dominate the public sphere.

The supporters of an independent and multiethnic Bosnia and Herzegovina usually see the war as the result of aggression. Their narrative refers to the political projects of "Greater Serbia" and "Greater Croatia" and draws on Bosnia-Herzegovina's legal rationale for independence at the onset of the war. Consequently, the collective memory of Bosnian Muslims and their national awareness as Bosniaks strengthened during the war in response to the rise of ethnonationalisms as well as the expansionist politics of Milošević and Tuđman and ethnic cleansing. "Sufferings" and ethnic cleansing produced a strong victimhood narrative and are constitutive of Bosniak ethnic identity. One of the distinctive traits of the narrative is its principle of (victim) exclusivity. This establishes a culture of impunity as a norm concerning the war crimes committed by the ARBiH, which are both taboo and tolerated because the country had to resist the aggressor. The culture is seen as a necessary evil that is widely known but is not discussed. This self-justification provides limited space for any nuanced narrative or acknowledgment that would challenge this version of the past.

This national "fortitude" is displayed in justifications for war crimes and violence against the enemies, whether they were soldiers or civilians. A good example is the response to the overturning of Naser Orić's conviction: more than five thousand people welcomed him home at Sarajevo airport after his release from jail (*Balkan Insight* 2008). In addition, an ARBiH commander, Mušan Topalović, alias Caco, who was responsible for the massacre of Serb civilians at Kazani, above Sarajevo, and who was later assassinated under controversial circumstances, was described by several high-profile politicians, including former BiH president Alija Izetbegović, as "both a hero and a criminal" (*Dani* 2002), a view widely held among Bosniaks.

Such sectarian legitimization of crimes was evident in the response to an indictment by the BiH State Prosecutor of eight persons responsible for torturing Serb civilians and prisoners of war in the Silos detention camp near Sarajevo. The indictment was denounced by the Assembly of Sarajevo Canton, whose delegates voted unanimously against "the manner and procedure of arrest of suspected members of Army of BiH" and agreed to provide "legal aid and all other forms of assistance to defendants" (*Balkan Insight* 2011). Mustafa Cerić, who has been an influential leader of the Islamic community for the past twenty years and who served as the Grand Mufti of Bosnia and Herzegovina from 1999 until 2012, also condemned the indictment and called for a "Muslim awakening" (Islamska Zajednica u Bosni i Hercegovini 2012). This is significant because religious communities in BiH dominate the formal political and social scene and ethnoclerical interpretations of the past shape suffering as an integral part of religious and ethnic identity. Cerić identifies aggression with Muslim hatred, or "Islamophobia," a term he often employs against public figures or journalists who are critical of his role or politics. Being labeled Islamophobes, they are viewed as enemies; their attitudes are taken as evidence of the continuity of aggression against Bosniaks (Islamska Zajednica u Bosni i Hercegovini 2011, 12–25). The emphasis on the genocide as a key constituent part of Bosniak identity is central to the Islamic community's ideological program.

The narrative of aggression castigates Republika Srpska as a perpetrator. The prevailing view is that this entity was born of sin—that is, formed out of genocide—and, therefore, its existence challenges any efforts of coexistence. This Bosniak nationalist narrative was most evident in the policies of the former member of the BiH presidency, Haris Silajdžić. Delegitimizing Republika Srpska and arguing that its raison d'être was the perpetuation of the genocide, Silajdžić based his political agenda on two central themes: abolishing the "entities" (Republika Srpska and the Federation) and transforming Bosniak victimization into state ideology. This perpetuated the conflict between the two entities, which continues to dominate the political scene (Oslobodjenje 2012).

In contrast to the narrative about Serb and Croat aggression, the most common narrative told in Republika Srpska focuses on the "civil war" or the "Defensive Fatherland-Patriotic War." The civil war narrative serves mostly to negate the demand for political and military accountability of the wartime Bosnian Serb leadership as well as to assign parity in responsibility for the war to Bosniaks and Croats. Republika Srpska, which encompasses the territories where most war crimes against non-Serbs were committed, is officially "seen as the greatest achievement of the Defensive-patriotic war" (Republic of Srpska Government 2012). This account engendered explicit strategies of memory politics, predominantly focused on advancing one ethnic truth by representation of war through, on one hand, the prism of the suffering of Bosnian Serbs (both during the war in the 1990s and during World War II), which is offered as a justification for the war and the inevitability of massacres and, on the other, an emphasis on the guilt and responsibility of other ethnic groups for the "civil war."

Serb victimization has been further accentuated by perceptions of international and local tribunals as "anti-Serb." This narrative relativizes guilt and violence and encourages denial, mostly evident in the discourse over key events such as the Srebrenica genocide. It gained currency after the far-right politician Milorad Dodik became prime minister of Republika Srpska in 2006.[1] He has stated several times that "Bosnian Serbs will never accept that the 1995 Srebrenica massacre of some 8,000 Muslims was genocide" and that "Republika Srpska does not deny that a large scale crime occurred in Srebrenica, but by definition it was not genocide as described by the ICTY" (Agence France-Presse 2010).

Dodik's government has contested all prior transitional justice efforts in Republika Srpska, including the work of the Commission for Investigation of the Events in and around Srebrenica between 10 and 19 July 1995, which was formed in 2003 to establish the truth, to locate mass graves, and to determine the identity of victims. The appointment of an official commission was a significant step, even if it was done under pressure from the Office of the High Representative in Bosnia and Herzegovina (OHR), an ad hoc international institution responsible for overseeing the implementation of civilian aspects of the Dayton Peace Agreement that ended the war in Bosnia and Herzegovina. Its members resisted public pressure and political interference; they established a list of 8,731 persons believed killed or missing between 10 and 19 July 1995, and provided a list of perpetrators of Serb military units, thus breaking for the first time the institutional taboo surrounding discussion of the militia's crimes (Commission 2004). The then president of Republika Srpska, Dragan Čavić, publically apologized to victims, saying that the "report makes it clear that enormous crimes were committed in the area of Srebrenica in July 1995" (Associated Press 2004). However, in 2010 the government initiated a revision of the report, claiming that it had been manipulated (Office of the High Representative 2010).

Here historical accountability proved a double-edged sword. For a brief moment it opened a window for acknowledgment, but it also fueled nationalist ideology. This is a political struggle, not merely an academic space for the production of knowledge. Historical accountability is a medium in which the legacy of convicted war criminals is fought. For instance, upon the release of Biljana Plavšić, who has been known for her racist statements about the ethnic superiority of Serb people and genetically deformed Muslims (Inic 1996), Dodik sent a government jet to pick her up and welcomed her in Belgrade (*Balkan Insight* 2009). Dodik's political program focused on the protection of

Republika Srpska by arguing for secession, refuting the legitimacy of BiH state institutions such as the Prosecutor's Office, and advocating war-crime trials at the level of entities (B92 2008; B92 2010; Isa Intel 2011; Vesti Online 2012). In November 2012 he also called for the disbanding of the unified armed forces of Bosnia and Herzegovina, which led Valentine Inzko, the High Representative of Bosnia and Herzegovina, to report to the UN Security Council that "Republika Srpska authorities continue to pursue a policy that is, as the president of the Republika Srpska has frequently expressed in public, aimed at rolling back previously agreed steps that have been taken to implement the [Dayton] Peace Agreement" (Reuters 2012). These constant tensions directly challenge the processes of reconciliation and peace building, which depend on legitimate and effective state institutions.

The third ethnic narrative is that of the "homeland war" or "war for independence"; it is shared by both Croatians and the majority of Bosnian Croats. By focusing on Milošević's nationalistic warfare project, this narrative has similarities with the "aggression" narrative, but, unlike the latter, it invokes the wartime legacy of the self-proclaimed Croatian Republic of Herzeg-Bosnia, the "breakup" of the state, and the Croat-Bosniak war. This narrative enflames the conflict among Bosniaks, Serbs, and Bosnian Croats because it is used to justify ethnic cleansing policies against the non-Croat population.

Convicted war criminals enjoy widespread political support among the Bosnian Croat establishment and victims' associations, and their hero image is a unifying emblem for the political mobilization of Bosnian Croats. The chief party representing Bosnian Croats—the Croatian Democratic Union (HDZ BiH)—used to be the political wing of the Croatian Defense Council, a military formation of Herzeg-Bosnia. It continues to cultivate its war legacy. For instance, during the celebrations of the nineteenth anniversary of Herzeg-Bosnia, in 2010, Dragan Čović, the president of HDZ BiH, invoked victimization as a justification for war crimes when denouncing demands for apologies for war crimes against non-Croats since "without Herzeg-Bosnia Croatian people wouldn't have a chance to fight for equality in Bosnia" (Croatian Democratic Union 2010). In addition, the articulation of ethnic identity still continues to be shaped by the factor of "territorial autonomy," or an additional "third (Croat) entity" that would be mostly based on the restoration of Herzeg-Bosnia. The dominant ethnonationalistic ideology still constructs the collective identity of Bosnian Croats around the image of the "homeland" or Croatian motherhood. Preservation of this liaison is not merely reduced to a symbolic, linguistic or cultural level but is present in all social spheres, from the media to the historical and educational fields (Lovrenović 2009).

Different in origin and historical context, these accounts produce selective memories in relation to the conflict by deliberately forgetting the crimes and remembering the heroes and the suffering of each ethnic community. Reciprocal accusation is a determining factor in the political power struggle between ethnonationalistic elites that "successfully use ethnic divisions to disguise their corrupt rent-seeking agenda" (Chêne 2009, 2). Nationalist narratives of victimization are regularly exploited by political elites to further their political and economic interests and to support corrupt practices by labeling corruption charges as hostile acts. Political power plays constitute the most visible space of the "memory conflict," but much of the identity formation is constructed by diverse civil society groups and stakeholders, from historians and educators to victims' associations, that compete over the legitimacy of representing the traumatic ethnic legacy of the conflict. The relationship between the psycho-cultural-legal discourse and the political is not always direct, but the affinity is clear.

Victims' Associations

There is a general view that the government ignores the needs of victims. Most survivors are displaced persons, unable to return to their homes or resolve their residence status. Many experience poverty and suffer from posttraumatic stress disorder. The high level of institutional corruption and power abuse, the inadequate implementation of the law, and the lack of transparency further deepen victims' feeling of insecurity and discrimination. Victims are remembered by politicians only when their support is needed to defend national identity or to gain political advantages (Bećirbašić 2011). There are more than two hundred survivors' organizations in BiH, mostly in Federation BiH. They represent family members of killed civilians and "disappeared persons," camp inmates, women victims of mass rapes, and war invalids and other veterans. The scope of those directly affected by war places an enormous burden on a financially weak, geo-ethnically fragmented and complex Bosnian bureaucracy. Many victims' groups provide crucial services, such as psychological and therapeutic aid to their members, counseling and peer support, and general assistance to the families and children of war victims. Victims' groups also play a leading role in the search for missing persons, commemorations, the collection of survivors' testimonies, the documentation of war crimes, database building, and support for witnesses in war crime trials; without the input of these groups, postwar justice would have been poorer.

At the same time, many victims' associations play a divisive role. Their representatives are often politically motivated and "have privatized" the associations with little concern for their members (Colo, Bozic, and Bubalo 2011, 22). As the core of vox populi, victims' groups contribute to the dominant mono-ethnic shaping of memory practices because of the emotional role they play in society. The lack of uniform legislation that would help prevent segregation and the categorization of victims on a religious and ethnic basis further contribute to the politicization of the victim discourse (Bećirbašić 2011). "Despite the fact that they should be the factors of cohesion and connection in the realization of the rights of all civilian war victims" (International Institute for Middle East and Balkan Studies 2010), victims' organizations appear as guardians of the ethnic conflict.

The most active stakeholders in the transitional justice process are organizations that represent former detainees in both entities and family members of victims of the Srebrenica genocide. The representatives of Srebrenica victims are most visible because of the particular status of Srebrenica in the collective memory of Bosniaks as a symbol of both massive ethnic purification and demands for international accountability. Moreover, since the war crimes in Srebrenica constitute the only legally acknowledged genocide during the war, the memory of Srebrenica has emerged as a key narrative of Bosniak victimhood. Therefore, Srebrenica victims' associations play an essential role in shaping ethnonational interpretations of the past and determining dominant political approaches to issues of transitional justice, reconciliation, and post-conflict identity. Their work is principally focused on documentation, the search for missing persons, commemoration, and the monitoring of war crimes trials. Politically, the common denominator of these associations has been their advocacy for the abolition of Republika Srpska, seen as a "genocidal entity" and forcibly occupied territory (*Bilten Srebrenica* 2006, 10–11; Camo 2009).

While their activities are crucial to the pursuit of justice and should be considered in the context of the widespread genocide denial in Republika Srpska, their political discourses contribute to cementing suffering as an idée fixe of Bosniak identity. Challenges to the formula "victimization equals virtue" are usually labeled hostile and are seen as an "offense to the memory of genocide." This was the case when the former president of the main Bosniak party, Stranka Demokratske Akcije (SDA, Party of Democratic Action), himself a former detainee in a camp run by the VRS, called for changes in Bosniak politics, "in which the focal point so far has been the victim philosophy, the story of aggression, genocide, war crimes and an injustice done to Bosnia and Herzegovina and the Bosniaks . . . a policy mainly based on the past, less on the present and the future" (BBC Monitoring International Reports 2008). The victims' associations, including the Association Woman–Victim of War and the Union of Detainees, organized a petition against his statement, accused him of being pro-Serb, of betraying the nation, and of offending Bosniaks (Orbus 2008). As argued elsewhere, the traumatic experience is never used as a driving force in creating progressive political and social values, but is employed only as a critical weapon of the dominant ideology, maintaining an aggressive and conflict-prone environment (Bećirbašić 2011).

In Republika Srpska, all victims' associations campaign for the abolition of the Prosecutor's Office and the Court of BiH and thereby support the government's obstruction of the state consolidation process. The most active association is the Union of Detainees of Republika Srpska, which was formed in 2002 to "establish the truth about the sufferings of Serb people during the Bosnia and Herzegovina civil war."[2] The claim of their representatives that fifty thousand Serbs were held in 536 concentration camps in the Federation, including 126 in Sarajevo, is considered highly exaggerated and part of nationalistic propaganda. However, most of their activities are focused on "deconstructing" popular knowledge about Sarajevo and Srebrenica, which is considered an "exclusively Muslim truth." Their perspective on the Srebrenica genocide is synonymous with the official narrative of the Republika Srpska government, since "they will never fully accept the genocide against non-Serb population till the Srebrenica No2, meaning the genocide against Serbs, is not equally recognized" (Vesti Online 2011).

The Reconciliatory Perspective—Knowledge Production by Civil Society Groups

Against this backdrop of a propaganda that focuses on the exclusive suffering of one ethnic group, several civil society organizations (CSOs) aim to bridge the ethnic divide through empirical research and balanced narratives. If historical dialogue is to develop, this is what it may look like.

The CSO sector flourished after the war, supported by international donors. It played a central role in the construction of public memory by ensuring the documentation of numerous war crimes and human rights abuses. A few independent media outlets have broken the dominant silences, exposed war crime perpetrators, and provided "other" victims with the opportunity to be heard despite the political and social pressure. For instance, the Kazani massacre was first reported by the investigative magazine *Dani*, whose journalists raised the issue of the BiH army's military and political accountability. Their Kazani dossier was introduced as follows: "At the same time we are making our own contribution towards the debate whether one should write about ones 'own' crimes and 'own' criminals. The only correct answer to this is that this is the right way. The killings in Kazan are a dark stain on the shining war history of Sarajevo. It is wrong to keep quiet about this stain" (*Dani* 2000). This is one of few exceptions to nationalist narratives.

Another exception has been the work of the Research and Documentation Center (RDC), which has systematically attempted to produce an unbiased and factual representation of the conflict. The flagships of the RDC's long-term research are ongoing projects on documenting war crimes: "Human Losses in 1991–1995"; the "Bosnian Book of the Dead," which lists the names of victims; and a digital "Bosnian Atlas of War Crimes," which could be considered a virtual war memorial. These projects are distinguished by their all-inclusive character, as they include victims of the war regardless of (but classified according to) their ethnic or religious affiliation or gender and regardless of whether they were civilians or soldiers. This is the only data-gathering project that relies on multiple sources, avoids the ideological classification of war casualties, and focuses on the victim as a person. Instead of focusing on numbers and ethnic affiliation, the RDC has shifted attention to victims as individual citizens. The RDC team sees the Atlas as the "geography of suffering of the entire Bosnian society rather than of one or the other ethnic or religious community"(Istrazivacko-dokumentacioni Centar 2010).

Impartiality has its costs. The RDC projects are subjected to harsh criticism mainly by Bosniak ethnonationalists—politicians, journalists and clerics—but also by victims' associations. The leading far-right Bosniak daily, *Dnevni Avaz*, criticized the RDC's director, Mirsad Tokača, for "pandering to Republika Srpska" (*Dnevni Avaz* 2012), while the Institute for Research of Crimes against Humanity objected to the RDC's calculations of the number of war dead and accused it of "manipulative amateur-quasi research" and of being "pro-Serb." In the political context this is viewed as support for "theses such as that of a 'civil war' or the reduction of the Bosnian genocide to 'ethnic cleansing'" (Čekić 2009, 116). Institutional and other difficulties have led to diminished activities by the RDC.

On the other side of the political spectrum, the Republika Srpska government is happy to exploit the results of the RDC research to back up its genocide denial. For instance, RDC research suggested that seventy-two persons buried in the Potočari Memorial Center were not killed in July 1995. Milorad Dodik used this to support his claim regarding the "Bosniak manipulation of Srebrenica death toll" (Arnautović 2012). The RDC example reflects the difficulty of conducting nonsectarian research and activism and the ways truth-telling efforts

Elazar Barkan and Belma Bećirbašić

may be challenged by nationalistic discourses. It is a case not of announcing the truth but of a political struggle to legitimize nonsectarian perspectives.

Another example of the efforts to establish impartial historical truth about the war is XY Films, based in Sarajevo. Its journalists and documentary filmmakers produced several films on postwar justice issues.[3] *Haški tribunal i zločini u BiH* (2004) is a five-episode documentary that follows investigations into war crimes in BiH, the handing down of indictments against perpetrators, and the subsequent proceedings before the ICTY; it uses archival material and testimonies from the Tribunal courtrooms. The first eighteen episodes of the *Otisci (Fingerprints)* series (2006–7) feature the testimonies of war survivors returning to the place where crimes had been committed, while *Otisci—15 godina poslije* aims to find out to what extent war crimes affect everyday life and portrays twenty-five sites of crimes and cities destroyed by war. This film includes testimonies of survivors from all three ethnic groups and was broadcast on national television. According to the filmmaker Aldin Arnautović, some communities refused to host debates and public screenings of the documentary because of their "unwillingness to talk about war crimes" (Vukušić 2008).

Some organizations use the shared narrative concept as a tool of rebuilding trust between communities and engaging the past through oral history projects, focusing on "positive" stories from the war. An example of a "positive story" as a catalyst for rebuilding interethnic trust is the commemoration of Srđan Aleksić, a VRS soldier who was beaten to death by members of his unit in Trebinje while trying to save his Muslim neighbor. Aleksić became a symbol of tolerance, humanity, and resistance to ethnic hatred and is commemorated across the former Yugoslavia. The production of knowledge about those who resisted the wartime hatred is an act of resistance to contemporary nationalism. It challenges the dominant perceptions about a fixed behavior prototype and exclusive ethnic guilt and might serve as a fruitful model for local community-based reconciliation.

The Regional Commission for Establishing the Facts about War Crimes and Other Gross Violations of Human Rights Committed on the Territory of the Former Yugoslavia (RECOM) is a network of nongovernmental organizations and victims' associations in the former Yugoslavia that has been calling for a regional truth commission to establish the facts about all war crimes in former Yugoslavia committed between 1991 and 2001.[4] The need for RECOM stems from the widely voiced frustrations that "the trials held before the [ICTY] and national courts . . . do not fully satisfy victims' needs for justice" (Coalition for RECOM 2011, 3), while victims are manipulated for political purposes. The RECOM initiative engaged in a four-year-long consultation process, organizing forums on transitional justice; bringing together members of all ethnic groups, law experts, journalists, artists, and representatives of youth organizations; and organizing public testimonies of victims. These activities finally led to the adoption of the Statute proposal, which assigns the commission the tasks of collecting facts about war crimes, missing persons, and victims and "researching the political and societal circumstances that decisively contributed to the outbreak of wars" (Coalition for RECOM 2011, 10).

Advocates for RECOM underline their belief that conflicts have to be investigated at a regional level, because the "same events produce different truths and meanings in different countries" (Božović 2011). The initiative, which so far has received only declarative political backing, faces a host of challenges. Some victims' representatives fear that the commission will further complicate the work of courts, which are already overburdened by cases and are unable to respond to survivors' long-term needs and ensure the protection of witnesses, who are "tired of repeatedly recounting their traumatic stories" (Ramulić 2011, 13). Others consider the courts as the only acceptable tools of justice in principle and therefore reject alternatives (for example, Nuhanović 2010). Last, there is the ethnic argument, which sees the initiative as a project driven by ethnic hatred that is reinforcing existing stigmas and unfair representations of victims and aggressors. In that sense, perceptions of the initiative in BiH have reflected conventional hostilities. For instance, while associations in Republika Srpska suggest that RECOM's hidden goal would be to further "cement the ongoing marginalization of Serb victims" and "reach a 'truth' according to which Republika Srpska will be declared an entity founded on genocide and ethnic cleansing" (Bojić 2010), Bosniaks and Croats see it as "Belgrade project" that would even out the guilt and deny the aggression.

The nonsectarian work of these organizations is noted at this stage for its exceptionalism and is illustrative of the challenges faced by efforts at peace building and historical dialogue; most organizations working in BiH avoid truth-telling activities that would validate the suffering of other ethnic groups or break silences surrounding the accountability of "our perpetrators."

Conclusion

Attempts to deal with the past in Bosnia and Herzegovina have mostly focused on direct victims and survivors with the aim of overcoming trauma and accessing justice. They have not addressed the issues of bystanders or of the cathartic aspect of survivors' narratives. There has also been little encouragement for historical dialogue or for attempts by dominant ethnic groups to acknowledge crimes committed in their name. While such initiatives are present within the NGO scene in Serbia and to some extent also in Croatia (examples include the Helsinki Committee, the Humanitarian Law Center, Women in Black, the Youth Initiative for Human Rights in Serbia, and Documenta in Croatia), they are mostly absent in Bosnia and Herzegovina, where their absence contributes to the increased tensions in an extremely divided society.

Notwithstanding the nationalist animosity, there is widespread interethnic and interentity cooperation at the cultural level within the women's and peace movements, primarily among activists, the younger generations, and "socially vulnerable" groups. Sometimes, the teamwork and citizen actions are motivated by calls for social change. For example, the Youth Initiative for Human Rights from Sarajevo (Federation BiH) and Oštra nula from Banja Luka (Republika Srpska) staged a joint public event in both cities on 1 October 2010 to remind citizens of the promises made by ruling political parties and to show that the problems of young people are identical throughout the country. Activists distributed packages with headings such as "better healthcare," "visa free regime," "education reform," "more jobs and youth employment," and "European standards of higher education." Interethnic solidarity was also reflected in the biggest antigovernment protests in Bosnia and Herzegovina since the end of the war (the so-called baby revolution), which took place in June 2013 (Associated Press 2013). In articulating their dissatisfaction and their anger in the face of corruption, low living standards, insecurity, and overall social instability, people consider one another equal citizens claiming their respective rights and not as members of hostile ethnic groups. Such forms of "connectivity" may challenge the conventional approach to addressing the past since they reveal that the public recognizes the artificial provocation of ethnic tensions as means of furthering the financial and political interests of power elites. However, these activities aim to address the future rather than the past.

The overwhelming nationalist domination of the historical discourse and the potential for interethnic/interentity cooperation on social issues show the value in a conflict-resolution methodology that ignores the past and is prudent in sponsoring specific activities that focus on citizens' participation, public policies, bridge-building forums, peace activism, and social/cultural/economic development. However, when it comes to nonjudicial transitional justice, intersectarian identity issues, activities related to education and textbooks, and knowledge of history, construction of public memory should focus on projects that explicitly address the past and break the dominant silences. The work of victims' associations should be contextualized, giving voice and representation to individual narratives, while emphasizing balanced and pluralist macro narratives. In that sense, the strategies for addressing the past should clearly divide activities related to the basic rights of victims (e.g., reparations, compensation, protection of victims in trials, or existential support) from those that deal with the construction of public memory and the production of historical knowledge by independent and multiethnic teams of scholars, activists, and journalists. Such trends will have to rely on international legitimization and funding, providing an alternative space beyond the sectarian voice.

The efforts of NGOs in Bosnia and Herzegovina have shown the potential for multiethnic work, but they have been overwhelmed by nationalist, often xenophobic, histories. Much work can be done by civil society, and the involvement of youth organizations in the region may be a cause for hope. Since the history of the conflict is a main source of contention, new stakeholders, including historians, among others, should become more involved in historical dialogue, which would highlight shared narratives and contextually engage existing judgments. Such an approach doesn't have to engender a conclusive version of the past that is acceptable to all. The goal of shared narratives doesn't mean the exclusion of different accounts of the same event but rather underscores an impartial, pluralist, and comprehensive construction of memory. Some authors introduce the notion of compatible narratives, suggesting "both acknowledgement and dialogue among people who would not necessarily tend to discuss or engage in dialogue." According to a report commissioned by the United Nations Development Programme, "The challenge of truth-telling is to make sure that these differing accounts can be told in ways that 'agree to disagree' even on major points of divergence" (Simpson, Hodžić, and Bickford 2011, 44; see also Barkan 2009).

Ethnic conformism affects the knowledge producers, whose discourses are valued according to their compliance with ethnic narratives. Usually, historical production by an author who is a member of the "other" ethnic group is welcomed as long as it corresponds to a suitable mononational narrative; however, the critical exposure of that same narrative can quickly turn that author into an enemy. Therefore, the ability of stakeholders to produce and promote knowledge that challenges the dominant "silences" or "ethnically" taboo topics in their particular geo-ethnic communities depends very much on evolving international norms. In this respect, victims' memories play as contentious a role in Bosnia and Herzegovina as they do in Northern Ireland, where the question of whether paramilitaries should be considered victims is controversial, and in Rwanda, where the victimization of Hutu is denied.

Notes

1. In October 2010, Dodik became president of Republika Srpska. Note that general elections were held in Bosnia and Herzegovina on 12 October 2014.

2. The organization's website is www.logorasi-rs.org.

3. The company's website is http://www.xyfilms.net/content/category/9/15/43/lang ,english/.

4. See http://www.zarekom.org/.

6

Memories in Transition

The Spanish Law
of Historical Memory

PATRIZIA VIOLI

S panish Law 52/2007, sometimes referred to as *Ley de reparación* (Law of Reparation) and more commonly, espe-
cially in the mass media, as *Ley de memoria histórica* (Law of Historical
Memory), was signed into law on 26 December 2007, more than three decades
after the election of the first post-Franco government.[1] The *Ley* is essentially a
measure to provide redress for victims of the Spanish Civil War and the Franco
dictatorship, ranging from symbolic and political recognition to material reparation. But the law also aims at a comprehensive rewriting of history and,
more generally, seeks to provide a new symbolic framework for the construction
of a shared historical memory. That this is one of the primary objectives of the
law is evident from the very first words of its preamble, which invoke "*El espíritu
de reconciliación y concordia*" (the spirit of reconciliation and concord).

These objectives suggest that the law counts as an act of transitional justice.
But the Civil War ended in 1939. Franco died in 1975, and the constitution of
the democratic government that replaced his regime was approved by a referendum in 1978. Transitions to democracy, together with their special processes
of both retributive and reparative justice, are often understood to be of limited
duration, brought to an end by the installation of a democratically elected
government and, if required, the ratification of a new constitution. According

to this understanding, the Spanish transition ended in 1978. Some scholars have argued that Spain's transition lasted longer: either until February 1981, when a coup against the democratically elected government failed, or until October 1982, when the Spanish Socialist Party, whose leaders had not compromised themselves during the dictatorship, first formed a government. The very fact that in 2007, twenty-five years after the establishment of this government, there was a widely perceived need for reparations underpinned by legislation suggests that the transition had not been completed.

Why the demand for a legislative intervention at such a distance from the end of the dictatorship, when, apparently, the transition should have been well concluded? Should it perhaps be understood as an element of a posttransitional phase, as has been suggested by Aguilar (2009)? Should we modify our way of thinking about what a transition can be? What is at stake here is a distinction between a transition as an *event* with definite limits and transition as a *process* that can last decades and cannot be precisely circumscribed. In the latter interpretation, which I adopt in this chapter, transition ceases to be predominately a matter of political change and becomes a much broader cultural transformation of society. Here, I am following Ruti Teitel (2000), who proposes a broader interpretation of transitional justice that focuses on the process rather than on the event. She emphasizes the symbolic power of legal and quasi-legal mechanisms in a postauthoritarian society and highlights the performative and public aspects of law that generate deep and long-lasting cultural effects. Stephanie Golob (2008) similarly suggests that a transition ought to be understood as a complex *culture*, an organized and systematic set of beliefs, practices, and norms. According to these writers' understanding, Spain is a paradigmatic case of an ongoing transition where a fully realized democracy did not emerge in parallel with a fully developed "culture of transition."

The gap between the well-established democratic forms of Spanish political life and the still problematic cultural elaboration of the traumatic past is the complex background against which the 2007 law has to be understood. Not only is it part of the transitional process in the broader sense I just defined; it is also representative of an ongoing conflict in Spanish society regarding key issues of memory and historical legacy. The tensions that characterize an unaccomplished culture of transition result from an underlying, still unstable system of values. This is not peculiar to Spain. During transitions to democracy, the values of peace, justice, and truth are always dynamically in tension with one another. Peace as a value projected into the future with the aim of mutual cohabitation implies a certain degree of forgetting. In order to foster a durable peace, past conflicts have to be pushed into the background if not buried and forgotten. Truth and justice, on the contrary, are mainly concerned with the past: with the need to remember what happened and to remedy the wrongs. In theory peace is not possible without justice and truth. But in practice it is difficult to reconcile these goals.

The Spanish law and its reception illustrate this difficulty. Despite its undeniable merits and positive aspects, the law did not succeed in constructing a unifying interpretative framework and precisely because of this weakness ended up dissatisfying everybody, both on the left of politics and on the right. The law remained precariously suspended between the memorial values of truth and justice and the future-oriented values of national reconciliation, without being able to reconcile the two or to move decisively in one direction or the other.

My analysis aims to highlight the system of values that underlies the law and its inherent unresolved tensions by providing a semiotic reading of the text framed within the larger context of its cultural background. According to Yuri Lotman (1990, 2005), the internal structure of any cultural system is organized by specialized semiotic resources—*modeling systems*—of different kinds. Though language is the primary modeling system, art, religion, architecture, and other cultural institutions contribute to maintaining the structural cohesion of a culture as well as its overall self-representation. Among these secondary modeling systems, the legal system plays a very important role, systematically defining what is allowed, forbidden, or mandatory in a given society. It constructs social reality by establishing, through its network of prohibitions and obligations, a powerful shared value system, legitimizing some narratives while excluding others, constructing a self-description of a culture and society, and filtering memories and thus operating as a *memory framework* in Maurice Halbwachs's sense (Halbwachs 1925). The law is thus a means of understanding wider social processes—a lens through which we are able to bring such processes into close focus.

Delayed Memories

The end of the Spanish Civil War in 1939 marked the beginning of a dictatorship by one party to the conflict. Although actual military actions ceased, Spain in the thirty-six years of the Franco dictatorship was never peacefully integrated; nor was it free from political violence and repression. Only Franco's death made a transition to democracy possible. This transition, however, was not accompanied by a transformation of collective memory or by a process of transitional justice, either retributive justice through courts or tribunals or restorative justice through truth commissions. Instead a general amnesty was proclaimed by the 1977 *Ley de amnistía*, popularly known as the *Pacto de olvido* (the pact of forgetting or pact of silence). This law represented both a consequence and a symptom of the serious "memory problem" that has afflicted Spanish society ever since its exit from the dictatorship (Silva et al. 2004; Vincent 2010).

To speak of a "pact of silence" is, however, rather misleading, since in the late 1970s the legacy of Francoism was still omnipresent in a country littered with monuments and symbols of the regime. By contrast, Republican memories were accorded little space in society and confined to an existence as marginalized countermemories. The *Pacto de olvido*, far from stimulating a generalized cultural forgetting, ended up silencing just one of the two opposing memory systems, thus preventing the development of a real "culture of transition" (Golob 2011), based on reciprocal respect for both parties involved in the past conflict.

Nevertheless, this law was Spain's solution to a common problem. Any transition to democracy after an authoritarian regime presents inevitable "memory management" problems, given the complicity with and even active support for the past regime among many members of civil society. There is always a clash between opposing and contrasting memories of different groups of social agents, not only victims and persecutors but also supporters of the regime who simply kept silent. Transition requires the ability to reconstruct a shared national narrative as a basis for the establishment of a new society, but in most cases this is extremely problematic, since it is unlikely that *all* experiences of the dictatorship can be integrated into a cohesive national discourse. It becomes almost impossible to agree on what Carsten Humlebæk (2011) has called a "historical master narrative," which can be semiotically defined as a coherent, convincing self-representation within which all members of society can reconcile their different memories.

One could argue that a "master narrative" of this kind is a utopian ideal, never likely to be realized. Though this might be the case, transition requires that something be done to manage the traumatic past. This can be done in different ways depending on whether a new regime wishes to emphasize or minimize the rupture between past and present. It might, for example, establish courts to try those responsible for past injustices, or it might instead pardon representatives of the former regime. Trapped between continuity and discontinuity, the solution is often a combination of different elements that are in an unstable equilibrium.

The *Pacto de olvido* was a response to a history of division and conflict.[2] The Civil War split an already divided Spanish society. The Franco dictatorship evoked as a justification for its rule the Civil War and the risk of a return to such chaos; it thus appealed to a widespread fear that also came to play a major role in the subsequent transition to democracy. Memories of the Francoist past recalled another, even more traumatic past: the Civil War, with its hundreds of thousands of dead, a phantom that must in no way be reactivated. No less important is the fact that democracy was not established in Spain by a revolution or by a collective activist movement, as had been the case in 1974 in Portugal. Franco died of old age, and it was only after his death that a transition process could begin, bearing all the hallmarks of an evolution, rather than a break with the past. Humlebæk (2011) made the observation that the new democratic state was born without foundation myths. A revolution, even if bloodless, is a collective break with the past that creates its own alternative narrative and gives rise to new legends that are often rooted in specific symbolic images (such as the carnations in the Portuguese army gun barrels). A marked discontinuity allows for the reformulation of key aspects of collective identity. This did not happen in the Spanish transition period. The establishment of democracy did not take place by way of what Lotman (2009) called *explosion*, a radical change that interrupts the regular course of events and allows new cultural forms to emerge. In Spain, by contrast, the transition to democracy happened by way of *extinction*, involving no real discontinuity with the past and thus offering no possibility of establishing a new set of broadly shareable meanings.

This cultural and political context determined the Spanish response to the difficulty of bridging the gap between memories of past suffering and present needs, between the demands of truth and justice and the desire for peace. Peace required a comprehensive agreement on a new democratic institutional framework authored by both opponents and supporters of the former regime. These two parties shared no common memory nor any political understanding of the past, apart from seeing the Civil War as a tragedy never to be repeated. The only possible option was to "forget" what had gone on during the Civil War and the dictatorship. The desire for peace prevailed, to the detriment of truth and justice.

The amnesty offered benefits to the (few) political prisoners of Francoism and to the (more numerous) left-wing Basque and Catalan nationalists, but it also guaranteed immunity to perpetrators who had committed crimes during the Franco dictatorship and to their collaborators. It was the latter who benefited most from the choice of silence and forgetting. The Spanish Socialist Party (PSOE), while in government from 1982 to 1996, never put the issue of dealing with a Francoist past or that of transforming the collective memories of the dictatorship on its agenda—perhaps because it was intimidated by the 1981 coup attempt and shied away from the risk of a return to the past. Spain's transition to democracy clearly gave priority to a consensus on democracy and its consolidation, rather than a condemnation of crimes and the search for historical truth. Nevertheless, by making peace the priority, Spain achieved a relatively peaceful transition to democracy.

Toward the turn of the century, the situation changed. In 2000 the first exhumations of mass graves took place, and in December of the same year the Asociación para le Recuperación de la Memoria Histórica (ARMH, Association for the Recovery of Historical Memory) began collecting oral and written testimonies of surviving victims of the Franco regime and excavating and identifying the remains of victims through DNA tests and other forensic methods.[3] But it was only during the first term of the government of PSOE prime minister José Zapatero (2004–8) that memory of the past was legitimized through specific legislative actions. For the first time official reference was made to the repression of the Franco regime and to the responsibility of Francoist insurgents for the outbreak of the Civil War. For the first time compensation was provided to victims of the War and of the Franco regime and associations of victims were publically subsidized, thus explicitly recognizing the importance of their work for the "recovery of historical memory." In an unprecedented initiative, 2006 was officially designated as the Year of Historical Memory. This was followed eighteen months later by the *Ley de reparación*.

The 2007 law was the culmination of a legislative process designed to reconfigure the historical narrative and its framework of values. The laws that came into being after 2004, up to and including the 2007 law, not only provide material compensation for victims but also reinterpret the meanings of their actions. They are no longer mere "victims" but are now "combatants for freedom and democracy." This reformulation forces a radical transformation of the discourse about Francoism, requiring a renegotiation of public narratives regarding the Civil War and the dictatorship.[4]

What made it possible after 2004 for such radical changes in memory politics to occur? Distance in time is a factor. Memories of the Civil War are now largely the "postmemories" of the grandchildren of the combatants—that is, memories that are not firsthand (Hirsch 1997, 2012). The reluctance of their parents and grandparents to deal with what for their generation was an all too recent trauma is superseded by a temporal distance that facilitates much more openness about the past. Moreover, *communicative memory*, embedded in personal memories of those who participated directly in the events and transmitted mainly through oral testimonies within families and friends, has evolved into *cultural memory*, a knowledge of history based on texts and documents of various kinds rather than on witnesses' accounts (Assmann 2011). The rise of memory politics as an international discourse has also had an influence on developments in Spain. The truth and reconciliation commissions in Latin America and South Africa and the extensive debate on Holocaust memory in Europe and North America have all contributed to a globalized sensitivity regarding public memories and to the emergence of a new human rights awareness. These developments call for a sense of history that is focused on victims and a form of reconciliation that requires acknowledgment of wrongs of the past.

Within this overall framework, civil society organizations that are fighting for the remembrance of the victims on the Republican side, the most important of which is the ARMH, have a powerful public presence. Their efforts to bring the past to light are complemented by those of international organizations such as Amnesty International, which between 2005 and 2006 published three different reports on the situation in Spain; the UN Human Rights Committee; and the Standing Committee of the Parliamentary Assembly of the Council of Europe, which in 2006 unanimously approved the condemnation of the Franco regime and called on the Spanish government to honor the victims of the Civil War and of the dictatorship.

The *Ley de memoria histórica*

Despite its popular title, the 2007 *Ley de memoria histórica* does not, according to its justifying reasons (*Exposición de motivos*), seek to "implant a particular collective memory." Nevertheless, it faces the issue of memory in an innovative way by recognizing an "*individual right of each citizen to personal and family memory*" (emphasis added). Emilio Silva (2008) argues that the emphasis put by the law on "individual" rather than "collective" memory leads to a privatization of memory. I suggest that his criticism is unjustified. It was after all the dominant narrative supported by Francoism that forced alternative public memories underground and thus privatized the memories of the Republican side. By recognizing the right to individual memories, the law makes such memories not only visible and speakable but also components of democratic discourse, as is explicitly recognized in the *Exposición de motivos*: "various aspects relating to personal and family memory, when they have been affected by conflicts of public nature, are *part of the legal status of democratic citizenship*" (emphasis added). The banished memories of victims thus emerge from the private sphere to which the Franco regime had confined them and enter public space. There is no precise distinction between individual memories and collective memories. The issue is which and whose memories are allowed to enter public discourse and which memories are considered legitimate. The

Franco regime made Republican memories illegitimate. In the face of this history, the law takes a correct stance by being cautious about any claims of a collective, unified memory—something that is not only beyond the reach of legislation but also quite problematic in itself. More appropriate is the goal of attributing dignity and space to alternative memories and narratives suppressed over the years, thus giving them recognition and overcoming the former imbalance between the opposing parties. The right to memory claimed in the *Exposición de motivos* is first and foremost a "right to biography" (Lotman 2005): according to Lotman, only some privileged subjects possess the right to a unique biography that will transmit their memory. The law's right to memory corresponds to the official recognition of alternative narratives that belong to subjects previously canceled and forgotten.

The law consists of twenty-two articles, the first three of which are of a general character. Article 1 describes the law's *objective* as the "recognition and extension of rights in favor of those who suffered persecution or violence, for reasons of politics, ideology, or for religious beliefs, during the Civil War or the Dictatorship." Article 2 declares completely unjust in nature "all convictions, punishments, or other forms of personal violence which took place . . . whether during the Civil War or during the Dictatorship." Article 3 is a *declaration of illegitimacy* for all the courts, tribunals, and organs constituted during the Civil War as well as for the penalties and punishments ordered during the dictatorship. The remaining articles can be categorized as follows:

- Symbolic and political recognition of the Republican victims and their heirs (Article 4: Reparación y reconocimiento personal) and material compensation of the same (Articles 5–10)
- Identification of nameless victims and the localization and reopening of graves (Articles 11–14)
- Transformation and/or destruction of Francoist symbols and monuments (Articles 15–17)
- Recognition of International Brigades volunteers and victims' associations (Articles 18 and 19)
- Termination of state secrecy and opening of archives (Articles 20–22)

The law affirms the rights of victims as specific individuals. But it also introduces measures that have implications for the whole of society. It provides moral and material compensation for victims. But it also engages in a project of historical reconstruction by affirming the activities and values of victims' associations and of those who fought on the side of the Republic in the Civil War. The value of those who opposed Franco and fought for democracy is indirectly recognized and thus, too, the values that motivated their actions.

The three final articles (Articles 20, 21, 22) sanction the ending of state secrecy and the opening up of the archives. This measure is of obvious importance to victims and their families and especially to the younger generations who are thus granted the possibility (and responsibility) of reconstructing not only their own past but also that of their predecessors. Articles regarding compensation of victims are directed to the past, to restoration of justice denied. Those regarding secrecy and historical truth are also directed to the future. However, the core value served by Articles 20, 21, and 22 is truth.

In dictatorial regimes secrets and lies are closely interrelated and imply the existence of each other. State secrecy denies access to all documents and records that would allow the truth to be known. At the same time, government propaganda spreads falsehoods. The opening up of the archives means the end of secrets and, at the same time, a revelation of the falsehood of propaganda and the possibility of knowing exactly what did and did not happen. Truth and secrecy also intimately concern the constitution of collective memory. A truth made inaccessible, an event kept secret, cannot belong to a public narrative. An essential step, then, is the reconstruction of truth or at least the facilitation of access to historical sources that will allow an approach to the truth, thus exposing what had been kept secret.

A second group of articles that are highly significant for the logic of memory has to do with the location and opening of mass graves, the identification of bodies, and their appropriate (re)burial. Historians now agree that during the Spanish Civil War, between seventy thousand and one hundred thousand opponents of Franco were executed (Juliá 1999; Casanova 2002) and for the most part buried in mass graves or left unburied. Executions and massacres were also perpetrated by the Republican side, but, unlike Franco's victims, those killed by the Republicans were located, exhumed, and commemorated during the dictatorship period with burials and monuments, the most famous being the controversial Valle de los Caídos, which is explicitly mentioned in Article 16 and where Franco's body is still buried. In the vast majority of cases, however, the dead on the Republican side remained nameless and without gravestones: disturbing ghosts in the symbolic political reconstruction process following the dictator's death. Here, there are parallels between the Spanish case and that of Argentina, where the *desaparecidos* have remained in the collective imagination with the ambiguous status of being both not-dead and not-living: uncanny witnesses of a traumatic past not yet overcome. The *desaparecidos* never belong entirely to the category of the dead, since no tangible remains of their bodies exist, nor were there rituals and practices that in our societies allow the transformation of a dead body into the social identity of a person no longer with us (Hallam and Hockey 2001).

Deprived of identity, recognition, and burial, the dead become phantoms, existent no longer on the plane of individual uniqueness but only as an indistinct group, as "social figures," points of intersection between history and subjectivity (Gordon 2008), as salient places of "unclaimed experience" situated at the very core of the trauma (Caruth 1996). In this context, the politics of burial and reburial assume a unique value: reburial not only restores the place of the dead in history but also allows new relationships to form between the living and the dead. As observed by Katherine Verdery (1999), the practice of reburial serves both to create and to reconfigure a sense of community.

The articles relating to the reopening of graves also sanction a particular form of compensation for the many nameless victims: the return of their individual identity. Identification is a very important and central part of an act of recognition, as it gives back their names to those who lost them and, with them, the traces of their actual existence. Deletion of names and historical oblivion are closely linked, as the Roman senators, who devised the *damnatio memoriae*, knew well: deletion of the name signifies disappearance from history. Conversely, restoration of the name signifies restoration of historical existence and, with it, a memory. Since the Napoleonic wars nations have remembered their war dead and victims of atrocity by means of a registration of names where these are known; a wall of names is often an integral part of contemporary mausoleums and memorials, from Yad Vashem in Jerusalem to the monuments to the fallen both in Vietnam and in Washington, DC. Identification and restitution of their names are thus profound acts of recognition of the victims.

These Articles are not only a way of recognizing the dead; they also have a meaning for society as a whole. Funerals serve as a means for the collective processing of loss and for the reestablishment of the conditions for coexistence. Here again, the law demonstrates careful attention to symbolic issues and to the construction of a sense of collectivity. But social processes of dealing with trauma are neither simple nor straightforward. The reopening of mass graves and the exhumation of bodies are highly emotional events because of the visual force of the associated images; they arouse contradictory collective passions that cannot be easily managed. In fact, not all relatives of victims have agreed to reopen such wounds, with some preferring to renounce the exhumation of remains and their eventual relocation (Silva 2005; Ferrándiz 2006, 2008; Jerez-Farrán and Amago 2010; Renshaw 2011).

Articles 15–17, having to do with the transformation or destruction of Francoist symbols and monuments, are less emotionally charged but in some ways more problematic. These Articles call for the undoing of what could be called "Francoist territorial semiotization": that is, the inscription of the landscape with the ideology of the Franco regime through monuments, effigies, and inscriptions. From a semiotic point of view, an operation to remove signs and symbols of a repudiated past raises questions not only about its effectiveness but also about its underlying ideology.

Can we return to the "authentic" or neutral character of a place or a building simply by eliminating the inscriptions left by its history? From a semiotic perspective, this is doubtful, since each subsequent act of inscription alters the original meaning of a text while also becoming an integral part of it, thus blocking any alleged recovery of the original. Not even the cancellation of traces guided by the best of intentions can escape this logic of a progressive accumulation and layering of meanings. Memory, once inscribed in a landscape and in space, is extremely difficult to regulate or even remove; what appears to be a recovery of the past always turns out to be a rewriting of it. There is an alternative to cancellation, namely a "reflexive conservation": the transformation of signs into *memory sites*, enabling and encouraging a continuous interrogation of the past one desires to eliminate. Traces of crimes carried out, which in any case are indelible, may then be restored to a logic of historical intelligibility, ensuring the passage of memories to future generations. Traces of the past are semiotically stratified inscriptions in complex palimpsests that manifest the history of a community, a history that, no matter how tragic it may be, can be endowed also with a positive sense, as both a memory and a warning for the future. For this purpose places of extermination and death such as concentration camps and torture centers are kept intact and turned into museums (Violi 2012).

Weaknesses Inherent in the Law of Historical Memory

"Forget, forgive, conclude and be agreed," says Richard II in Shakespeare's play, suggesting a way out from a past of endless fratricidal wars that is not unlike that of the *Pacto de olvido*. With the Law of Historical Memory a different option was adopted: revisiting the traumatic past to reestablish neglected rights, to validate countermemories of victims, and, even more important, to generate an alternative narrative of the past based on a different value framework. This latter goal, however, was not completely met. This partial failure was the result not least of the contradictory values underlying the law. In order to understand this, it is useful to position the Law of Historical Memory in relation to other means that have been used to deal with a traumatic past, ranging from truth and reconciliation commissions to international courts. Adapting a classification proposed by Aleida Assmann (2009), we can

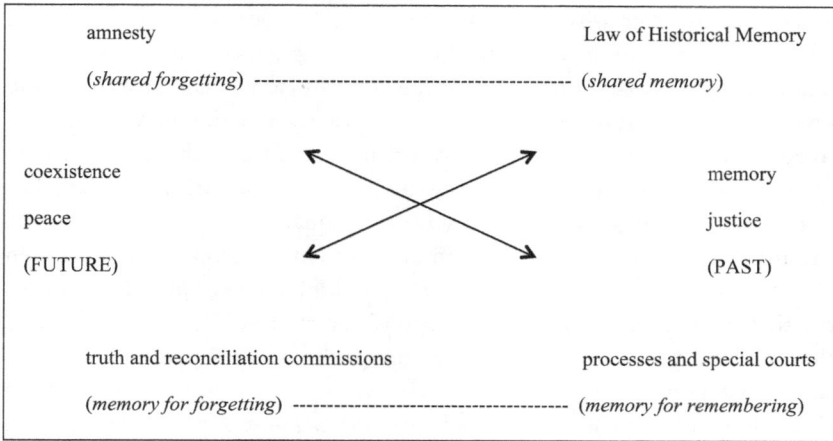

```
amnesty                                    Law of Historical Memory

    (shared forgetting) ------------------------------------ (shared memory)


coexistence                                              memory

peace                                                    justice

(FUTURE)                                                 (PAST)



    truth and reconciliation commissions     processes and special courts

    (memory for forgetting) ----------------------------- (memory for remembering)
```

Figure 1

show the relationship between these processes and the way they deal with memory by means of the semiotic square shown in figure 1.

Though transitional justice in all its different forms is much more nuanced than this schema suggests, the semiotic square has the advantage of schematically representing the system of semantic relationships that relate individual terms to one another, thus making visible aspects of their signification function that would otherwise be left implicit and less visible. In particular it enables us to see the inherent tension between the values that lie at the heart of the 2007 law and thus helps us to understand why it did not succeed in unifying an unstable system of values in reciprocal tension.

Amnesty, with its accompanying covenant of silence, requires shared forgetting and in this sense is directly opposed to the 2007 law, which at least in intention, if not in outcome, aims for "shared memory." On the diagonal axis of contradiction, amnesty opposes the "obsession with remembering" that, according to Assmann, characterizes the memory of the Holocaust but is also present in the will "not to forget" that underlies legal processes and special tribunals. Presenting the work of truth commissions as contradictory to the law is more problematic but is justified by the focus of truth commissions on reconciliation and peaceful coexistence, rather than on creating a shared memory.

The transitional justice processes on the left side of the diagram are oriented toward *peace* and *coexistence* and those on the right toward *memory* and *justice*. These two value orientations differ in a significant way: while peace and coexistence are temporally "progressive" in that they point to the future, memory and justice are "regressive" in the sense that they are oriented toward the past. The semiotic square thus exhibits the value ambiguity on which the law was built. In its very declaration of intent the law states as its main goal the will to produce "reconciliation and concord," thus placing its action on what appears to be the left side of the square, which is also the one facing the future. On the other hand, however, the law is clearly situated on the pole of values that relate to memory and justice on the right side of the square and therefore is oriented toward the past. A tension, if not an outright contradiction, exists between the explicit declaration of intent in the law and the values of justice and memory that the law aims to establish in opposition to the oblivion that followed the amnesty. A similar tension also permeates the law in its temporal orientation, leaving open an unstable balance between past and future, memory and oblivion, that the law is unable to fully reconcile. This tension is probably one of the main causes of the partial lack of success of the Law of Historical Memory.

In fact, the 2007 law pleased nobody, either on the right or on the left (Aguilar and Humlebæk 2002; Aguilar 2009; Humlebæk 2011). A common criticism advanced by those on the left, especially by those involved in the historical memory movement, was that the law was "not enough": it incorporated too many compromises and, most important, did not foresee any punishment for perpetrators. Impunity is indeed the most controversial aspect of the law, since the law did not require trials in court for those responsible for crimes and other offenses or any other quasi-juridical form of redress, such as a truth commission. Other critics, such as the historian and polemicist Santos Juliá (2006), who could not be suspected of sympathy for the Franco regime, questioned the very appropriateness of legislative action on issues of memory. Regarding the efficacy of the law, evaluations have not been unanimous either: Emilio Silva has voiced his doubts about its usefulness (Ángel Marfull 2008; Silva 2008). International organizations such as Amnesty International have also taken critical positions, claiming that the Spanish state is still disregarding its obligations to provide for reparations and justice.

The criticism from the right—that a recuperation of memory is unnecessary, undesirable, and even harmful, as it evokes past traumas with a risk of exacerbating conflicts—is predictable. But the right has also been able to position itself as the defender of the transition to democracy. Accusing the Socialists of failing to observe the founding pact of silence at the core of Spanish democracy, the right engineered a semantic turn within the political debate, first equating "memory" with "vengeance" and then contrasting "historical memory" (increasingly read as "social vengeance") with "democratic coexistence." This led to "memory" and "democracy" being opposed to each other, with "democracy" acquiring positive connotations, while "memory," equated with

Patrizia Violi

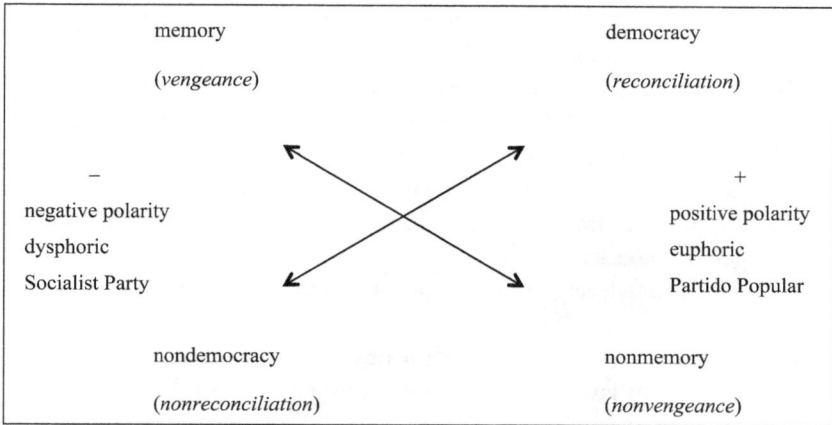

```
        memory                              democracy

       (vengeance)                       (reconciliation)


  −                    ↖        ↗                      +
  negative polarity         ╲  ╱              positive polarity
  dysphoric                  ╳               euphoric
  Socialist Party           ╱  ╲              Partido Popular
                        ↙        ↘

      nondemocracy                         nonmemory

   (nonreconciliation)                   (nonvengeance)
```

Figure 2

vengeance, became a negative term. This semantic turn allowed the right to identify itself with the positive value of democracy and to identify the left with the negative value of memory. Another semiotic square (figure 2) delineates the system of semantic oppositions that came into being.

Making use of this framework of meaning, the rightwing Partido Popular (People's Party) managed to achieve three important semantic transformations within the political debate: first, it validated a negative image of memory as a source of potential division and conflict; second, it attributed this negative image to the left; and, finally, it regained for the right the positive legacy linked to the memory of democratic transition. The "bad" memories of the Civil War with their symbolic baggage of hate and vengeance were pushed onto the side of the left, while the "good" memories of the democratic transition were appropriated by the right. Such a complex political strategy was successful, at least in part, because both the center and the moderate left were concerned about possible negative consequences of reopening conflicts regarding historical memory.

Conclusion

At the time of writing, six years after the passing of the Law of Historical Memory, Spaniards, much like other Europeans, are preoccupied with economic issues. The *Indignados* movement has not been particularly concerned with issues of memory. But it is difficult to imagine that the painful work of dealing with the past will remain forever in the background in Spain, because the relationship between past memories and democracy is far too crucial to be underestimated and neglected.

It should be noted, however, that the People's Party government, which took over from Zapatero's PSOE government in 2011, did not try to change the law. This could be interpreted as an acceptance of the principles stated in the law or at least a will not to reopen a discussion on this matter. This was coupled with a disappearance from the political agenda of memory issues in the face of more cogent economical needs.

Despite the low level of public approval[5] and the partial failure of the law to facilitate a sharing of traumatic memories of the Civil War and of the dictatorship, the law has merits. Besides the obviously positive action of opening up the archives, the law proposed an alternative narrative of the past based on a different value system, thus changing the semiotic frame of reference. The 2007 law was innovative in three respects: first, by postulating a right to memory for victims and insisting on the social and public validation of their memories; second, by reframing the historical discourse and proposing a new value system in which those who suffered or were persecuted are seen as both victims and fighters in pursuit of a legitimate cause; third, by unambiguously declaring the Franco regime illegitimate.

The 2007 law does not provide and even less prescribes a univocal memory but rather reestablishes and vindicates the dignity and historical value of narratives of marginalized and forgotten "others." It has done so by political means in the performative form of legislative discourse, rather than through individual judicial processes. For all these reasons the law can be seen as an important, albeit controversial and partly unsuccessful, step in a longer transition.

This brings us back to the relationship between memory and transitional justice. The 2007 law shows how, even years after the formal establishment of democracy, memory and related human rights issues can reenter the political agenda, especially when new generations and new social actors such as civil society associations appear on the scene. Not only can transitions be long-term processes; they are often also complex asynchronous and nonlinear processes in which remembering and forgetting alternate over time. Legislation can influence such processes. However, a "culture of transition" is not only a matter of transitional justice; it also requires the generation of alternative narratives, which inevitably coexist and confront each other in the longer run.

Notes

1. The full title of Ley 52/2007 is *Ley por la que se reconocen y amplían derechos y se establecen medidas en favor de quienes padecieron persecución o violencia durante la*

Guerra Civil y la Dictadura (Law to recognize and broaden rights and to establish measures in favor of those who suffered persecution or violence during the Civil War and the Dictatorship); see http://www.boe.es/boe/dias/2007/12/27/pdfs/A53410-53416 .pdf.

2. On the politics of memories in Spain, see, among others, Aguilar 2001, 2002, 2008, 2009; Aguilar and Humlebæk 2002; Ranzato 2008; Bernecker 2009; Alonso and Muro 2011; Humlebæk 2011.

3. In semiotic terms, ARMH represents a "social addresser" (Greimas and Courtès 1979), the abstract narrative role of the social instance that establishes the set of values that will govern the actions to be carried out. The appearance of a civil society organization as social addresser marks an important cultural shift, since in general the role of social adresser is performed by institutional entities, such as the government or the judiciary.

4. According to Louis Hjelmslev (1954), meaning is a stratified entity, whose more profound level is represented by "collective appreciation," that is, by an attribution of collective values. What is apparently "one and the same thing" can be endowed with very different social and cultural values; dogs, for example, are sacred animals in some societies, despised in others, and familiar domestic presences in others. Thus, they are no longer one and the same thing.

5. In the only available survey (Metroscopia for *El País*, February 3, 2008, cited in Aguilar 2009, 148), appreciation measures only 5.3 on a scale of 1 to 10, even lower than the controversial law on homosexual marriage. In light of such data, we can instead contrast the high appreciation attributed to memory of the transition, positively evaluated by 80 percent of Spaniards (see the studies by the Centro de Investigaciones Sociológicas, commented on in Aguilar and Humlebæk 2002, 153). From these data we can draw two conclusions. In the first place, while there is a widely approved positive shared memory regarding the democratic transition, the memory of past traumas is still highly controversial and a source of conflict. Second, the amnesty, despite all the ethical problems it entails, has managed to create agreement about memory in the period since 1975.

7

How Can Truth Telling Count as Reparations?

MARGARET URBAN WALKER

International human rights discourse now encompasses a "right to know" or "right to truth" about the occurrence, circumstances, causes, and perpetrators of all gross human rights violations and serious breaches of international humanitarian law (Méndez 1997a, 2006; United Nations 2006a, 2007). The right is both individual and collective. The rights bearers are victims, their families and representatives, and "society" or "a people." Obligations fall upon governments not only to protect human rights but also to effectively investigate gross violations of human rights and to make the information discovered available. The right is currently described as "inalienable," "autonomous," and "non-derogable" (United Nations 2006a). The right to truth has achieved visibility over the past decade as truth commissions and other investigative mechanisms burgeoned (Rotberg and Thompson 2000; Borer 2006; Bickford 2007; Hayner 2011). The right is recognized and elaborated progressively by international treaties and instruments; national legislation in some countries; national, regional, and international jurisprudence; and international and regional intergovernmental organizations.

Two distinct sets of international norms feature a right to truth. Principles for "combating impunity" of human rights violators have enshrined a "right to know" from their earliest formulation (United Nations 1997). The most recent 2005 update of these principles describes the "right to know" not only as the "imprescriptable" right of victims and their families but also as the "inalienable" right of "a people" to know the "history of oppression" that is "part of its heritage" (United Nations 2005, Principles 2, 3, 4). States are obligated to preserve "collective memory from extinction . . . guarding against the development of revisionist and negationist arguments" (United Nations 2005, Principle 3). Effective measures to get to the truth and make it available are needed both for "recognition of the dignity of victims and their families" and to combat denial (United Nations 2005, Principle 6). Rights to the truth also figure in the "Basic Principles and Guidelines on the Right to a Remedy and Reparation for Victims of Gross Violations of International Human Rights Law and Serious Violations of Humanitarian Law" (United Nations 2006b). While access to "factual information concerning the violation" is a core remedy for individual victims (alongside access to justice and reparation for harm in Article VII), rights to truth also appear in a second role in the same document as rights to a distinct kind of *reparations*. Under the category of reparations through "satisfaction," at least four of eight diverse measures are related specifically to truth telling: "verification of the facts and full public disclosure of the truth"; search for the whereabouts and identities of the executed, the disappeared, and abducted children, and assistance in recovery, identification and reburial of remains of murdered victims; public apology, "including acknowledgment of the facts and acceptance of responsibility"; and "inclusion of an accurate account of the violations that occurred in international human rights law and international humanitarian law training and in educational material at all levels" (United Nations 2006b, Article IX). Arguably, two other measures of "satisfaction" are related to establishing the truth as well: commemorations that remember victims and their fates and official declarations "restoring the dignity, the reputation and the rights of victims and of persons closely connected with the victim" (United Nations 2006b, Article IX).

Finding and telling the truth about grave wrongs is obviously a *condition* of remedies and reparations. Establishing the facts of a violation is necessary in order to redress it, that is, to make the case that remedies and reparations are required and to decide which are appropriate. It is not so obvious that finding and telling the truth about violations is itself a kind of remedy or a kind of reparation. Richard Falk (2006) comments on the emergence of truth telling as reparation in a deflationary tone; he suggests that among the obligations that states might recognize in postauthoritarian or postconflict settings, "satisfaction" through truth telling might be favored on grounds of expediency. Falk notes that the post–World War II era witnessed an historically unprecedented movement from a purely "state-centric" orientation in international law toward an acceptance of state responsibility to *individuals*, rather than to other states (see also Colonomos and Armstrong 2006). But, he adds:

Such a drive for corrective justice was tempered by resource constraints and by the search for normalcy or social peace, tending to produce compromise approaches, especially encouraging an approach to feasible levels of "satisfaction" for victims by reliance on truth and reconciliation processes adapted to the particularities of a given country. The end result is an acknowledgment of the past, but without great efforts either to punish perpetrators or to compensate victims. Symbolic forms of redress prevail, with both corrective and deterrent goals. (Falk 2006, 490)

Falk's point is politically plausible, but it does not answer the question. Truth commissions, documentation of massacres, or truth trials might be cheaper and more feasible, financially and politically, than criminal prosecutions, civil litigation, or massive material reparations programs. Even so, can a case be made morally for truth telling itself as one form of genuine reparations rather than a less costly substitute?

I defend the status of politically implemented modes of truth telling as a kind of reparations (see Walker 2010 for an earlier version of this argument). I do not claim that truth telling alone is sufficient reparation for serious wrongs or that the effectiveness of orchestrated truth telling as a form of reparations is independent of whether other forms of reparations are given. Like other particular vehicles or modes of reparations, the meaning and effectiveness of truth telling as a form of reparations is affected by whether other kinds of reparations (or other measures of redress or institutional change) are also offered or attempted. In this respect, truth telling does not differ from other measures readily recognized as reparations. Monetary compensation, for many the paradigm of reparation, is also insufficient in and of itself without acknowledgment or apology. My argument provides an account of the aim of reparation that particular reparations measures serve and of four conditions that specific vehicles used to provide reparations must meet. I use this account to defend concerted tellings of certain truths as a suitable and significant vehicle for reparations in particular situations. In conclusion, I note three challenges for truth telling as reparations that have become apparent as truth recovery in the face of human rights abuses becomes a common practice: epistemically effective truth dissemination, accessible truth preservation, and institutional disaggregation of the search for and preservation of the truth.

The Nature and Aims of Reparations Measures

Reparations are intentionally reparative actions in which goods (material and interactive) are tendered to victims of wrong by parties that acknowledge responsibility for wrongs or for their repair and whose reparative

Margaret Urban Walker

actions are intended to redress those wrongs as a question of justice. It is not in itself what is given to or done for a victim of wrong, the person or entities that give or do it, or even the act of giving or doing it that constitutes reparations. It is rather the roles these play in the giver's attempt at a communicative act with a particular content: a message of acknowledgment, responsibility, and intent of rendering just treatment deserved by a victim who has been wronged. Regardless of the particular vehicle, the vindicatory message—the message of acknowledgment, responsibility, and intent to do justice—is the "expressive" dimension that is essential to constitute the act as reparations rather than simple indemnification, charitable concern, or a purely forwarding-looking redistributive effort.

For this reason, a now common distinction between "symbolic" and "material" reparations, where the term "symbolic" is meant to cover any reparations measures, individual or collective, that do not have monetary value, can be misleading (de Greiff 2006, 452–53). An act or object is "symbolic" if it is or involves a representation of something else not actually present, so that what is symbolic is opposed to what is real or actually present. Using "symbolic" to denote acts or objects without monetary value to victims implies that it is monetary or other materially valuable acts and objects that are the only "real" reparations and that reparations such as memorials or apologies are acts and objects just "standing in" for the unavailable "real" goods that are necessarily ones of monetary value.

Yet *all* reparations are symbolic and cannot be otherwise in being reparations. What I have called the expressive dimension—the communicative act of expressing acknowledgment, responsibility, and intent to do justice—that constitutes an interaction or tender of goods as reparations is a necessary feature, no matter what measures, including money or monetarily valuable instruments, goods, or services, are offered. To call an apology or a memorial "symbolic" might imply that such measures or interaction aren't themselves effective transactions in real time with very concrete effects among human beings. Apologies necessarily use words, and memorials use visual, tactile, and verbal materials in representative ways in order to conduct this transaction; so too is the monetary payment the symbolic use of a financial instrument to conduct the same kind of transaction. In every case, however, the transaction is a real event or process aimed at an alteration in the relationship and standing of the parties. If the transaction is successful, it produces real effects of psychological, moral, social, or political kinds; if it misfires or is poorly executed, the very real effects can include resentment, outrage, bitterness, despair, and cynicism, as well as continuing legal and political action to secure meaningful reparations.

In order to redress a wrong, the truth about that wrong must be uncovered and acknowledged. Because all reparations depend upon the expressive dimension that acknowledges offense, responsibility, and intent to do justice, truth telling about a wrong is also a constitutive element of that expressive function. So, truth telling is clearly both a *condition* and a *constituent* of reparations measures. I want to defend the further distinct proposition that truth telling *in itself* in the appropriate context can be an act of reparations. I begin with an account of the goal of reparation at which specific reparations measures aim. I then offer an account of how a particular "vehicle" of reparations embodies and sustains the expressive dimension that acknowledges violation, responsibility, and the need for justice.

First, what aim or end do reparations embodied in various vehicles serve? Recent work on reparations, filtered through diverse practical and disciplinary contexts, invokes different idioms of damage and repair. Psychosocial perspectives address relieving the suffering, distress, anger and sense of violation experienced by victims (Herman 1992; Walker 2006a; Hamber 2009). Legal approaches focus on restoring the status quo ante or making the victim whole. Political discussions speak in terms of equal citizenship, parity of public status and recognition, and civic and social trust (Brooks 2004; Roht-Arriaza 2004; de Greiff 2006; Walker 2006c; Satz 2007; Gray 2010; and, on civil litigation and reparations, Malamud-Goti and Grosman 2006). The moral idiom in discussions of reparations usually refers to the restoration or recognition of the dignity of victims and the reaffirmation or reconstruction of a moral order. "Material" harms are distinguished from the "moral" or "dignitary" harms of insult, disrespect, disregard, and abuse from which they are inseparable and that thus require responses that do more than offer material relief. As Bernard Boxill (1972) said decades ago, reparation requires not only acknowledgment of wrong but an affirmation of the dignity and moral equality of the wronged party and a rejection of the imputation of deserved ill treatment, inferiority, or lack of standing that the wrong implies.

Drawing on my own work on moral repair, I understand reparations as governed by moral aims, while recognizing that these aims are implemented politically and expressed socially. By moral repair I mean the attempt to reconstruct or introduce recognizably moral patterns of relationship after wrongdoing. I identify three central conditions of functioning moral relations that are threatened or damaged by serious wrongs (Walker 2006b, 23–28). One is the *confidence* that there are mutually recognized and defensible shared standards that define roughly aligned normative expectations between parties. A second is *trust* that parties may rely on each other to be responsive to these standards, either by conforming to them or by acknowledging that failure to conform creates liabilities and possibly obligations. The trust in question may

Margaret Urban Walker

be either rather general or specific to relationships with distinct histories. Third, and less commonly recognized, parties must sustain *hopefulness* about the defensibility and mutual acceptance of moral standards and about the trustworthiness of individuals to respond to them. Discussions of reparation often focus on restoring trust in authorities and institutions and creating confidence that shared standards are (now or once again) ones that protect citizens and affirm their dignity. I argue that hopefulness is an even more fundamental condition of moral relations. The hopefulness that sustains moral relations involves a motivating belief that there is a possibility, even if uncertain or slight, that defensible standards are shared and that individuals are disposed to respond to what the standards require. Hopefulness can be essential to restoring trust, because the trust we repose in each other in acting on coordinated normative expectations set by shared standards is often disappointed. Hence, the mutual reliance involved in trust needs to be maintained by hopefulness at least about the general reliability of fellow moral actors, whether or not future reliance on wrongdoers is possible or wise. The centrality of hope has important consequences for understanding repair and, more specifically, reparations measures.

All reparative gestures, I have suggested, are inevitably *symbolic*, even when they tender monetary compensation, material goods, or property. Their reparative force is carried in part by how clearly they exemplify the "right relationship" that wrongdoing has denied or broken. Reparative gestures, however, are particular actions at a particular time; they are necessarily promissory, tokening the possibility of morally acceptable relations henceforward. So while reparations measures invite trust, what they offer immediately, if they seem genuinely motivated, is hope. They demonstrate the possibility of a respectful interaction in light of shared standards, and they aim to motivate and energize thought, feeling, and action toward making that form of interaction reliable, that is, toward building or rebuilding trust based on shared standards.

The question then becomes: how do reparations carry the vindicatory message of acknowledgment, responsibility, and intent to do justice? How do they model a kind of moral relationship that assures those formerly disregarded, disrespected, and grossly mistreated that wrongs are acknowledged, standards shared, responsibilities accepted, and obligations of repair perceived as requirements of justice? I argue now that specific features of the vehicles or measures offered as reparations sustain (or where absent defeat) that message. Appropriate vehicles of reparation are ones that, in context, open a genuine interaction, are useful to victims, fit the specific nature of the wrongs and harms suffered, and are effectively designed to reach victims. I offer this account as a normative framework; these are conditions of success that reparations vehicles must approximate to carry the constitutive message. They are the dimensions of success or failure of the specifically expressive burden of reparations.

1. *Interactive*. The vehicle is suitable to be the focus of an *interaction* between responsible parties and victims. Responsible parties include the actual perpetrators of wrong but also parties otherwise responsible (for example, by complicity or culpable inaction) and always in some ways the communities that are the reference point for the norms violated and for the reaffirmation of norms and of the victims' deservingness of repair. Victims are construed for the purposes of this interaction as those who have suffered intentional harms directed at them. In keeping with current legal and political understandings, however, reparations may be offered to others unavoidably and severely affected by wrongs, such as families, close relations, and dependents of direct victims. This interactive aspect crucially represents *acknowledgment of relationship and the intent to repair it*.

2. *Useful*. The vehicle is *useful* for victims in this sense: it is suitable to the victims' own use in coping with the harms inflicted by the wrongdoing. It might be used to replace what was lost; as a means to pursue interests otherwise thwarted by the wrong and its harms; as a means to pursue interests that replace and in some degree compensate for those interests that can no longer be pursued because of the wrong and its harm; or to provide some degree of satisfaction or relief for the pain, suffering, and grief caused by the wrong and its harms. The limiting case is restitution, where the very thing lost or destroyed is returned or restored. More commonly, reparations offer something the victim of wrong can use to deal with the irreversible loss and damage the wrong has caused, and, because these losses and harms are various, so may reparative measures vary. This element represents the *acknowledgment of the victims' experience of suffering and loss while demonstrating respect for the victims' agency*.

3. *Fitting*. Crucially, reparative measures must be *fitting*. The vehicle is related to the wrong and harm that were endured in such ways as to seem *appropriate and deserved*, especially to the victim but also to others in their community. It must be recognizable as a response to the particular wrong and loss in question, to the diminished opportunities and well-being it caused, and to the pain, suffering, and grief inflicted. It must make a statement to the victim but also to the society or community of the seriousness of the violation and the urgency of addressing it as a matter of justice. Fit is intimately and intuitively related to justice. The common requirement of "proportionality" of compensation to injury in corrective justice is one kind of fit. The fittingness of the vehicle represents an *appreciation of the nature, meaning, and magnitude of what is "due" as a matter of justice*.

4. *Effective*. The vehicle must be carefully considered and ideally negotiated so that victims of wrong are *able to access and use it* and so that they can take up the intended interaction and experience what is given as fitting and

Margaret Urban Walker

deserved. Care in selecting a vehicle for its effectiveness represents the *seriousness and sincerity* of amends makers in the attempt at reparation. It expresses their acceptance of responsibility and their focus on the victim's concrete experience of repair.

These four criteria typically operate implicitly. Questions or contests surrounding proposed reparations from the side of victims or advocates are usually about whether particular measures in fact fulfill these conditions. That these conditions express reasonable expectations of reparations is assumed. A formulaic or evasive reparations measure, like a public pronouncement of regret that does not engage the wishes or require the awareness or response of victims or that does not come from the appropriate authorities, violates the first *interactive* condition and may aggravate the victims' sense of being disregarded. The sad and tangled case of women enslaved in brothels by the Japanese Army in World War II illustrates repetitive failures of interaction. The so-called comfort women sought and failed to achieve a direct response from the Japanese government as a condition of accepting monetary reparation, a question of appropriate interaction and accountability (see Iida 2004; Fackler and Sang-Hun 2007; Onishi 2007). The second and third conditions, *value* and *fit*, address victim perceptions of whether a reparations vehicle acknowledges and expresses appreciation of the nature of the loss victims have suffered. The Lakota Sioux do not accept the proposed compensation payment by the US government for the unconstitutional taking of the Black Hills; the loss of the Black Hills is not a question of economic value for the Lakota, and payment for them does not fit the offense of cultural destruction, genocidal dispossession, and denial of sovereign nationhood (Barkan 2000; Tsosie 2007). A question about the *effectiveness* condition arises, for example, for women who might receive lump-sum payments as victims of atrocity or torture in patriarchal societies in which women will realistically have no effective control over the economic resources tendered (Rubio Marín 2006, 34–35).

I claim that defending a particular vehicle as a kind of reparations requires that a good enough case can be made for it in terms of these conditions and that vehicles in fact offered or used as reparations are *correctly* vetted and contested on roughly these grounds (see Walker 2013). What now of truth as reparations?

How Truth Telling Functions as Reparations

The kinds of truth telling that can serve as reparations are concerted acts or processes of recovering and revealing truths in cases of severe and violent abuses and extended eras of oppression or repression. While a truth commission process has become a paradigm of concerted truth telling in the aftermath of mass violence and injustice, concerted and official truth telling that can function as reparations includes at least the following: investigating abuses and making the results of investigations about wrongs, actors, and institutions publicly accessible; making formerly secret documents public; exhuming human remains with the assistance of forensic experts; facilitating the access of victims to information; giving victims a public voice in articulating their experience of violence and injustice; and taking measures, especially educational, archival, or memorial, to disseminate and authoritatively promulgate truths and to preserve truths for future generations (Minow 1998; Rotberg and Thompson 2000; Teitel 2000; Thompson 2002; McCarthy 2002, 2004; Gibson 2004; Bilbija et al. 2005; Borer 2006; Freeman 2006; Walker 2007; Blustein 2008; Brudholm 2008; Hamber 2009; Wiebelhaus-Brahm 2010; Olsen et al. 2010; and Hayner 2011).

The power of truth telling as reparations derives from the way that oppressive and abusive power arrangements, both episodic and prolonged intergenerationally, require extensive coordination of social and epistemic orders (Walker 2007, especially chapters 3 and 7; see also Mills 1997, 91–109, on the "epistemology of ignorance" involved in racial domination; and Fricker 2007 on epistemic injustice). When people are invested in the conviction that their society is well ordered, they must be able to sustain certain beliefs that support their acceptance of and confidence in aspects of their social order and also be able to ignore or reject beliefs that are incompatible with that confidence. Where there is or has been violence, persecution, or oppression within a society, shared convolutions in belief, both gross and subtle, usefully create epistemic diversion and deniability in place of acknowledgment and accountability for those who *need others or themselves not to know* the truth. Convolutions include outright denial; defensive reinterpretations; "double discourses" that simultaneously deny facts and provide justifying minimizing explanations and euphemisms for the very thing denied; and protective incuriosity sustained by tacit agreements not to know more or not to say publicly what some or many people know (see Cohen 2001, 235, on "double discourses"). Elliot Jaspin, writing on largely unresearched racial expulsions in the post-Reconstruction United States, speaks of "the fable" that offers "a different and far more pleasing story of what happened"; shared euphemisms misname what has occurred and reduce systemic violence, communal action, and policies of repression to unfortunate "incidents" (Jaspin 2007, 238). Similarly, Iwona Irwin-Zarecka speaks of the "displacement (or replacement)" of one version of the past by "an alternative and morally comfortable vision" (Irwin-Zarecka 1994, 118, 120).

Margaret Urban Walker

These defenses against acknowledgment and accountability have profound effects on communities and societies as well as specific and destructive effects on victims of wrong and often on their survivors or even their descendants in unresolved histories of injustice. Reparative truth telling addresses two intertwined harms that often befall victims: their *epistemic impeachment* and their *degradation from the moral status of a credibly self-accounting actor*. These harms constitute a fundamental form of moral disqualification. They add a morally annihilating insult to the original injury.

Victims of political violence and repression or systemic oppression are often treated with the intent to degrade them. They are, at least, treated as if they deserved a form of treatment that would be unacceptably abusive if undeserved or are treated purely instrumentally without regard for their humanity and dignity. Significant parts of abusive and oppressive practices are invariably devoted to creating diminished statuses and stigmatized social identities that make it easier to justify the practices, to conceal certain treatment or effects, or to fabricate support for treatment that would otherwise be patently unacceptable. In the case of historical injustice, to be a member of a group subjected to unredressed systemic and intergenerational oppression is typically to live both with the inertial effects of this kind of diminished status and with widespread and normal social denial of either the detailed history of the oppression or the persisting effects or both. The result is that it becomes difficult and even unreasonable for many others to believe what one knows is true; victims labor under excessive burdens of proof, are deprived of basic credibility in giving their own accounts, and find their standing to demand accountings of others ignored or rejected. The most profound disqualification from participation in the practices of mutual accounting that make up moral life is to be unable to command an accounting from others and to lack the standing credibly to give accounts of oneself. Where this occurs, even with respect to a particular matter, this is a disqualification, at least locally, from the relation of accountability itself (Walker 2014).

The concerted official truth telling that is becoming part of the standard menu of internationally recognized best practices following conflict and repression is an attempt to intervene and disrupt the momentum toward epistemic impeachment and degradation of the moral status of victims that so commonly results from denials of grave wrongs. Because of this common situation, truth telling can in fact be an interactive, useful, fitting, and effective vehicle of reparations in the following ways.

1. *Interactive.* Concerted tellings of truths about violence and injustice intentionally provide information meant to circulate publicly and to be

subject to discussion and evaluation or made the basis of other actions such as demands for additional investigation or revelation, criminal prosecution, or other reparations. Truth telling puts important and previously hidden or undiscovered evidence and testimony into circulation and at the disposal of victims, parties responsible for wrongs or their repair, and their societies. It potentially opens a field of epistemic and moral interaction. It enhances the power of victims and witnesses to speak with basic credibility about what victims have suffered and its effects; it closes off some routes of escape for their listeners through denial or diversion.

2. *Useful.* Monetary compensation or services or scholarships can obviously be put to use by victims to make good for certain kinds of losses and to satisfy the sense that choices must be given in response to lost freedoms and powers to act given in response to victims' having been powerless. By comparison, speaking of the "uses" of truths and their tellings might seem metaphorical. I believe it seems so, however, only to those who do not themselves suffer the consequences for their own agency and credibility of silence, denial, and distortion. The moral and epistemic effects upon individuals of silence, pervasive denial, and massive distortion in the aftermath of wrongs are profound physically, psychologically, socially, politically, and morally.

In cases where there is a need for the truth, it is common to speak of the problem as "denial." Governments and individuals seek actively to cover up policies and events for which they prefer not to have to account, and "deniability" is a widely practiced strategy in institutions of many kinds. Yet denial is but one aspect of constructing and maintaining an alternative story or "fable" that partakes of lies and silences but also of strategically altered or edited truths. Those useful fables and edited or fabricated histories often have sufficient currency to constitute a reflective equilibrium of widely shared beliefs in society. Where this is true or to the extent that this is true, the reported experience of victims of and witnesses to violence and injustice—whether torture survivors, people who live with daily racism or hetero/sexism, or witnesses to an atrocity— becomes dubious if not literally incredible to many others. More insidious, the attempt by victims to report what they have experienced places upon them a disproportionate if not impossible burden of proof, and it discredits them as reliable knowers or testifiers in the eyes of those for whom some version of the fable is a touchstone. In cases of historical injustice there is a peculiar depth and opacity to the fable, which acquires, ironically, the prestige of history: "After all, it survived the test of time, and only truth is powerful enough to remain in its purity. We humans love to believe in the power and resilience of truth" (Bilbija 2005, 113). Denial, fabulation, distortion, and epistemic diversion suffice to preempt certain questions, to make certain inferences unavailable, or to render

Margaret Urban Walker

certain truths incredible and those who tell them untrustworthy. Authoritatively declared truths about violence and injustice can be used by victims to substantiate their assertions of injury and, more broadly, to buttress their credibility and their claim upon others to take their accounts seriously.

3. *Fitting.* The truths that need to be told and will be sought by victims are those about the reality, nature, extent, and authorship of the policies and acts of violence they have suffered. In this dimension, when authorities or processes tell too little about what needs to be understood, admit to generalities while withholding details, or admit to instances while obscuring patterns, the resentment or bitterness of victims may be greater than in cases of flat silence or denial. So "fit" in truth-telling reparations is about the scope, detail, and net effect of what is told on what and whom it is reasonable to believe. Fit also involves the occasions and the authority of particular tellings. Official apologies for violence and injustice, in particular, are correctly scrutinized for their characterization of offenses, their mode of addressing those wronged, the nature and extent of the responsibility they claim, the authority and publicity with which they are offered, and by whom they are spoken. Fit is intimately related to justice and to perceptions of justice: punishment is to be proportionate to crime, compensation proportionate to injury, and reward proportionate to achievement. The scope, authority, and consequences of truth tellings need to fit the type and size of the epistemic distortion and moral disregard that prompt the need for truth telling in the first place.

4. *Effective.* The issue of effectiveness in reparative truth telling is whether the truths that are told and the ways they are made public are going to have a lasting impact on common socially shared presumptions. Truths lay claim on us communally only if they are defended in authoritative places and to the extent that a wide array of surrounding beliefs holds them firmly in place. It is never just a question of establishing one thing but rather one of entrenching and continuing to fortify a rough reflective equilibrium of common belief that makes it reasonable to believe what in fact is true and reasonable to credit those who say it and assume it. Discrete exercises in truth telling are subject to contestation and are threatened with irrelevance, forgetfulness, and intentional or unwitting distortion over time. Thus, truth telling as a form of reparations entails a commitment not only to discover, announce, and archive facts but also to create conditions under which it is reasonable and remains reasonable to believe what is in fact true about episodes of violence or oppression. This means a commitment to creating an alteration in common belief comprehensive enough to shift burdens of proof and credibility, and it requires a concerted effort of dissemination, education, and continuing discussion and defense of what is true.

The Challenges for Truth Telling
as Reparations

Truth telling has multiple values as a reparative activity. Truth telling is obviously a *condition* of other kinds of reparations, identifying what there is to remedy, and thereby grounding assessments of the usefulness and fit of various reparations measures, individually and in concert. I have argued that orchestrated truth telling itself is a reparations *measure* of independent importance. To take the view that truth telling can itself constitute reparations is not to assume that truth telling alone can suffice as reparations for serious wrongs. But neither is it true that material reparations, such as compensation programs, are alone necessarily sufficient contributions to the larger process of reparation. No specific measures of redress—criminal trials of major figures, monetary payments to victims and their survivors, institutional reforms aimed at prevention—are guaranteed just by themselves to produce and maintain the moral conditions of confidence, trust, and hope and the political embodiment of these conditions in voice, recognition, civic respect, and guarantees of equal standing and protection. As Pablo de Greiff has argued, transitional justice measures such as reparations are weak relative to the transformations they intend; it is their coordinated implementation and their multiple relations to each other and to the idea of justice that are more likely to give them force as justice-promoting (de Greiff 2012, 34–39).

Truth telling, just like any other suitable reparations vehicle, has the potential to effect quite real and profound changes in our intertwined epistemic and moral worlds. In order to fulfill the conditions of a viable reparations vehicle, however, more is required than that the truth about violence and injustice simply be published or spoken. In conclusion, I note three factors of particular importance to the reparative powers of truth telling: dissemination, preservation, and disaggregation of truth recovery projects. All three bear on how fully interactive, useful, fitting, and effective an episode of concerted truth recovery can be.

Simply affirming the truth uncovered (for example, in an official report, the necessary culmination of a truth commission) is not enough and should ideally be only the beginning of a wider process of public awareness, reflection, and discussion. Findings that do not circulate, that take forms that are not widely accessible, or that are not explicitly backed by credible authorities are not likely to stimulate the kind of private reflection, public debate, and local engagement that might reshape widespread assumptions. The truth must reach diverse populations with different perceptions and experiences of the conflict, repression, or violence investigated. Effective dissemination is necessary

Margaret Urban Walker

to initiate and sustain individual, interpersonal, social, and political processes of acknowledgment and reckoning. An interview with the Chilean truth commissioner José Zalaquett gives a good example of how an institutionally commissioned truth-telling process can receive concerted dissemination. Zalaquett describes briefly the process surrounding the Chilean National Commission on Truth and Reconciliation:

> Even though Aylwin [the newly democratically elected president of Chile] himself had opposed the military regime and certainly was not in any way associated with its crimes, he appeared on national television when the commission's report was made public, and, in the name of the Chilean state, he atoned for the crimes that were committed. He sent a copy of the Commission's report to all the victims' families with a personal letter. More generally, President Aylwin decided to give this whole process the proper ritual. Nationwide public television appearances marked the establishment of the Commission, receipt of its report, and communication of its results. After that, the report was circulated in newspaper supplements; it was published in book form; and it was news in the papers every day for four weeks. . . . There was a great deal of discussion at the community level in churches, annual meetings of professional associations, university campuses, and the like. (Zalaquett in Roht-Arriaza 1999, 198–99).

South Africa's famed Truth and Reconciliation Commission (TRC) televised many public hearings and testimonies, and South African and world media provided daily coverage of the TRC that made it impossible for South Africans, in particular, not to know what the TRC claimed to find. Peru's truth commission staged a photography exhibition and produced a forty-page popular version of its report; Sierra Leone's created a video summary and child-friendly version of its report (see Freeman 2006, 36; Hayner 2011, 38, 59). Multiple modes of transmission (written, oral, visual, dramatic, and through artworks) and diverse sites of dissemination (popular media, journalism, museums, schools and universities, and cultural institutions) are essential to disseminate effectively recovered truths about human rights abuses.

The transitional moment (or an upsurge of political pressure or public interest in the past) that propels truth recovery will pass. If truth telling is to be more than an orchestrated episode, it is necessary to secure the results of truth recovery for future study, history, and instruction, as well as supplementation, correction, and reconsideration. Preservation of findings, under appropriate conditions of public accessibility and the safety and privacy of individuals, is essential (United Nations 2007, 2009). Yet what is required is more than a matter of creating secure but accessible archives of information, although this is necessary in every case (Bickford 1999). A project of truth recovery needs to try to secure an enduring epistemic impact: to transform the terms of discussion of the past going forward and to entrench its findings widely enough that the burden of proof and credibility shifts to those who would deny what has been established. There is no simple recipe for accomplishing this. One categorical approach, adopted by several countries, criminalizes denial of the Nazi Holocaust and other crimes against humanity in an attempt to fix some parts of common social belief, at least for purposes of public discourse (Cohen 2001, 268–69). This approach can pose dilemmas for societies committed to freedom of thought, speech, and association (Teitel 2000, 105–8). Textbooks and educational curricula are obvious candidates for bearing recovered truths into the future; yet the classroom can be a fraught arena for teachers, students, and parents when dealing with a violent and contested past (Shriver 2005; Cole 2007). Other measures include public education through media programming and events, academic and popular history, consistent official discourse and symbolism, and memorialization.

Finally, while international guidelines regarding truth telling in the aftermath of political violence and repression are directed to states as their responsibility, there are substantial and crucial roles for varied nonofficial or local truth-telling, dissemination, and preservation initiatives. Truth commissions have become emblematic institutions in contexts of political transition (and in some instances of historically silenced injustice), but many limitations of truth commissions are receiving critical attention (Chapman and Ball 2001; Mendeloff 2004; Shaw 2006; Chapman and van der Merwe 2008; Hamber 2009; Olsen et al. 2010; Wiebelhaus-Brahm 2010; and Braithwaite 2011). Even if truth commissions have a central role to play in the fulfillment of state responsibilities, they cannot be all things to all interested parties (Walker 2015; see also United Nations 2013). Specifically, they cannot capture all the macro- and micro-truths that it might be important to tell for various purposes or meet all the hopes and expectations of recognition, respect, validation, information, and redress that victims and survivors, especially, might seek. The psychologist Brandon Hamber warns of the gap between the pace of transition and the longer uneven process of individual recovery generally and of South African victims' disappointed expectations for additional information about their lost relatives from the TRC (Hamber 2009). There is no reason for truth commissions to monopolize the political and social project of truth recovery, and there are good reasons to think beyond this short-term, state-level, state-dominated, and quasi-juridical format. Stressing the insufficiency of nation-level initiatives, Laura Arriaza and Naomi Roht-Arriaza report local truth-telling initiatives in Guatemala, a country that had one unofficial and one official truth commission, both publicly prominent and thorough undertakings that extensively documented a decades-long national conflict. Yet the effects of the conflict varied widely among different regional and ethnic communities. The authors recount a project in more than twenty communities to generate a communal map of the conflict by and for divided and nonliterate communities. Communities created a process of individuals' knotting ropes to define personal timelines, braiding multiple rope lines together, drawing maps of where conflict events took place and where people were killed and displaced, and showing how the community was transformed, socially and geographically, with a pace and direction set through community involvement (Arriaza and Roht-Arriaza 2010, 212–13). This single example of a community-specific and locally shaped response to the needs for truth and memory of victims and communities provokes the imagination. If truth telling as reparations needs to be interactive, useful, fitting, and effective, the necessary devices might be vastly more varied than we currently envision.

Note

An earlier version of the argument updated, revised, and expanded in this chapter first appeared in "Truth Telling as Reparations," *Metaphilosophy* 41 (2010): 525–45.

8

Promoting Historical Justice through Truth Commissions

An Uneasy Relationship

ONUR BAKINER

Societies are built on the legacies of past injustices. Histories of slavery, economic exploitation, colonialism, institutional racism and discrimination, gender-based violence and exclusion, and gross bodily rights violations shape citizens' sense of political belonging and interpersonal relationships in the present. Those who strive for a just society increasingly acknowledge that past wrongs cannot be reduced to questions of social or criminal justice in the present, precisely because the underprivileged status of individuals and groups often results from past injustices. Therefore, the quest for historical justice has a special place in contemporary struggles for recognition, reparation, and justice.

The causes, patterns, and consequences of past injustices exhibit enormous variation across political and cultural contexts. So do the official and unofficial mechanisms to rectify them. Official apologies, reparation programs, symbolic acts of recognition toward identity claims and victimhood, affirmative action legislation, political-institutional reform to overcome institutional discrimination, criminal and noncriminal sanctions for human rights violations, museums, memorials, revised history textbooks, and fact-finding commissions are among the chief mechanisms to reckon with past wrongs. One should also not forget unofficial attempts, such as apologies by nonstate actors (e.g., churches), works of art and literature that take issue with historical injustices, and truth-finding efforts led by civil society.

This chapter explores the ways in which truth commissions, among the most widespread mechanisms for addressing the legacy of gross human rights violations since the 1980s, conceptualize and enable historical justice. Why and how do truth commissions narrativize national history? Which conceptions of justice do they adopt? How do they combine the backward-looking task of identifying past wrongs, their victims, and those responsible, with the forward-looking project of national reconstruction? In what ways have they contributed to historical justice? What are the limitations of promoting historical justice through truth commissions?

I argue that truth commissions have been exceptionally accommodating—much more than other transitional justice measures such as human rights trials, apologies, and removal of perpetrators from public office—to the demands for redress and reconstruction through the prism of a historically informed conception of justice. Most commissions combine forensic investigation of human rights violations with a historical narrative that explores the causes, patterns, and consequences of political violence. In addition, they use testimonies, mostly collected from victims' relatives and victim-survivors, to make sense of the national past. This opens a space for the inclusion of hitherto silenced and marginalized voices in the social contestation over the meaning of the past, while exposing official lies, propaganda, and widely held misconceptions about past violence and violations.

Needless to say, coming to terms with the past through truth commissions has its own limitations and ambiguities. Not all commissions are eager to complement human rights investigation with a comprehensive account of physical, structural, and discursive forms of violence that unfolded in the longer trajectory of national history. Even when they are, their success in promoting retributive and restorative justice depends on a host of political, institutional, and judicial variables. Although most commissions have been remarkably accurate in their descriptions of the massive and systematic nature of violations of human rights and international humanitarian law, presumed perpetrators and the political groups representing them have often resorted to delegitimizing truth commissions' efforts, instead of adopting an attitude of acknowledgment and responsibility.

Moreover, commissions constrain as much as enable historical justice: they are mandated to investigate a specific period and a specific list of violations, which inevitably exclude other experiences of victimhood and demands for recognition. They constantly negotiate the ethics and politics of writing national history by choosing to characterize the past in different ways. Some commissions portray past violence as radically alien to the present process of democratic and civic reconstruction, while others highlight the extent to which past injustices constitute and therefore problematize social relations and political institutions in the present. Thus, commissions find themselves policing the boundary that separates the present from the incursions of past wrongs that keep haunting contemporaries.

This chapter is organized as follows: first, I define historical justice and lay out the major ethical and practical issues that preoccupy the scholars and practitioners of historical justice today. Then I provide an account of the variety of contexts in which truth commissions were established and show that their peculiar engagement with past human rights violations as a matter of national historiography *and* justice brings the perspective of historical justice into social and political debates on postconflict reconstruction. Finally, I discuss the promises and limitations of advocating historical justice through truth commissions.

Before proceeding, a caveat is in order. I do not argue that truth commissions have developed a unified approach to historiography or that they have provided a univocal, monolithic response to the challenges of postconflict justice. In fact, nothing would be more misleading than to analyze institutions that exhibit so much cross-national variation as though they were uniform. Commissions adopt distinctive approaches in terms of how they explain the underlying causes of past wrongs, assign responsibility both to particular actors and to society as a whole, and make recommendations to build a just and peaceful society. Throughout the text I highlight these different responses, even as I identify the common threads that unify some or most truth commissions.

What Is Historical Justice?

A wide range of violent and nonviolent incidents, policies, institutions, and social structures is considered historical injustice. Violation of bodily integrity rights, slavery and other forms of coerced labor, transfer of political sovereignty and land ownership through military occupation, all forms of exclusion and discrimination based on race, gender, ethnic background, and place of origin, and cultural misrecognition are among its many forms. Even when scholars, civil society activists, and politicians agree on what constitutes historical *injustice*, it remains difficult to define and conceptualize the notion of historical *justice*.

Historical justice refers to the distribution of rights and (material and symbolic) entitlements in line with a conception of fairness that seeks to (i) identify and remedy present exclusions and deprivations resulting from illegitimate past actions (which may necessitate the transfer of commitments and resources across generations) and (ii) assign moral, political, and (if possible) criminal responsibility for such actions. The fundamental premise of historical justice is that individuals and social groups were illegitimately deprived of their fundamental rights, livelihood, and social standing and that there is an ethical obligation to recognize their past suffering and to restore their well-being and status, to the extent possible. Thus, it involves acknowledging past injustices and their victims; compensating for the material, mental, affective, and cultural losses suffered by individuals and social groups; and holding those responsible for injustices morally, politically, and legally accountable, if possible. Needless to say, contemporary societies have not reached consensus on which past actions should be considered illegitimate—which is one of the chief justifications for the creation of investigation commissions. It is generally accepted that the prosecution of human rights violations, reparations for victims and their descendants, historical investigation commissions, affirmative action programs, official (and occasionally unofficial) apologies, and other symbolic acts and gestures that acknowledge past wrongs and offer redress for the affected are policy tools that serve historical justice.

Historical justice addresses past wrongs *in the present*. It should not be understood as an attempt to restore the status quo ante, since complete restitution is unfeasible in all but a few cases and may prove undesirable for the members of the existing society, including many of the victims (Maynard 1999). For example, dispossessed and displaced rural communities might not benefit from land redistribution in a fast-urbanizing economy. Especially in contexts where the social relations before the latest wave of violence and injustices were already deemed unjust, idealizing the status quo ante might perpetuate illegitimate power dynamics and institutions. Historical justice is a creative engagement with the past to construct a just society in the present. Moral repair is about "restoring or creating trust and hope in a shared sense of value and community" (Walker 2006b, 28).

Historical justice is firmly embedded in present political and judicial struggles, but it is important not to reduce it entirely to present aspirations, such as distributive justice and social reconciliation. It is true that demands for socioeconomic justice often result from the unjust distribution of rights and entitlements in the past. The beneficiaries of present redistribution and historical justice mechanisms are likely to coincide. However, the moral justification for each conception of justice remains distinctive, and redress may still target different individuals and social groups.[1] A similar point needs to be made about reconciliation: commentators agree that proper reconciliation is tied to historical justice and recognition (Schaap 2004; Verdeja 2009), since the acknowledgment of past wrongs and responsibility should inform efforts at building mutual trust. The overlaps notwithstanding, historical justice is not merely an element of reconciliation, and the two goals are based on different moral justifications. Reconciliation may have to go beyond historical justice to include future-oriented dispute resolution and trust-building practices, while historical justice may or may not involve reconciliation efforts. For example, advocates of historical justice in a particular context might reject reconciliation with former wrongdoers and their contemporary supporters. In other words, the justification for and the practical implications of historical justice are distinct from present ethical obligations and social struggles, which may generate tensions, as well as overlapping policy agendas.

The widespread use of apologies and reparatory policies (Olick and Coughlin 2003; Olick 2007; de Greiff and International Center for Transitional Justice 2006) is relatively new in world history, not least because until recently the conventional wisdom was to "let bygones be bygones" and to reconstruct political community through the forced silencing of troubling past legacies. The idea that remembrance and self-reflection, rather than social amnesia, should lie at the foundation of lasting peace underpinned German efforts to come to terms with the legacy of World War II and the Holocaust. But the idea rose to global salience only in the late 1980s and 1990s, in the wake of dictatorship and civil conflict in Eastern and Central Europe, Latin America, Africa, and parts of Asia. While the argument for leaving the past behind still has traction, it no longer enjoys unquestioned authority. Activism on the part of victim-survivors, victims' relatives, and human rights organizations has brought along an alternative discourse that considers the acknowledgment of the past a precondition for the nonrecurrence of political violence. The call of "never again" has resulted in the incorporation of human rights as a key component of recent transitions from authoritarianism to democracy and/or from conflict to peace. It has been suggested that an honest engagement with the national past, an emerging international norm (Barkan 2000), may reflect positively on a country's international standing, as well.[2]

Yet accepting the moral and practical desirability of coming to terms with the past does not necessarily mean that contemporary societies have an *obligation* to take responsibility for past wrongs (Wyman 2008). In other words, historical injustice may be morally relevant but not binding. Jeremy Waldron points out that uncertainty about what would have happened in the absence of past wrongs undermines the case for a binding conception of historical justice: "Why should the exaction of specific reparation in the real world be oriented to what the idealized agents of rational choice would have secured for themselves in a hypothetical world?" (1992, 13; see also Fishkin 1991; Winter 2006). Likewise, the pressing needs of present redistribution may invalidate claims based on historical wrongs, especially if the violators of yesterday find themselves in need as a result of today's changing circumstances (Lyons 1977). In the face of skepticism, proponents of historical justice have defended the notion that historical wrongs should be addressed in the present insofar as they leave "morally relevant traces in the present" (Collste 2010, 89), referring to those individuals or relationships that carry the weight of past injustices. Others point to the transgenerational nature of present commitments and obligations (Thompson 2002; Boxill 2003; Sepinwall 2006)—a point that I will discuss in further detail.

In what follows, I highlight some of the challenges and dilemmas that accompany debates on historical justice. I identify five such challenges: (i) the ontological limits of doing justice to the past, (ii) identification of (individual and collective) victimhood, (iii) identification of responsibility, (iv) the adequacy and appropriateness of historical justice measures, and (v) competing social/political agendas.

First and foremost, there is an ontological limit that puts into question the very possibility of justice in the wake of past wrongs: justice invokes the dream of restoring that which can never be restored. The dead cannot tell their stories to seek recognition or enjoy the restitution of their rights and entitlements.[3] Survivors may no longer feel that they belong to the world of the living (Minow 1998, 62). Lives, life stories, families, interpersonal relationships, and community networks are lost forever. Taking note of the unrepentant attitude of Nazi criminals during the Nuremberg trials, Hannah Arendt's *Eichmann in Jerusalem* ([1963] 2006) points to the possibility that some wrongs simply defy commensurate punishment—and forgiveness, which she elaborates in *The Human Condition* (Arendt [1958] 1998). As argued earlier, historical justice is not a process of restoring the (real or imagined) status quo ante but rather the creation of new social relations in the face of irretrievable personal and interpersonal losses. As such, procedures and institutions of justice operate in *present* society, and they evoke the memories of loss only in the service of that which exists. The project of redemption, which Walter Benjamin describes as recovering the "fullness of [mankind's] past" (1968, 254), lies beyond the reach of historical justice. The ontological limit does not invalidate the quest for historical justice. Rather, it acknowledges the inherently finite nature of human action in the face of past wrongs.

Another difficulty concerns the identification of those affected by past injustices, especially in cases where the illegitimate actions took place in the distant past and few (if any) of the survivors and victims' relatives are still alive. Who, among the living, can legitimately demand redress? Should victimhood be attached to individuals or communities? It may be tempting to individualize victimhood and to seek justice only for those who were personally affected by past wrongs. However, this strategy makes little sense when the injustices in question go beyond the violations of individual rights. Social and political structures, such as apartheid, institutional racism, patriarchy, and colonialism, have aftereffects that diminish the prospects of direct victims as well as those of individuals born into underprivileged communities and social roles. An African American man who is not the descendant of former slaves is still likely to suffer the effects of socioeconomic inequality, social prejudices, and institutional discrimination that characterize the relationship between his immediate surroundings and the broader society—and, given their roots in past legacies, these are problems of *historical*, as well as *present*, injustice. The analytical distinction between backward- and forward-looking justice breaks down in practice, and strict individualism in identifying victims runs the risk of perpetuating structural injustice. Historical justice, therefore, "may be rendered at the individual, collective, and structural levels" (Berg and Schaefer 2009, 2).

The identification of responsibility further complicates historical justice efforts. Moral, political, and criminal responsibility rests with those who devised and implemented past policies, but this category is applicable only to perpetrators of human rights violations in the somewhat recent past.[4] In most cases, one needs to ask whether the ethical obligation for redress falls upon the descendants of perpetrators, all members of privileged social groups, society as a whole, or the state as the sovereign actor capable of representing social values and interests. Again, strict individualism does little to illuminate the nature of obligations in addressing past wrongs. Janna Thompson states that political community is constituted through series of commitments that presume transgenerational responsibility. If the most basic rights and benefits in a society, starting with citizenship itself (Thompson 2009), are granted through transgenerational transfers rather than through individual choice, then it follows that the ethical responsibility to rectify past wrongs should be comprehended as a transgenerational commitment (Thompson 2002). The state emerges as the main actor that should assume the ethical responsibility for implementing policies of redress in order to fulfill citizens' shared obligation: "although citizens inherit the obligation to make reparation for the wrongs committed by their political predecessors, they cannot fulfill this obligation directly. Instead, the obligation must be fulfilled by a proxy, and this is the role of the state" (Blustein 2012, 23).

Yet the politics of historical justice rooted in these premises carries along new tensions. Thompson's defense of transgenerational ethical obligations and her (and Blustein's) account of the state as the primary (but not unique) site for administering historical justice provide solid justification for state-led justice efforts. However, state-sanctioned gestures of contrition, such as official apologies, may invite accusations of insincerity and political instrumentalism (Cunningham 1999; Mills 2001). Politicians' admissions of fault in the name of the collective do not necessarily encourage unrepentant perpetrators or bystanders to do the same. Observers note that the transformation of social relations away from past injustice and discrimination, rather than mere state apology, is the genuine test for historically informed justice (McGregor 2012; Thompson 2012). Contemporary debates on migration, asylum seekers, race relations, gender equality, and so on in many countries seem unaffected by the avalanche of state apologies and reparation programs in the past fifteen years (Neumann 2011), which raises the suspicion that the existing historical justice mechanisms are rather inadequate when it comes to identifying society-wide moral obligations and promoting transformation in attitudes. As I will argue later, truth commissions grapple with the implications of promoting a victim-centered approach to truth finding and recognition in contexts where the identification of moral, political, and criminal responsibility remains a divisive political issue.

Historical justice, insofar as it is a present attempt to deliver justice in light of the past, confronts a host of competing ethical and practical objectives, such as social reconciliation and peace, improvements in the country's international standing, economic efficiency, and redistributive justice. As argued earlier, historical justice may have a mutually reinforcing relationship with these present goals, but the possibility of conflicting agendas cannot be ignored. Victims of past violations may seek retribution, if not outright revenge, which may put their understandably punitive approach to historical justice at odds with social peace. The "complete truth" about past violations, an indispensable element of historical justice, is often compromised in negotiated transitions, as truth commissions and similar investigatory bodies refrain from identifying alleged perpetrators by name as a result of political pressures and the need to uphold procedural fairness. Moreover, there are competing economic and moral claims on the allocation of scarce resources: citizens might prioritize improving the present distribution or fostering future economic development over rectifying past wrongs.

The practical challenges and ethical dilemmas notwithstanding, historical justice is fundamental to contemporary struggles for recognition (Honneth 1995), preservation of cultural identity (Cunningham 1999), and the conduct of national and international politics (Barkan 2000; Hazan 2010) in the contemporary world. The powerful claim for backward-looking restitution and reconstruction cuts across the boundaries that separate the past and the present. The challenges and aporias described earlier do not invalidate the need for historical justice; rather, they caution contemporary citizens against the dangers of self-righteousness and complacency in their relationship to a past that they cannot fully rectify. In the spirit of Theodor Adorno's suggestion for a working through (*Aufarbeitung*) rather than a mastering (*Bewältigung*) of the past,[5] I argue that historical justice is not something that can be *delivered* once and for all; rather, it *calls for* the reordering of present social relations in light of a past that necessitates an attitude of solemnity and responsibility.

Truth Commissions, History, and Justice

Truth commissions (also known as truth and *reconciliation* commissions) are ad hoc panels established to investigate past human rights violations, identify the patterns and causes of violence, make recommendations for political-institutional, legal, and social reform, and publicize the findings and recommendations with a final report (Bakiner 2011).[6] These commissions, alongside similar unofficial truth-finding projects, have become the most widespread mechanism to address past wrongs during the political transitions of the past thirty years (Hayner 2011). While the pioneering commissions in the 1980s and 1990s reflected the priorities of difficult regime transitions, even nontransitioning polities use truth commissions today to investigate past injustices that range from the violation of bodily integrity rights to the legacies of colonialism and slavery. Although definitional differences fuel disagreements on which panels should count as truth commissions, it is safe to state that more than thirty countries have established them.

At first sight it may appear that truth commissions, the archetypal transitional justice tool, have little connection to historical justice.[7] They mostly investigate human rights violations committed in the recent past by identifiable (though often purposefully unidentified) perpetrators, leaving behind identifiable victims, whereas historical justice explores the transgenerational implications of assigning moral and political responsibility for wrongs in the distant past. Furthermore, professional historians have served on truth commissions in no more than a few countries. Yet a closer look into truth commissions' topics of investigation, methods, and objectives reveals significant overlaps with the discourse and practice of historical justice. In what follows, I sketch some of these overlaps.

The global evolution of truth commissions shows that the topics of investigation increasingly include wrongs in the distant past—bringing commissions' considerations in line with those of historical justice. The first truth commissions dealt with forced disappearance and extrajudicial killing during military dictatorships. Argentina's Commission on the Disappeared (1983), Nepal's Commission of Inquiry to Find the Disappeared Persons (1990), and Chile's Truth and Reconciliation Commission (1990) are chief examples. The incorporation of truth commissions into peace processes in the 1990s and 2000s in settings as diverse as El Salvador and Liberia, East Timor and Sierra Leone, expanded their topics of investigation, as well as their goals. Especially the worldwide attention to the South African Truth and Reconciliation Commission (1995–98) popularized this institutional form as an appropriate mechanism to deal with past wrongs in the context of transitions from authoritarianism to democracy and/or from internal conflict to peace. The use of truth commissions during transitions soon triggered their adoption by nontransitional regimes, which sought either to remedy the shortcomings of earlier transitional justice efforts (e.g., Chile, Uruguay, Panama, Brazil) or to deal with the injustices of the relatively distant past (e.g., South Korea, Mauritius). Some of the new truth commissions investigate violations of bodily integrity rights during political violence (Brazil) just as earlier ones did; yet one also observes the expansion of investigation themes to slavery and colonialism (Mauritius) and to Indian Residential Schools (Canada). Therefore, a new generation of truth commissions addresses the difficult questions of responsibility and entitlements arising from offenses in the not-so-recent past.

Whether investigating the recent or the distant past, commissions perform historiographical tasks in at least two ways. First, almost all truth commissions view their topic of investigation as a problem *from* the past: a host of deep-rooted political, institutional, social-structural, and moral shortcomings underlie the context in which human rights violations become possible. Truth commissions first and foremost conduct forensic investigation in order to document past human rights violations. Yet few commissions have limited themselves to fact-finding, since they are almost always expected to provide an account of the underlying causes of political violence, the institutional and systematic nature of violations, and their consequences for individuals and for society as a whole. Since most commissions did not or were not allowed to name individual perpetrators, they were attentive to moral and political responsibility at the level of state institutions and society as a whole. Some commissions have produced short context chapters or even paragraphs to accompany forensic investigation (e.g., Argentina's 1983 National Commission on the Disappearance of Persons), whereas others have published in-depth studies of the political, legal, socioeconomic, and cultural factors that spark, perpetuate, or result from a period of political violence (e.g., Peru's 2001 Truth and

Reconciliation Commission). Some of the later truth commissions' publications, such as the Interim Report of the Truth and Reconciliation Commission of Canada (2012), provide very little individual-level data, focusing instead on the broader patterns of historical injustices (the Indian Residential Schools system in the Canadian case). Overall, therefore, truth commissions have conceptualized past violations as systematic and institutionalized and responsibility for these violations as collective and institutional, rather than strictly individual.

Second, truth commissions constantly negotiate the boundaries between past horror and present national reconstruction. In that sense, they ensure that human rights violations are *of* the past: they make historiographical (and inevitably ethical) choices in characterizing the relationship between past and present. Commissions are mandated to investigate a circumscribed period, which determines the contours of forensic research, historical explanation, and who counts as a victim. The periodization triggers controversy about their exclusion of incidents that would have shed light on the nation's conflict history and grounded legitimate justice claims but remain outside the mandate.

Furthermore, commissions' narrative construction of a better future in light of the past speaks to the moral complexity of advocating justice at the confluence of time horizons. Some commissions portray political violence as a period of breakdown that is essentially alien to the civic traditions of the nation, as Chile's 1990 Truth and Reconciliation Commission does, whereas others, like Guatemala's 1998 Historical Clarification Commission, regard physical and structural violence as endemic to the nation-building project itself (Grandin 2005). As a result, national reconstruction is understood as a process of restoring peaceful social norms and democratic institutions in some transitional contexts, whereas other commissions invite citizens and the political elite to rethink their deeply held assumptions about the basic values and institutions that uphold national unity. Naturally, the extent to which a commission characterizes past wrongs as exceptional or foundational depends on the other historiographical task, namely that of identifying (or not) the root causes of violence. No matter what the specific choices are, the fact that truth commissions make such historiographical choices about whether and the extent to which human rights violations should be historicized makes them an important actor in contemporary historical justice debates.

Commissions have emerged as practices of (self-)critique for nation-states that have failed to provide citizens with adequate protection from violations by state agents and/or nonstate combatants and misinformed the public systematically about this failure. Yet their objective is to explore the possibility of reimagining a cohesive nation in the wake of violence and social dissolution, not merely to expose failures. In this sense, they face the at once historiographical, political, and ethical choice of what Deena Rymhs calls the "deconstruction of national master-narratives" or "a reconstruction of one" (Rymhs 2006, 106) as acts of reconciliation. The difficult choice between reconstruction and deconstruction in truth commissions' historical narratives reflects the deeper questions of justice and responsibility. Should truth commissions put victims' demands for justice above all other considerations? Or should their orientation toward national reconstruction and reconciliation set limits on commissioners' self-identification with victims? Should contemporary citizens' responsibility toward the past be one of taking lessons to overcome legacies of violence in which they took no direct part? Or should citizens be urged to hold a mirror to see themselves as products and producers of various forms of violence and injustice in the present? These considerations echo the complexities of determining agency/structure dynamics in assigning responsibility for past wrongs and of categorizing the scope and depth of justice demands (Gordon 1996; Berg 2009).

Not surprisingly, this orientation toward the past has accentuated truth commissions' pioneering role in reinvigorating academic and political debates at the turn of the century around the key terms of historical justice, such as memory, truth, justice, recognition, and reconciliation. Victim-survivors, victims' relatives, human rights groups, leaders of armed groups, politicians, bureaucrats, and all concerned citizens participate in struggles over social memory around questions such as: What happened in the past? Why did it happen? What meaning should contemporaries make out of it? What should be done to avoid its recurrence in the future? What moral obligations do past events impose on citizens in the present? How important and appropriate is it to take issue with the legacies of the past? The contestation over social memory, a pluralistic process characterized by the multilayered effects of past and present social hierarchies and power relations (Stern 2004), often precedes and shapes a truth commission's work and is in turn shaped by the findings, conclusions, and recommendations of the commission.

In what ways does commissions' backward-looking orientation promote justice? Commissions claim to serve a combination of three different conceptions of justice: (i) retribution, (ii) material and symbolic restitution/repair, and (ii) truth-as-justice. While retributive and restorative justice are somewhat familiar notions, the idea that the complete truth about past wrongs, which refers to a truthful and accurate record of the past (i.e., forensic truth), accompanied by an account of the causes and consequences of a period of political violence (i.e., historical truth), constitutes a form of justice in and of itself is relatively new.[8] In the next section I discuss the social and political implications of including historical truth as a crucial form of justice.[9]

Do truth commissions serve or undermine retribution? Do they provide sufficient compensation, material and symbolic, for the victims of past human rights abuses? Does the "truth" produced by commissions amount to an accurate and comprehensive account of past violence? While various truth commissions have claimed to serve some or all of these conceptions of justice, victims' groups and human rights advocates often base their objections on the grounds that they fail to address past injustices adequately. The relationship between truth commissions and criminal justice has sparked enormous controversy, especially in reaction to the South African commission's amnesty procedure. While I stress the extent to which a commission can exert agency in promoting justice in the wake of past wrongs, it is nonetheless necessary to point out that success and failure depend critically on factors outside the commission itself, such as political will, judicial activism in the area of human rights, and society-wide acceptance of past injustices. To this day, only two commissions, namely those in South Africa and in Liberia, have had amnesty procedures, and even in those cases the majority of the perpetrators failed to secure immunity from justice through the commission's amnesty. In other words, impunity owes less to truth commissions than to lack of political and judicial will. Most commissions have recommended reparations to restore the well-being and dignity of the affected, but few governments have actually implemented them. Likewise, the striving for the right to truth has faced adversaries (in particular the perpetrators and institutions representing them) almost everywhere, as there have been attempts to discredit commissions' findings and conclusions, no matter how accurate or comprehensive they were. Therefore it is more meaningful to ask how truth commissions enable or constrain historical justice than to analyze their achievements and shortcomings in isolation from the broader political, legal, and judicial contexts in which they operate.

The Promises and Challenges of Promoting Historical Justice through Truth Commissions: General Observations

The rejection of state denial regarding past human rights violations has been a lasting contribution of almost every truth commission. I argued earlier that disagreements over what constitutes past injustice are central to contemporary historical justice debates. The post–World War II period has seen a dramatic increase in intrastate political violence as a result of conflicts over class, identity, material resources, and political control in the context of socioeconomic development, postcolonial reconstruction, and the Cold War. Whether in the form of a repressive dictatorship, foreign occupation, or civil war, armed state and nonstate actors have been committing atrocities against civilians and combatants massively and systematically. Political violence targets (mostly unarmed) citizens, even though winning the hearts and minds of citizens has become indispensable to military and political victory. Therefore, hiding atrocities, silencing dissent, official propaganda, and psychological warfare have become integral to contemporary political conflicts. From the perspective of historical justice, the injustice is twofold: the violation of many persons' fundamental rights to life, liberty, and well-being, accompanied by the denial of their suffering.

It is against the latter injustice that truth commissions have provided an effective response. Even the "dry" truth commissions that emphasize forensic investigation at the expense of comprehensive historical explanation and victim-centered performances (such as public hearings) have played a crucial historiographical role by establishing a foundation of facts that would ideally facilitate an informed debate about the national past. Facts by themselves have not eradicated denialism, as can be evidenced by vocal apologists for past policies whose inability to refute facts does not stop them from attacking truth commissions. Nevertheless, these findings have revealed the inconsistencies and blatant lies in the discourse of denial, put into question the legitimacy and respectability of deniers, and consequently made it possible for the broader society to recognize the injustice of ignoring past human rights violations. Commissions are rightly criticized for the constraints they place on what they consider to be relevant facts and how they contextualize them, but when it comes to the veracity of what they publicize as facts of human rights violations, neither sympathetic critics nor vicious adversaries have found serious and systematic errors.

Commissions open a space for dialogue in which members of the political community, particularly the most vulnerable ones, come forward and narrate their experiences. They are portrayed as a victim-centered mechanism that offers a corrective against the violent and exclusionary nature of making and writing official national history. Victims' memory narratives, alongside documentation in government and civil society archives, provide the raw material out of which the nation's history is rewritten. Various commentators have even argued that truth telling may have a healing effect on victims, although this notion has been widely criticized (Minow 2000; Soyinka 2000; Freeman and Hayner 2003; Humphrey 2003; Laplante and Theidon 2007). Especially commissions that publicize victims' detailed testimonies through public (and sometimes televised) hearings seek to offer a remedy for one of the key factors that contributed to the twofold injustice of violation and denial: the geographical, cultural, and emotional gaps between the societal mainstream and the victims. It is definitely wrong to exaggerate commissions' service to victims, who often find themselves deeply dissatisfied by the bureaucratic procedures of testimony taking and by the disconnect between the commission's findings and the political or judicial decisions that determine the fate of retributive and reparatory justice. However, it is safe to argue that if experiences of victimization at the hands of armed political actors (chief among them the state), far from being considered an unfortunate by-product of history, constitute in today's world a key element of how polities understand themselves and their relationship to the past, truth commissions are to be credited for shifting the focus of justice away from victors and toward victims in postconflict settings.

Truth commissions also invite society as a whole to assume a self-reflective attitude toward the violent past. Commission processes are presented as opportunities for the recognition of victimhood, apology, and even forgiveness. In Argentina, Chile, South Africa, Guatemala, Nigeria, Peru, and Sierra Leone, top political leaders have endorsed a truth commission's findings, albeit with delays, thereby granting official recognition of past violations. Some individual and institutional actors have likewise apologized for their behavior during a period of political violence, although the overwhelming majority of presumed perpetrators, as well as the institutions representing them, have rejected the findings and conclusions of truth commissions. Just like any other mechanism that seeks to promote historical justice, truth commissions face selective gestures of acknowledgment on the part of the political class and the failure to admit responsibility on the part of most perpetrators.

The increasing sensitivity to past suffering has resulted in the official recognition of victimhood and some form of material and symbolic reparation. As argued in the previous section, the state serves as the chief (but by no means only) collective actor that lends an ear to grievances and assumes responsibility for past injustices. The practice of transitional justice in general and of truth commissions in particular has exhibited all the promises and shortcomings that accompany the salience of the state as the promoter of historically informed justice. The fact that truth commissions urge governments, rather than individual or institutional offenders, to pay reparations to victims raises questions about whether reparatory justice punishes wrongdoers and how public funds should be spent. Similarly, fact-finding bodies have facilitated practices of acknowledgment and apology on the part of public authorities, but the individuals who make such gestures are rarely the perpetrators or their former supporters.

The uneasy relationship between political authority and truth commissions, which results from the peculiar nature of these quasi-official truth-finding panels, highlights many of the shortcomings of institutionalized mechanisms of coming to terms with the past. Commissions' legitimacy is not based on the procedures and discourses that normally bestow authority upon public institutions. The commissioners are appointed on an ad hoc basis; therefore, they do not enjoy the democratic legitimacy of elected lawmakers or the legal-rational authority of bureaucrats. They conduct investigation on grave human rights violations, yet have little, if any, judicial power (Freeman 2006). Although various commissioners and staff members explore the underlying causes, as well as the consequences, of political violence, their inquiry is evaluated less on the standards of social-scientific research than by their capacity to please, persuade, and perhaps transform victims, perpetrators, political elites, and the broader national and international audiences. Thus, commissions base their authority over the "truth" about the nation's past on the good will and incorruptibility of commissioners (which has proven right in almost all cases), and on the hope that their findings and conclusions will satisfy sympathetic sectors, delegitimize opponents, and convince skeptics. This notion of legitimacy is *performative* in the sense that the commission process itself and the postcommission reception of the findings and recommendations, in other words a commission's dynamic interactions with outside actors during and after the commission's duration, account for its authority and reputation.

Truth commissions' performative legitimacy highlights a deeper tendency in contemporary efforts to reconstruct politics in the wake of historical injustice. The incoming political elite during a transition cannot simply assume that the state enjoys widespread authority and respect in a cohesive and peaceful society after a period of political violence that was destructive (and also constructive in its own way) of civic bonds, especially because the military, political, and judicial institutions of the state were parties to the conflict through active participation and/or complicity. Representatives of state authority need the mediation of truth commissions as ad hoc public bodies that build their reputation on good will and a disposition to incorporate the memories and demands of some of the most vulnerable members of the population, that is, victim-survivors and victims' relatives. Ideally the state recognizes victimhood, and in turn victims and other participants in the truth-finding effort reaffirm the state's role as the primary site where truth and justice are to be sought.

The possibility of official endorsement grants a truth commission considerable authority in its effort to bridge the gaps between the state and citizens, as well as those that divide various groups of citizens. However, the "contract" between the state and a truth commission is nonbinding: politicians and courts may refuse to acknowledge the findings and conclusions or to implement recommendations. The downside of truth commissions' position as outsiders to political authority is inefficacy. From the perspective of historical justice, then, truth commissions reflect an innovative approach that has made a forceful intervention on behalf of recognition and (restorative, if not retributive) justice in the face of past legacies of violations, but the inherent limitations of this approach reveal that contemporary political-institutional arrangements have proven incapable of incorporating historical justice as a binding, indispensable aspect of reconstructing social relations. Thus, historical justice remains an option, not an obligation, in contemporary politics.

Conclusion

In postmetaphysical times we no longer have the certainty that history will march toward freedom or justice, nor can we rest content with the idea that the bright future will justify past injustices as the side effect of progress (Torpey 2009). Truth commissions have a strong appeal in transitional democracies insofar as the provision of truth, justice, and reconciliation—not ignoring the fact that each one is an essentially contested concept—is expected to contribute to democracy, human rights, the rule of law, prevention of violence, the preservation of historical memory, good governance, political liberalism, domestic and international peace, international legitimacy, and so on. It is unfair to expect these ad hoc, often underfunded, and politically toothless institutions to deliver all socially desirable goals. Their lasting contribution has been to set an accurate record of past human rights violations in the face of official lies, propaganda, and societal apathy. It is no small achievement that when citizens in many countries discuss postconflict *justice*, they have an accurate picture of what the *injustice* was. Especially those commissions that have mobilized human rights groups, victims' associations, and intellectuals to produce and disseminate a comprehensive and pluralistic account of national history (among the completed commissions, I have in mind the Peruvian, Guatemalan, East Timorese, Sierra Leonean, and, to a lesser extent, South African ones) have reinvigorated social debates on past wrongs and facilitated policies of acknowledgment and reparation.

Yet commissions depend on key political actors' cooperation and endorsement to produce changes in politics and society. Their findings do not enjoy the coercive force of judicial truth, and their recommendations are not binding. Moreover, they face vicious adversaries, which forces the ex-commissioners to become increasingly vocal in the public sphere in order to ward off (often unjust and uninformed) criticisms and to forge political alliances. The ex-commissioners, ideally appointed to fortify an ethical position for truth and justice, end up politicizing their stance in the face of a hostile environment where they lack electoral legitimacy, governmental resources, and strong political allies. Insofar as the government chooses to honor its nonbinding contract with the commission, the postcommission process may culminate in the relatively successful incorporation of commission findings into political practice. Even then, the government may choose to comply with some items of the recommendations program and not others. This dependence on political will defeats the very purpose of the truth commission—reconstructing the nation in the light of critical history—when political exigencies push the commission's findings and recommendations into irrelevance or vulnerability before political contingencies.

Truth commissions are here to stay. Between 2009 and 2013, eight countries (Mauritius, Kenya, the Solomon Islands, Canada, Togo, Brazil, Thailand, and Côte d'Ivoire) created truth commissions to investigate a variety of past injustices and violations, while civil society groups and politicians in other countries (such as the Philippines and Turkey) proposed commissions to no avail (yet). Political elites may have an incentive to establish a commission to gloss over, rather than address, questions of historical justice. A truth commission may be designed to be the last, rather than first, step in coming to terms with the past. Politicians may establish one as a cheap way of dealing with compensation demands or simply because it has become a "fad," a marker of regime transition and international respectability in the age of official soul-searching. Yet, whatever the motives of their designers may be, truth commissions have proved capable of reinvigorating debates over social memory, political and moral responsibility, and justice, beyond the initial set of expectations that brought them into existence.

Notes

I would like to thank Annikki Herranen, Klaus Neumann, Pilar Riaño-Alcalá, Janna Thompson, and Peter J. Verovsek for comments on the previous drafts of this chapter.

1. For example, Robert Nozick's (1974) "principle of rectification" clearly exemplifies a conception of justice that warrants redress for illegitimate past acquisitions while finding no justification for redistribution to address present inequalities resulting from just acquisitions and transfers in the past. Other influential conceptions of justice, such as the one developed in John Rawls's *A Theory of Justice* (1971), pay little attention to the history of acquisitions and transfers, focusing instead on the fairness of the present distribution of basic goods.

2. For a critique of the notion that apology is a necessary condition for peaceful and effective foreign policy, see Lind (2008).

3. My claim seeks to acknowledge the limitations of contemporary political-institutional practices of coming to terms with the past. Admittedly it does not discuss alternative ontologies and cultural practices that consider the restoration of the world of the dead a central element of justice. I thank Pilar Riaño-Alcalá for this insight.

4. The strict separation of victim and perpetrator is untenable in most cases. Although one-sided historical injustices, such as slavery, colonialism, and state-sponsored human rights violations, frame the contemporary discourse, there are many cases where the line between victim and perpetrator is blurred. Child soldiers, often abducted from their communities and subjected to various forms of abuse by elder combatants, commit atrocities themselves (Baines 2009). Ethnolinguistic and cultural communities may subjugate dissenting in-group members and persons seen as "outsiders," even as they rightfully protest mistreatment and discrimination by other groups and the state.

5. Adorno's famous 1959 lecture "What Does Coming to Terms with the Past Mean?" (Adorno 1986) begins with the observation that the West German society has achieved spectacular political and economic recovery at the cost of citizens' emotional detachment and alienation from politics. His terminology is instructive in grasping the subtleties of the general notion of *coming to terms with the past*. In a Freud-inspired discussion, he argues for *Aufarbeitung* (working through), counterpoised to *Bewältigung* (mastering): the former connotes active and continuous engagement with the past, whereas the latter notion suggests that an endpoint, a moment of mastery over the past, is achievable.

6. I follow the consensus in transitional justice scholarship in defining truth commissions as officially mandated panels that investigate past human rights violations, whether or not the panel is formally called a truth commission (Brahm 2006; Freeman 2006; Hayner 2011). NGO-based truth-finding efforts do not fit into this definition, although their role in promoting awareness for past violations should be acknowledged (Bickford 2007).

7. Paige Arthur notes the reluctance of historical justice scholars to accept overlaps between historical and transitional justice: "Indeed, many working in the field of historical justice have flatly rejected the relevance of anything so narrow as transitional justice. For these critics, transitional justice is intimately linked with measures specifically designed for the brief duration of a political transition. They emphasize the importance of long-term efforts at transformation that involve some element of social

Onur Bakiner

restructuring, such as affirmative action or land reform, which they see as fundamentally different from the limited aims of prosecutions, reparations, and the like" (Arthur 2009, 362). See also Minow (1998); Teitel (2000).

8. International courts and organizations have been increasingly recognizing the "right to the truth" as a fundamental right, which imposes obligations on states alongside the responsibility to deliver criminal justice (Méndez 1997; Naqvi 2006; Walker 2010).

9. The analytical separation of forensic and historical notions of truth should not be overstated. Investigating facts of human rights violations always presupposes a narrative framework (the invocation of human rights norms at the least) and some degree of contextualization. The forensic investigation in turn makes it possible to establish broad patterns and causal relationships. While it is true that some commissions have prioritized forensic over historical truth, the interrelatedness of the two conceptions suggests that the variation across commissions' truth-telling strategies should be examined along a continuum, rather than as a binary.

9

Historical Justice in Postcolonial Contexts

Repairing Historical Wrongs and the End of Empire

DANIEL BUTT

t is a truism to say that we live in a world that has been deeply shaped by imperialism. The history of humanity is, in many ways, a story of the attempted and achieved subjugation of one people by another, and it is unsurprising that such interaction has had profound effects on the contemporary world, affecting cultural understandings of community identity, the composition of and boundaries between modern states, and the distribution of resources among different communities. This chapter addresses the claim that some contemporary states may possess obligations to pay reparations as a result of the lasting effects of a particular form of historical imperialism: colonialism (Ferro 1997, 1–23; Larsen 2000, 23–40). Claims about the harms and benefits caused by colonialism must make some kind of comparison between the world as it currently is and a counterfactual state in which the injustice that has characterized so much of the historic interaction between colonizers and the colonized did not occur. Rather than imagining a world where there was no such interaction, this chapter maintains that the appropriate counterfactual is one in which relations between different communities were characterized by an absence of domination and exploitation. This means that current states may possess reparative duties that are much more extensive than is often supposed.

Quite what it means for a form of interaction to be "colonial" is disputed. While some use the term to refer to a specific historical type of imperialism involving settlement and foreign rule, others employ more expansive definitions, which have the potential to characterize a wide variety of contemporary forms of international interaction as colonial (or "neocolonial") in nature. In broad terms, we can follow Lea Ypi in describing colonialism as "a practice that involves both the subjugation of one people to another and the political and economic control of a dependent territory (or parts of it)" (2013, 162). It is clear that a very wide range of practices could be described in such terms, even if we restrict our attention to those cases from the sixteenth century on that are often described in terms of the "colonial period": Robert Young writes that colonialism "involved an extraordinary range of different forms and practices carried out with respect to radically different cultures, over many centuries," and lists examples including settler colonies such as North America, Australia, and New Zealand (Britain), Algeria (France), and Brazil (Portugal); administered territories established without significant settlement for the purposes of economic exploitation, such as the Philippines and Puerto Rico (United States), India (Britain), the East Indies (the Netherlands), Togo (Germany), and Taiwan (Japan); and maritime enclaves such as Guantánamo, Cuba (United States), and Gibraltar, Hong Kong, Malta, and Singapore (Britain) (2001, 17). I have written elsewhere that three characteristics frequently emerge in descriptions of colonialism: domination, cultural imposition, and exploitation (Butt 2013a). Definitions typically place the greatest emphasis on domination: Osterhammel, for example, defines colonialism as "a relationship of domination between an indigenous (or forcibly imported) majority and a minority of foreign invaders" and notes that "the fundamental decisions affecting the lives of the colonized people are made and implemented by the colonial rulers in pursuit of interests that are often defined in a distant metropolis" (1997, 16–17). Ypi speaks of the wrong of colonialism as being that of "the creation and upholding of a political association that denies its members equal and reciprocal terms of cooperation" (2013, 158). This idea of domination is undoubtedly key to understanding what it is that makes a relationship between different communities colonial in character. As will be seen, however, the frequency with which colonial practice led to the forceful imposition of the culture or customs of the colonizer onto the colonized and of a wide variety of different forms of exploitation is also of great significance when it comes to assessing present obligations stemming from the wrongs of the colonial period.

My focus in this chapter is primarily on historical cases that lie some distance in the past, since it is often assumed that the combination of the character of colonial exploitation and the effects of the passage of time together combine to undermine the case for contemporary reparative obligations. The examples employed generally refer to the colonial activities of West European powers, but the general argument could equally be applied to a range of other past cases, such as Japanese colonial expansion in East Asia prior to World War II (see Kwak and Nobles 2013). The logic of my position, however, is equally applicable to present cases of international domination and exploitation: such instances are in a sense less complicated because claims for reparation do not have to deal with temporal concerns, but they do nonetheless need to engage with questions of the right way to employ counterfactual reasoning in the face of exploitative interaction.

While there is great variety in terms of the historical experience of colonized peoples, it is nowadays commonplace to maintain that the domination that they suffered at the hands of colonizing powers was unjust. Such claims have a long tradition in both anticolonial and postcolonial writing, but recent years have seen the emergence of something approaching a consensus on this point in international political discourse, as evidenced by the condemnation of historical colonialism agreed to at the World Conference against Racism, Racial Discrimination, Xenophobia, and Related Intolerance in Durban in 2001, Article 13 of which reads:

> We recognize that colonialism has led to racism, racial discrimination, xenophobia and related intolerance, and that Africans and people of African descent, and people of Asian descent and indigenous peoples were victims of colonialism and continue to be victims of its consequences. We acknowledge the suffering caused by colonialism and affirm that, wherever and whenever it occurred, it must be condemned and its reoccurrence prevented. We further regret that the effects and persistence of these structures and practices have been among the factors contributing to lasting social and economic inequalities in many parts of the world today. (United Nations 2001)

This chapter is concerned not with the justification but rather with the implications of this verdict of past wrongdoing. Contemporary movements for reparations can have varied justifications and seek remedies of differing types. Miller and Kumar list the different forms of "reparations" as including "money, land, apologies, public memorials and museums, changes in the law, changes in political institutions, enhanced educational opportunities, [and] the introduction of policies designed to educate the general public about the character of past injustices" (2007, v). This chapter is primarily concerned with the subset of these approaches that involves the compensatory redistribution of resources in response to the ongoing effects of historical colonialism. This is perhaps the most controversial of modern reparation claims and has led to substantial disagreement both between and within states that were historically colonized, as witnessed, for example, by the disagreement on financial reparations at the 2001 Conference among countries such as Nigeria, Zimbabwe, and Senegal (see Chakma 2003). Some of the most prominent contemporary claims of this kind, such as those of the Herero tribe in Namibia against Germany in response to the genocide of 1904–7, have been advanced by civil society groups, with at best limited support and in some cases genuine opposition from state governments (for discussion, see Torpey 2006, 134–42; Sarkin 2009). Compensation of this type necessarily corresponds to some sort of loss, and calculating such a loss necessarily involves counterfactual comparison between the status quo and a nonexistent possible world that could have come about in the absence of injustice. The key question, then, is that of the lasting wrongful harm caused by colonialism: how should this be characterized and calculated?

It is crucial here to be clear as to the rationale under which claims for reparations stemming from the lasting material effects of colonialism are advanced. Many historical persons had their lives directly impacted by the actions of colonial powers, at times suffering grievous harms and losses. At some times and in some places, colonial domination involved multiple instances of genocide, slavery, rape and sexual enslavement, murder, torture, displacement, and the misappropriation and destruction of property, alongside many other serious moral transgressions. Ypi cites the observation of Bartolomé de Las Casas, written in 1542: "No account, no matter how lengthy, how long it took to write, nor how conscientiously it was compiled, could do justice to the full horror of the atrocities committed at one time or another" (2013, 162). One set of questions concerns what is owed to the direct victims of such actions. In the immediate aftermath of injustice, these are the most pressing questions that corrective justice must answer. As time passes, however, and fewer direct victims remain, a further set of questions gains prominence. Colonialism has had significant effects on many present communities. Different people would live in different modern states, with different advantages and disadvantages, had colonial exploitation never taken place.

This chapter argues that insofar as present communities have benefited and others have suffered relative to a counterfactual state in which their historical interaction was characterized by an absence of domination and exploitation, they possess contemporary duties of reparation. It maintains that many

developed states are guilty of serious wrongdoing in failing to fulfill their reparative obligations and puts forward principles that suggest a case for a potentially
massive redistribution of resources. It may fairly be asked what use such theoretical argumentation, expressed in terms of ideas of morality and justice, is to
legal practitioners and political activists at the sharp end of campaigns for the
redress of historical wrongdoing. It need not be contended that such redistribution is likely in the short term or maintained that pursuing such distributive arguments would be the most effective way of seeking to repair the most
pressing harms caused by colonialism. Much contemporary campaigning in
relation to colonialism has goals that are not primarily distributive in character.
At times, a focus on material compensation may not only obscure other more
important ends but prove counterproductive, either by deterring officials from
engaging in reconciliatory processes such as apologizing or by apparently in-
sulting the victims of colonial injustice by belittling or mischaracterizing their
suffering.

This chapter is not a critique of existing political campaigns or public ra-
tionales for reparations. Its argument is theoretical—it argues that justice
requires extensive redistribution in the present day, but it is a further question
whether this should form a significant part of the agenda of those involved in
seeking the repair of historical wrongs. It is this question that takes center stage
in the extensive contemporary literature on transitional and reparative justice
(Teitel 2000; Thompson 2002; de Greiff 2006a; Walker 2006b). Instead, my
purpose is to determine what modern distributive rights and obligations are
entailed by historical colonial practices. It may be that claims based on such
arguments are currently politically infeasible or that distributive questions are
not the most important issues facing those communities that seek redress for
historical wrongdoing. It might also be pointed out, however, that some of the
poorest countries in the world are former colonies of some of the richest. For
such countries, a conclusion that the developed world is failing to fulfill its
distributive duties of rectification in relation to them is of not only theoretical
but also potentially practical importance. A number of writers have suggested
that rectificatory justice has a powerful motivating force: it is easier to make
arguments in favor of international redistribution that make reference to past
wrongdoing than to appeal to controversial accounts of international distributive justice, such as global egalitarianism (Tan 2007, 290; Butt 2009a, 16; see
also Pogge 2002, 132). In cases where symbolic reparation is what is most
desired by the descendants of victims, the neglect of distributive concerns may
be unproblematic. But there are other contexts where the monetary aspect of
reparations is key to the future prospects of many current and future people.
In such cases, a proper understanding of how past actions affect present
entitlements is vitally important.

Historical Injustice:
The International Dimension

Much discussion of historical injustice has traditionally focused on domestic cases, where citizens of a given state, typically belonging to an identifiable group, make a claim against their own government that stems from wrongs perpetrated against their ancestors. In the United States, for example, claims have been made by Native Americans in relation to the historical dispossession of indigenous peoples, by African Americans with regard to slavery and its aftermath, and by Japanese Americans in relation to wartime internment (Brooks 1999; Barkan 2000). The groups involved have often pursued both legal and political strategies—seeking redress through the courts but also trying to influence public opinion in favor of the rectification of historical injustice. Reparative claims have met with mixed judicial results—while there have been notable successes, other claims have largely been rebuffed or ignored. Recent years have seen growing interest in a different set of cases, in which the perpetrators and the victims of historical injustice were members of different modern states. Legal strategies are often not viable in such cases, owing to the fact that international legal prohibitions on various forms of unjust international interaction have a relatively recent genesis and generally do not have retrospective force (Reshetov 1990; Butt 2009b). Such cases frequently have a political character—the aim is to pressure or persuade the modern polity in question to apologize for and/or pay reparations in response to the actions of its forebear. Two sets of claims have achieved particular prominence: one arising from the actions of the Axis powers in World War II and one relating to the wrongs of the colonial period and of European colonialism in particular, including the slave trade. This chapter focuses on this second set of claims. To what extent do modern polities owe rectificatory duties to others as a result of actions originating in their imperial past? Specifically, how does the fact that the historical interaction between two polities was colonial in character affect conventional arguments relating to the rectification of historical injustice?

To answer this question, it is necessary to consider the relation between distributive and rectificatory or corrective justice. Any account of rectificatory justice, which seeks to reallocate or redistribute contemporary resource holdings in response to historical injustice, must engage with ideas of distributive justice, which seeks to determine the fair distribution of benefits and burdens in a given society. If we are, for example, to return misappropriated possessions to their rightful owners, we need some reason to hold that the owners are indeed in some sense entitled to the property in question, that their title is at least legitimate. As Jules Coleman writes: "In order for a scheme of rights to warrant protection under corrective justice . . . they must be sufficiently defensible in justice to warrant being sustained against individual infringements. Entitlements that fail to have this minimal property are not real rights in the sense that their infringements cannot give rise to a moral reason for acting" (1992, 352).

In broad terms, efforts to rectify the distributive effects of historical injustice have the greatest significance in contexts where distributive justice has a significant backward-looking context—where the actions of previous generations make a difference to the entitlements of persons in the present. If history is not of great importance to the question of who owns what in the present, then there will be little reason to suppose that past wrongdoing will cast a shadow over contemporary property holdings. So if, for example, one advocates highly redistributive, egalitarian principles of distributive justice that (say) allocate an equal share of resources to each individual at the start of each new generation and prohibit the transfer of advantage from one generation to another by mechanisms such as inheritance, then one's concern for backward-looking rectificatory justice will be very limited. Although there may still be good reasons to care about the past, if, for example, it affects modern ideas of group identity, arguments in favor of reparations will typically be grounded in the symbolic effects of making amends for the past—the distributive injustice of the past wrongdoing will have been, to use Jeremy Waldron's terminology, superseded (Waldron 1992). By contrast, if one thinks that it can be legitimate for property to be transferred from one generation to the next, so that one's social background makes a significant difference to how well one's life goes, then the provenance of one's advantages becomes much more significant— and the case for rectification, in contexts where these advantages have come about unjustly at the expense of others, much stronger (Nozick 1974, 231).

The relevance of historical injustice to present distributions, then, turns on the backward- or forward-looking character of one's account of distributive justice. It is not unusual to oppose the rectification of historical wrongs on the basis of a forward-looking account of distributive justice—rather than seeking to restore potentially suspect historical distributions, it might be asked, should we not look forward and seek to bring about just distributions of benefits and burdens (Waldron 1992; Vernon 2003; Wenar 2006)? It is here that the distinction between domestic and international injustice becomes significant. Many writers and real-world actors support quite different principles of distributive justice in domestic and in international contexts, advocating broadly egalitarian principles when it comes to relations with fellow citizens but much less redistributive principles in relation to persons living in other political communities (Rawls 1999; for discussion, see Caney 2002). A range of reasons can be given for this difference in approach—rooted in, for example, the shared nationality of members of particular nation states (Miller 2007) or the fact that citizens of specific states are all subject to the same coercive laws, which do not apply in the same way to those living in other countries (Blake 2002; Nagel 2005)—but the fact remains that for such writers, there is a much more compelling rationale for redistribution within, rather than across, state boundaries. The result is that there is widespread endorsement of forward-looking principles of distributive justice, stressing egalitarian principles such as equality of opportunity, at a national level but that international distributive justice is generally portrayed in primarily backward-looking fashion, with an emphasis on collective responsibility and self-determination. If one holds that the state in which one lives makes a difference when it comes to who should have what, then one necessarily needs a distinct account of international rectificatory justice—and this account will have to take seriously the question of how contemporary resource holdings have come about. This opens the door to reflection on the distributive legacy of historical colonialism.

The observation, however, that present advantages and disadvantages are rooted in historical injustice does not in itself establish the existence of present reparative obligations. The problem here concerns the effects of the passage of time. It is one thing to maintain that a given political community possesses reparative obligations immediately following an act of international injustice. Such a claim is itself controversial in terms of its willingness to hold people collectively responsible for the actions of their leaders, but the principle is widely accepted, particularly if the community in question has at least some kind of democratic character (Glenn Gray 1998, 198–99; Miller 2004, 262; Butt 2009a, 178–83; Pasternak 2011). This need not represent a claim that the people as a whole are morally responsible for the commission of injustice. The point is more simply that they face an obligation to put right the actions of their leaders. Things are more problematic when we consider events that took place a long time ago. Why should present communities, not alive at the time of the original injustice, be obliged to pay for the sins of their ancestors? A range of different answers has been put forward in response to this question. Some writers suggest communitarian approaches that focus on the fact that individuals are members of communities that persist through time in a way that their individual members do not and suggest that membership in a given community unavoidably comes with preexisting commitments (for discussion, see Fabre 2007, 150–55) or stress the ongoing responsibilities of political institutions, which similarly can have an ongoing identity across different time periods, analogous to a corporation (Tan 2007). Others suggest mechanisms by which individual members of one generation can come to have remedial responsibility to right another's wrongs (Thompson 2002; Abdel Nour 2003; Butt 2006).

Perhaps the most straightforward pro-reparations argument, however, is based on the idea of unjust enrichment. It holds that those who benefit from the wrongdoing of others can possess reparative obligations to the victims of injustice, even though they are not responsible for the original wrongdoing. Such an approach is controversial in its nonvoluntarist methodology (see Fullinwider 1975; Anwander 2005), but some scholars, at least, are willing to accept that the beneficiaries of injustice can have such obligations (Thomson 1986; Butt 2007). The claim is often made in environmental contexts in support of the "beneficiary pays" principle, which holds that those who benefit involuntarily from certain forms of harmful pollution can justifiably be held responsible for its costs (Gosseries 2004; Page 2012). Strikingly, the "benefit" rationale was explicitly invoked by the Group of 21 in their draft declaration for the 2001 UN World Conference, which argued that reparations to victims of colonialism should be contributed to by "States, companies and individuals who benefited materially from these practices" (Tan 2007, 280). Suppose it is granted that it is possible for rectificatory duties to arise by these sorts of mechanisms, such that we can construct a paradigm case of historical international injustice in need of present rectification, where we assign reparative duties to the present community or communities that have benefited from the historic wrongdoing (who often will be the direct descendants of the transgressors) to restore to some degree the condition of those harmed by a historical wrongdoing. Let us accept that in this type of case there is a moral basis for reparations as a result of (a) the generally backward-looking background account of distributive justice, (b) the presence of ongoing harm caused by the historical wrongdoing, and (c) the existence of a class of persons who have benefited from the harm in question. How does the shift to the colonial context complicate things?

The Colonial Dimension

In keeping with the paradigm case outlined earlier, many claims arising from historical colonialism are international in character—they are made by members of one present state against another. Even if there are multiple linkages between the communities in the present day, such as the existence of significant migrant communities in either or both states, close trading relationships, or formal structures such as the British Commonwealth, there is no single overarching authority with the power to redistribute resources from members of one state to members of another. In this regard they are members of separate, backward-looking schemes of distribution—even if this may not have been the case in the past (Ypi, Goodin, and Barry 2009). Clearly, the precise sovereign entities that exist in the present may well be different from those that existed historically. There are currently 192 states that are members of the United Nations. By contrast, 51 states were represented at the first UN General Assembly in 1946. For a range of reasons, notably including processes of decolonization, the set of states that currently exists is very different from that of fifty or a hundred years ago. This certainly complicates the legal case for reparations, but it is less problematic from the perspective of the "beneficiary pays" model. It does not matter, on this approach, if the language we use to describe different political communities changes with time, so that we speak of nations at one point and states at another, for example (for discussion, see Butt 2009a, 23–24). The key question here is not whether a particular political entity, such as a people or a state, had a sufficient degree of collective political agency at a given point in time such that it is fair to hold it responsible for the actions of its leaders or whether it has continuously existed in a particular sort of way such that it bears an appropriate kind of morally relevant similarity to its forebear. Instead, the question is straightforwardly that of who has benefited and who has suffered as a result of historical injustice, a question that can be asked both between and within particular political communities.

It is this issue, of the nature of the purported modern harm caused by colonialism, that complicates the case for reparations in postcolonial contexts. The extent to which colonialism has indeed had lasting harmful consequences is the subject of heated debate among historians in many different countries. Does historical colonialism continue to cause harm to persons living in the present—and, if so, how much? This question is typically framed in terms of the *net effects* of colonialism and asks whether particular former colonies might now be better off than they would have been had colonialism not taken place—or, at least, if there might not be *some* sense in which they have benefited. This need not serve as a defense of colonialism per se; the claim may simply be that present members of the former colony are not worse off as a result of the historical treatment of their ancestors than they would have been had their ancestors not been treated in the way they were. This issue is a recurrent theme of historical debate relating, for example, to the British Empire. It once again came to the fore in April 2011, when British prime minister David Cameron addressed a group of schoolchildren in Pakistan and appeared to question the Empire's legacy, stating: "As with so many of the problems of the world, we are responsible for their creation in the first place." A familiar debate unfolded in the British media. The BBC contrasted the views of two historians,

Nick Lloyd and Andrew Thompson. Lloyd argued that Cameron's comments revealed "a disappointing lack of historical judgment"; he described the British Empire in India as "the greatest experiment in paternalistic imperial government in history," maintaining that British rule left a still persisting legacy of "a number of priceless assets," including the English language, governmental structures, and logistical infrastructure, and concluding that, "far from damaging India, British imperial rule gave it a head start." While Lloyd held that "the empire gave its colonies real, tangible benefits," Thompson instead focused on "the inheritance of colonial violence" in places such as Kenya, Palestine, Malaysia, Zimbabwe, and Northern Ireland and questioned whether "the violence that characterised . . . counter-insurgency operations during decolonisation then set the scene for the way in which independent, post-colonial African and Asian governments dealt with political dissent from their own peoples," concluding that "the imperial past is far from being dead. On the contrary it is actually very much part of contemporary politics" (BBC News 2011).

Such debates, of course, are not exclusive to Britain. One finds, for example, similar discussions in historical writing on the character of French colonialism, reflected in the French government's legislation of 2005 requiring that colonial history be taught in a "positive" manner in French schools (Tyre 2008, 152) and holding that "School courses should recognise in particular the positive role of the French presence overseas, notably in north Africa" (Henley 2005); in debates over the lasting effects of Japanese colonialism in areas including China and Korea (Sand 1999); in the "history wars" in Australia concerning the effects of British colonialism on Australian Aborigines and Torres Strait Islanders (Macintyre and Clark 2004); and so on. The effects of colonialism on imperial powers as well as on those subject to their subjugation are similarly disputed, with some challenging the assumption that historical colonialism has necessarily led to modern advantage for states such as Spain and Portugal (Landes 1998). One might also look at the extensive literature in the social sciences that seeks to use comparative analysis to quantify the differential effects of different forms of colonization (Sokoloff and Engerman 2000; Lange, Mahoney, and vom Hau 2006). Feyrer and Sacerdote, for example, use this form of analysis to study the effects of colonialism via a database on islands in the Atlantic, Pacific, and Indian Oceans. They identify "a robust positive relationship between the years of European colonialism and current levels of income" (which, they suggest, is at least partly causal in nature), while also differentiating between the effects of different colonial powers and eras. Thus, they claim that "there is a discernable pecking order amongst the colonizers. Years under US and Dutch colonial rule are significantly better than years

under the Spanish and Portuguese," and "later years of colonialism are associated with a much larger increase in modern GDP than years before 1700"
(2009, 256).

It might be thought that such questions map directly onto the reparations
debate. The suggestion is that compensation is due only if it can be shown
that members of former colonies are still suffering a net loss as a result of the
experiences of their ancestors. Even if it is accepted that there is a net loss, it
still may be maintained that the positive effects of colonialism should be taken
into account when calculating what is owed—that they should, as it were,
offset the bill for reparations. This issue can be differentiated from the debate
over apologies, where it can be claimed that there should be apologies for each
and every moral transgression, regardless of the net overall impact of colonialism as a whole. But as the benefit model does not seek to hold modern parties
responsible for historical injustice, the "net loss" approach appears to be appropriate. The historical debate over the extent of this loss, of course, is deeply
contentious. In a British context, while some writers follow Lloyd in pointing
to purported institutional and cultural benefits to former colonies (Ferguson
2002), others have argued that such a perspective massively underestimates
both the historical damage wrought by the colonialists and its long-lasting
effects (Newsinger 2006). In seeking to conduct a "moral audit" of the British
Empire, Piers Brendon first observes that "the moral balance sheet of the British
Empire is a chaotic mixture of black and red," before arguing that "all balance
sheets require interpretation; but it seems clear that, even according to its own
lights, the British Empire was in grave moral deficit," pointing not only to the
historical "catalogue of gross imperial wrongdoing" but also to the fact that
"much of the imperial legacy was failed states and internecine strife" (Brendon
2007). The fundamental rationale of this type of assessment—that the current
state of the postcolonial communities is being compared with some kind of
world where colonialism did not take place—is rarely scrutinized. Although
there is huge disagreement as to the relative weight of benefit and loss, it is
commonplace even among advocates of reparations to find acknowledgments
that colonialism had some positive aspects: witness Tan's statement that "the
history of colonialism is, of course, a highly complex one. There is no denying
that colonized people have also benefited in different ways from their encounter
with the colonizing power" (2007, 281). Such an acknowledgment opens up a
vulnerability in the pro-reparations argument, as it seemingly makes the case
for reparations dependent on the resolution to the historical debate on net
loss. It is this move that should be resisted.

The question of what it means to benefit or suffer as a result of wrongdoing
is key here. In everyday discourse relating to compensation, reference is

sometimes made to the idea of the status quo ante. One compensates someone for something, it is supposed, by restoring the state of affairs obtained prior to the act of injustice. This is problematic, since it is not hard to think of cases where trying to turn back the clock in this way leaves the victim worse off than she would have been had the act of injustice not taken place. Thus the point of compensation is seen as being to redress the difference between a victim's current state and the state she would have been in had the act of injustice not taken place. As Nickel writes, "Compensatory justice requires that counterbalancing benefits be provided to those individuals who have been wrongly injured which will serve to bring them up to the level of wealth and welfare that they would now have if they had not been disadvantaged" (Nickel 1975, 537). The problem here is that, unlike in the status quo ante case, there is no fact of the matter as to how a victim would have fared in the absence of injustice, and so reference has to be made to some possible state of affairs that might have come about in the absence of the unjust action. How should this counterfactual be calculated, given the countless number of ways in which history might have unfolded? The standard response appeals to the most likely outcome—what would most probably have occurred had the injustice not taken place. We measure the difference between someone's current state and the state she would probably be in had injustice never occurred and hold the perpetrator responsible for making up the difference between the real world and this possible world.

In many cases, this is indeed the right kind of comparison to employ. However, in some situations this leads to intuitively unacceptable consequences, and so calculations of just compensation instead make use of a quite different mode of counterfactual comparison. Feinberg employs the example of a businessman who is injured as a result of his driver's negligently reckless driving but as a result misses a flight that goes on to crash (Feinberg 1992, 8; for discussion, see Butt 2009a, 108–11). Rather than asking what would have been the most likely outcome had the driver not acted wrongly, he claims we should consider a "doubly counterfactual" alternative in such cases in which the driver acts properly and the plane does not crash (Feinberg 1992, 11). It might be highly unlikely that such an outcome would have actually come about had the driver acted properly, but nonetheless compensatory justice requires us to suspend our disbelief and use this possible world as the basis for assessing the harm that the wrongdoing has caused. Similarly, a mugger cannot escape his duty to compensate his victim by observing, however accurately, that had he not attacked his victim, another, more brutal mugger would have done so—instead, we construct a doubly counterfactual case in which there was no mugging at all (Feinberg 1992, 8). The common element to both examples is the idea that thinking about the most likely outcome in the absence of the intervention of the wrongdoer does not seem to be the right way to isolate the harm done by the wrongdoing in question. Though it is likely in such cases that the net interest of the victim is not lower than it would have been had there been no interaction between wrongdoer and victim, we nonetheless want to maintain that the victim has not just been wronged but wrongfully harmed and so is entitled to compensation.

The construction of the doubly counterfactual formulation is particularly appropriate when it comes to the consideration of cases of exploitation. The specification of what constitutes exploitation is controversial philosophically, but different accounts typically reflect the idea that to exploit someone is, in some sense, to take unfair advantage of him or her (Goodin 1987, 166; Wertheimer 1996, 16; Logar 2010, 333). Exploitation typically arises in cases where one party takes wrongful advantage of another in a context of unequal power relations, and such unequal power relations were evidently the norm in colonial contexts defined by relations of domination and subjugation. Indeed, to a large extent, the desire to take wrongful advantage provided the rationale for colonialism itself: as Young writes, "colonisation was not primarily concerned with transposing cultural values. They came as a by-product of its real objectives of trade, economic exploitation and settlement" (2001, 24). In cases of exploitation that involved labor and material production—literally, the blood, sweat, and tears of the victims of injustice—to invoke the most likely outcome in the absence of interaction badly mischaracterizes the appropriate counterfactual. Instead, a counterfactual should be employed that includes this labor but imagines a way in which it could have come about through nondominated cooperation—however unlikely this would have been in practice. As argued earlier, historical colonialism took many different forms, and we can delineate a wide variety of different forms of interaction between the colonizers and the colonized. But, insofar as these are instances of colonial interaction, they take place, by definition, within a context of domination. Even if the historical interaction appears to have been consensual, if one party stood in an unequal power relation to another as a result of unjust colonial expansion, the potential for the unjust taking of advantage and thus for exploitation was there. Insofar as this led to one side gaining more and the other less than it should have had the relationship been fair and nondominated, there is a case for reparation—and this stands regardless of the likely fate of the exploited party in a possible world where there was no interaction between the colonizer and the colonized.

One way to think about this is to consider forms of contemporary international interaction that some observers hold to be exploitative, such as instances of trade between the developed and the developing world in commodities such as coffee. Take the claim of fair trade advocates that certain seemingly consensual trade practices are unjust since they do not pay workers a fair price for their labor. Such a view need not depend upon a claim that the workers in question are actually worse off given the practice than they likely would have been if there had been no interaction with the exploiting corporation. The fair trade advocate can maintain that the transaction is unfair since the worker is underpaid relevant to a counterfactual in which the worker is paid what is deemed a fair wage. It may well be that such an advocate might accept that it is likely that the workers would actually be worse off had they never been contracted: this counterfactual, however, fails to take into account the production that has been generated by their exploitation but that would not exist in the most probable possible world where exploitation is absent. If we affirm that exploitation is unjust and gives rise to rectificatory obligations, the appropriate counterfactual is not one in which the exploitee had no interaction with the exploiter at all but rather one in which the exploitee was a nonexploited partner in the collaborative enterprise and so was paid a fair wage. The exploitative character of the fair trade case is controversial, since it rests upon the claim that exchanges in which one party accepts a price that is less than some externally derived fair benchmark price are exploitative, even in the absence of any kind of coercion or rights violation (see Wertheimer 1996, 10–12). The wrongful character of colonial exploitation, however, is significantly more straightforward insofar as the difference in power relations emerges as a result of colonial domination.

If we hold that colonial domination was unjust, then it follows that taking advantage of the unequal power relations that resulted was wrongfully exploitative. This claim, it should be noted, is perfectly compatible with an observation that this kind of taking unfair advantage represented (or represents) the norm in international relations. It might even be that such exploitation is so commonplace that it is hard to imagine what past or present consensual cooperation that did not take unfair advantage would look like or to think of examples of when this has actually taken place. The morally relevant counterfactual in such cases is nonetheless one in which production occurred in nondominated circumstances—however unlikely it is that this would actually have taken place in practice and however hard it is to envisage. The claim, then, is that the domination characteristic of colonialism results in an inequality of power relations that is particularly problematic from the viewpoint of transactional justice. There is still a further question as to what form of cooperation would be just in the presence of inequality but in the absence of domination, and the answer to this question will likely depend on one's background account of distributive justice. (There are then further questions still about whether choosing not to cooperate in a context of inequality might be wrong: is there a positive duty on affluent states to interact?) The key point, though, is that the wrongness of taking advantage of colonial domination stands regardless of whether it is generally wrong to take advantage of inequality.

A striking example of the misapplication of counterfactual reasoning in relation to colonialism is found in the recent work of the historian Niall Ferguson (2002). Ferguson explicitly links his assessment of the question of whether the British Empire was a "Good Thing" or a "Bad Thing" to the reparations debate. Ferguson does not explain the meta-ethical character of his assessment but seems to favor a crude form of utilitarianism, writing, "Prima facie . . . there seems a plausible case that the Empire enhanced global welfare— in other words, was a Good Thing" and noting that the arguments against imperialism can be "summarized . . . under two headings": "those that stress the negative consequences for the colonized; and those that stress the negative consequences for the colonizers" (2002, xx). Despite observing that "the imagination reels from the counterfactual of a world without the British Empire," he nonetheless proposes a balance sheet that lists both the good and the bad of the Empire, strongly suggesting that the net balance was positive. He first invokes a status quo ante argument—"To imagine the world without the Empire would be to expunge from the map the elegant boulevards of Williamsburg and old Philadelphia; to sweep into the sea the squat battlements of Port Royal, Jamaica; to return to the bush the glorious skyline of Sydney; to level the steamy seaside slum that is Freetown, Sierra Leone; to fill in the Big Hole at Kimberley; to demolish the mission at Kuruman; to send the town of Livingstone hurtling over the Victoria Falls" (Ferguson 2002, xxi)—before invoking a counterfactual grounded in probability: "It is of course tempting to argue that it would all have happened anyway, albeit with different names. . . . Yet there is reason to doubt that the world would have been the same or even similar in the absence of the Empire. . . . Would other empires have produced the same effects? It seems doubtful" (Ferguson 2002, xxi–xxii).

There is much here that might be disputed, as the work of anti-apologists such as Newsinger makes clear. But, crucially, the reparations advocate need not be drawn into this debate about what would likely have happened in the absence of Britain's imperial misadventures. To oppose reparations claims on the basis of this kind of reasoning is straightforwardly mistaken. The appropriate counterfactual here is not that which would most probably have come about in the absence of any interaction between colonizers and their colonies nor that in which the colonies are subject to even more brutal treatment at the hands of a different power. Instead, we should imagine a possible world— however unlikely—where there was productive interchange between the different political communities but where this was consensual and nonexploitative. Ferguson concludes his preface by posing the following rhetorical question: "For better, for worse—fair and foul—the world we know today is in large measure the product of Britain's age of Empire. The question is not whether British imperialism was without a blemish. It was not. The question is whether there could have been a less bloody path to modernity. Perhaps in theory there could have been. But in practice?" (2002, xxv).

It is sufficient for those who argue in favor of reparations for colonialism that the less bloody path is there in theory. However unlikely it is that various forms of development would have emerged in the absence of egregious wrongdoing, this is nonetheless the appropriate counterfactual to consider in assessing present levels of benefit and disadvantage stemming from the colonial past. There are, of course, many such possible worlds, and a full account of rectificatory justice will have to come to a conclusion as to which is the most appropriate in each given case. A full determination here will inevitably be messy and may not be expressed simply in terms of a debt that is payable from one group to another, particularly when we remember that some members of historically wronged groups may themselves have benefited substantially from the misfortune that befell their fellow members, as may members of quite separate groups with no direct link to the wrong in question. Whichever possible world is deemed most appropriate, however, it will be one that imagines fair cooperation between colonizer and colonized in a mutually beneficial context of nondomination. Writing in 1955, Aimé Césaire characterized the African colonial experience as follows: "The great historical tragedy of Africa has been not so much that it was too late in making contact with the rest of the world, as the manner in which that contact was brought about; that Europe began to 'propagate' at a time when it had fallen into the hands of the most unscrupulous financiers and captains of industry; that it was our misfortune to encounter that particular Europe on our path, and that Europe is responsible before the human community for the highest heap of corpses in human history" (Césaire, in Olaniyan 2000, 269).

From the perspective of modern compensatory justice, it is not the fact of contact but precisely the tragic and morally horrific manner in which contact was brought about that stands in need of redress.

Conclusion

This chapter has argued that modern communities should ask themselves whether they are better off and others are worse off than they would have been had the historical productive interaction between them been consensual and cooperative in character. A situation in which they are advantaged and others disadvantaged relative to this counterfactual is unjust and gives rise to rectificatory obligations. How such obligations should be met is a difficult question. One possibility, of course, is simply to suggest a straightforward transfer of resources, such as a cash payment, but there is a range of other alternatives, including debt relief, the granting of advantageous access to markets, development assistance, and forms of exemption from free trade agreements (Tan 2007, 280–81). It may be that the disadvantage in question is unlikely to be easily resolved by a one-off payment and that, instead, what is indicated is the need for an ongoing commitment on the part of the advantaged party to correct the distributive distortion caused by both the initial wrongdoing and the subsequent failure to fulfill rectificatory obligations. It is important, however, that this not be seen as some kind of reasonable compromise between acknowledging one's duties and straightforwardly avoiding them altogether. The mechanisms outlined here should generally be pursued only when it is genuinely believed that they represent the best and most effective way of fulfilling reparative obligations: the test to be employed is that of which approach best aids those to whom reparation is owed. This is not likely to happen overnight. Most former colonial powers have not even begun to come to terms, in any sort of meaningful way, with their imperial pasts—frequently refusing to compensate even surviving victims of terrible and obvious wrongdoing, such as torture at the hands of the British in the Kenyan Emergency or sexual enslavement by the Japanese military during World War II. But a key conclusion of this chapter is that the rectificatory obligations of such countries are not limited to surviving victims.

The ongoing failure to do what can be done to repair such terrible injustices is a grievous wrong that can never be righted (Boxill 2003; Sher 2005; Butt 2006, 2013b). But this failure to fulfill rectificatory duties does not get former colonial powers off the compensatory hook as time passes. The passage of time does mean that a particular set of reparative obligations—to the direct victims of injustice—lapses. But this need not lead to the conclusion that all that is needed can be found in the nondistributive domain of apology, education, and symbolic action—even if that is all we feel can be realistically achieved, even if we fear that pursuing the reparative agenda might actually be counterproductive to the pursuit of more modest goals. For as long as we continue to live in a world where the distribution of resources is literally of vital importance, the failure of colonial powers to fulfill their reparative duties to the peoples they have wronged is a continuing injustice, which cries out for rectification. It is tragic if it really is the case that we must sacrifice the pursuit of justice for

the achievement of more pressing or easily realizable goals as a result of a refusal on the part of some of the world's most affluent people to acknowledge
the tainted origins of their contemporary advantages.

Note

This chapter is a significantly revised and expanded version of a paper originally
published as "Repairing Historical Wrongs and the End of Empire," *Social and Legal
Studies* 21, no. 2 (2012): 227–42. I am very grateful to Klaus Neumann and Janna
Thompson and to two anonymous reviewers for their helpful comments on this new
version.

10

Historical Dialogue

*Beyond Transitional Justice and
Conflict Resolution*

ELAZAR BARKAN

his chapter explores the discursive space between transitional justice on the one hand and conflict prevention
and resolution on the other. It argues that while the memory of historical
enmity is often a factor in instigating conflict, no professional community
today that is engaged in the promotion of human rights, peace building, or
international justice attempts to address the political challenge presented by
the memory and history of conflicts. Historical dialogue provides a methodology that bridges scholarship and advocacy with the goal of contributing to
conflict prevention.

Memories of victimization are a primary cause of retaliation and vengeance.
The question of whether suffering occurred in the recent or the distant past is
often secondary. From East Anatolia to Nanjing to the Battle of Kosovo,
examples of the desire for recognition and, at times, revenge abound. Yet
memories of suffering as a result of conflicts do not necessarily become an
ongoing bone of contention; in fact, many violent enmities in history have not
been protracted. Often the memories of sufferings are contained, and the
dispute subsides or even disappears from view—not because it is deliberately
silenced but because the parties to the conflict coexist peacefully or have even
reconciled and resolved their differences.

In other cases violent pasts have not been reenacted because the memory of violence has served as a deterrent, rather than an incitement, and history is subsumed by politics, rather than neglected. In the 1990s in Eastern Europe, there were all imaginable reasons for conflict, including a tradition of ethnic cleansing, frontiers without historical legitimacy, and memories of eternal national conflict (Snyder 2003). One could have expected the region comprising the Baltic countries, Poland, Ukraine, and Belarus to descend into violence after the Soviet bloc disintegrated. But, although conflicting historical memories abounded, political considerations have prevailed and averted major national or ethnic conflicts. However, the 2014 violence (war) in Ukraine exposed the ethnic fissures, and indeed both Russia and Ukraine resorted to historical justifications in their claims to Crimea and Eastern Ukraine.

Memories of suffering tend to loom large particularly when they become instrumental for national(ist) identities. Identities of nations and peoples are vested in their histories. Nationalists perpetuate their own versions of history, which often include xenophobic and sectarian myths. While this is recognized discursively, however, it is rarely incorporated into conflict resolution or conflict prevention policy.

Beyond Peace Building and Transitional Justice

In this chapter I argue for a particular form of intervention in historical discourse: historical dialogue. Elsewhere (Barkan 2009) I explored the methodological and professional considerations for historians who participate in historical debates. Here I examine further the policy implications of addressing or ignoring the memory of historical violence in contemporary conflicts. The approach I am advocating differs from that of conventional conflict resolution on the one hand and transitional justice on the other. The former is future oriented and focuses on charting a road map to end violence, leaving aside considerations of justice, accountability, and impunity. Its refrain is "let bygones be bygones." It was the realist orthodoxy for decades, especially during the Cold War, and still informs international efforts led by the United Nations.[1] There are no international mechanisms or recognized instruments that include historical clarification as part of the process (Responsibility to Protect is one clear example); instead, the focus is on incentives and sanctions and on military and diplomatic action (Woocher 2009). Experts in the areas of peace building and peacekeeping mediate between warring parties and try to address the immediate reasons for a given conflict, rather than seeking its root causes or how the history of the conflict has become—through its memorialization—a political factor in its own right. Their task is to achieve a cessation of violence and a prevention of its recurrence, and they are neither willing nor equipped to deal with the historical causes of conflicts.

Transitional justice practitioners, in contrast, claim that without accountability for past violence there can be no lasting peace, nor can there be genuine reconciliation: in order to establish respect for the rule of law and to prevent a recurrence of crimes, perpetrators, at least the most prominent among them, have to be prosecuted. In some cases punishment is avoided, as in South Africa, but experts increasingly agree that the dispute between peace and justice has been resolved in favor of peace *and* justice. These experts generally march under the banner of "never again!" The relationship between these efforts to reconciliation is much more ambivalent (Tolbert 2013). While the conflict resolution professionals privilege peace over accountability, the transitional justice experts see peace as complementary to, if not dependent on, justice.

Transitional justice practitioners focus on the immediate past rather than on chronologically more distant memories. They see in commemorations and acknowledgments of past violence a form of reparations. Their goal is to "unsilence a topic that might otherwise be spoken of only in hushed tones" (Hayner 2011, 20), to counter denial, and to prevent the repetition of horrendous acts of violence and cycles of revenge. The focus is on the immediate victims who are at the heart of the narratives, but little or no attention is paid to the impact these specific narratives have on conflict resolution.

Both the conventional conflict resolution and the transitional justice approaches have their merits, although the jury is still out on the precise efficacy of either (see, for example, Snyder and Vinjamuri 2003; Sikkink 2011). Even a cursory survey of various conflicts suggests that overcoming historical animosity at times demands overcoming the past. One has only to look to the relationship between Poland and Ukraine or to the transition to democracy in Spain, where the past was overlooked for more than a generation after 1978, to recognize how historical memories and animosity can be put aside. Peace building and peacekeeping are crucial in cases in which conflicts are ongoing. But even protracted conflicts are often continuations of historical violence. In those cases, history and contemporary issues are closely intertwined and are of similar prominence. The Palestinian-Israeli conflict is a good example: although current issues may seem to dominate it, its resolution requires a better understanding of its historical aspects, such as dispossession and whether Zionism as a national movement or colonialism was responsible for the 1948 war and the Nakba.

When conflict erupts, the outside world pays attention and in doing so often emphasizes the historical context and the role of ancient hatred. The

Balkan wars are a paradigmatic case; here even people who learn from their history are said to be condemned to repeat it. This perception shaped the West's belated response to the breakup of Yugoslavia. On the other hand, when peace prevails, historical animosities are ignored or at least judged to have been overcome. Yet the need to address the past is viewed as necessary even in the most successful recent case in which peace superseded long-standing animosities, namely the integration of Europe. In France and Germany, the construction of a mutually empathic historical narrative is considered a factor that has contributed to strengthening the relationship between the two nations.

Both conventional conflict resolution and transitional justice approaches become more problematic when the conflict is long lasting, when most of the perpetrators and, somewhat later, the survivors have died, when the tensions are informed by historical distrust and group animosity more so than by on-going violence, and when nationalist narratives fan the flames of hostility. In these cases, an approach that responds to the desire for acknowledgment and recognition of historical injustice and suffering, while shifting the focus away from accountability, may be necessary.

Conventional conflict resolution instruments tend to be ineffectual where historical memory is the main vehicle for expressing animosity and appears to cause the conflict. What I am referring to as "historical conflicts" are character-ized by memories of a violent history that are at the core of the conflict while other contemporary causes are represented as secondary; in northeast Asia, the conflicts between Korea and Japan and between China and Japan focus on Japanese crimes while the contemporary disputes, such as those over the Senkaku (Diaoyu) and Takeshima (Dokdo) Islands, are filtered through and subsumed under either the traumatic past or the memory of the historical violence. In these cases, the conflict has a past that reaches into the present, and contemporary causes are overshadowed by the contested interpretation of the historical conflict, the legacy of which remains part of the identity of the victims and, sometimes, also of the perpetrators. Such historical conflicts neces-sitate a bridging of the protagonists' historical narratives in order to reduce distrust and to create space for reconciliation.

The Armenian genocide is a prime example of a historical conflict in this sense. There are contemporary causes and manifestations of the dispute, such as the conflict between Turkey and Armenia, the dispute over Azerbaijan, or even the diaspora's role in Armenian politics. But the memory of historical injustice driving the descendants of the victims to pursue acknowledgment and redress is the focus of the contemporary dispute, channels contemporary distrust, and filters the interpretation of contemporary events and politics. Here, the transitional justice approach of accountability and the conflict resolution option of overlooking the past are inadequate.

When conflicts are inflamed by history, they are often fanned by partisan memories: that is, by myths that are intentionally manipulated by nationalists, rather than by critical sophisticated history. Professional historians have long been aware of the methodological and epistemological limitations for producing objective history. By undertaking critical empirical work and by taking account of narratives constructed from alternative perspectives, what are sometimes referred to as intersubjective histories aim to present nonpartisan narratives, where the descriptions of the disagreements are based on professional analysis and do not stem from the identity of the historians. In contrast, much nationalist history aims to glorify by mythologizing national claims.

Thus far, we know relatively little about the conditions that inflame or repress historical conflicts: about why some historical myths give rise to violent conflicts, whereas others are contained. While there is a growing attention to the past in contemporary politics, there is little knowledge of the relationship of historical memory to conflict, conflict resolution, and peace building or to the historical roots of conflicts. We still know too little about the circumstances under which historical conflicts come to the fore rather than remain dormant, and we have no satisfactory answers to the question of how protagonists and experts ought to act in an active historical conflict to diminish its volatility and to prevent it from escalating. Yet there are sufficient examples to suggest that it is possible to alter the nationalistic perspectives of a conflict and thereby to change the attitudes of previous enemies.

Historical Discourse in Conflict and Nonconflict Areas

Demands for historical redress occur in conflict, postconflict, and nonconflict situations. Often the avalanche of historical discourse obscures these critical distinctions and, as with human rights, the legitimacy of demands for redress and accountability is viewed as "universal" and "indivisible." For example, the Office of the UN High Commissioner for Human Rights sees the right to truth "about gross human rights violations and serious violations of human rights law" as "an inalienable and autonomous right, linked to the duty and obligation of the State to protect and guarantee human rights, to conduct effective investigations and to guarantee effective remedy and reparations." According to its "Study on the Right to the Truth," this right "has both an individual and a societal dimension and should be considered as a nonderogable right and not be subject to limitations" (United Nations 2006a). Similarly the right to redress places the victims at the center and is also nonderogable (United Nations 2006b; see also van Boven 2005).

Such expansive expectations have been informed in particular by historical redress cases in postauthoritarian situations, making it seem that addressing the past, and even acknowledging and accounting for historical root causes, is also a necessary tool not only for redress but to bring a conflict to an end. Advocates of redress see this as a new norm and a growing moral and legal obligation. Yet these examples do not extend to ongoing conflicts among groups (nations, ethnicities), and redress is more of an aspiration than a reality, even in historical conflicts.

If we limit conflict to mean an ongoing violent military or paramilitary conflict, not the memory of a conflict or a political conflict, then the assertion that redressing the past is a necessary condition is aspirational rather than based on empirical evidence. Few violent conflicts have been resolved outright by paying attention to historical dialogue between the sides. Therefore, the lack of engagement with the past by the conflict resolution and peace-building communities is understandable. Yet it is at the same time frustrating because the role of history in inciting conflict suggests that it is necessary to engage such history, albeit within a different time scale, and possibly with different actors.

What does the evidence tell us? One approach to historical disputes and the memory of violent conflicts that continues to haunt contemporary society calls for a silencing of history, that is, ignoring or denying contentious historical issues and suppressing historical discussion. Another approach is to engage in dialogue: to discuss the issues, investigate, but not inflame or create a conflict or controversy, while being prepared to acknowledge responsibility. The reopening of a dialogue requires the group or nation to reexamine its past. It may involve an acknowledgment of victims, which goes beyond a search for individual accountability.

These two categories are along a spectrum and tend to shade into each other. Each of them is locally and temporally specific, and efforts to resolve a particular historical dispute may evolve from relying on one approach to utilizing the other over time. Spain, for example, moved from repression of historical issues immediately after the transition to democracy to a reengagement with some of these issues three decades later (see Violi's chapter in this volume). Spain maintained its ethnic heterogeneity, and the legacy of the Civil War could easily have been reawakened and strengthened regional rivalry. Instead, the time span between the 1970s and the early 2000s served to legitimize the political system and to routinize elections and transfers of political power. Initially, only some aspects of the Civil War have been investigated, while the dictatorship itself remains largely out of bounds. This has been slowly changing. Consequently, the reengagement with history has carried painful emotions but has not presented a challenge to the political system.

Elazar Barkan

Examples of efforts to silence historical discussion include Rwanda, Cambodia, and East Timor. In each of these cases, transitional justice instruments such as commissions, courts, museums, and memorials have addressed aspects of the memory of the conflict, but historical redress and a national dialogue remain at best an aspiration pursued by a few NGOs. In Rwanda, the production of history as propaganda and the repression of all contesting voices seem to risk inspiring a resurgence of ethnic conflict. The Hutu try increasingly to have their suffering recognized, and the categorical identification in this case of one group as historical victims and the other as historical perpetrators may not be sustainable, and is slowly challenged with the aid of international actors. Could it perhaps be argued that Rwanda is at an early stage and that once the political system stabilizes, critical historical examination will become feasible? Could there be a rationale for delaying a discussion of horrific violence, analogous to what happened in Spain? However, unlike in Spain, in Rwanda there is no ongoing process of political legitimization, and together with the lack of democracy, the limits on civil society NGOs, and the ongoing and renewed civil war in the Congo, present conditions do not bode well for a historical dialogue. Interviews by reporters often reveal the frustration of citizens with the regime, especially concerning the repression of free speech, which is often manifested in the repression of dissenting opinions about history. The Gacaca trials are often hailed as an adaptation of transitional justice mechanism to local traditions and demands, yet local antigovernment testimonies are not recorded out of fear, and the local history written through these records is reifying the victory of the Tutsi (Clark 2010).

One variable that should be examined is whether there is any correlation between a willingness to engage and investigate the past, regardless of the success of the investigation, and reduced prospects for conflict. While at times the line between a conflict and a postconflict situation can become blurred, the proximity to mass violence is critical. The paradigmatic case of successful reconciliation between old enemies is that of Germany and France. Following hundreds of years of conflict, including three major wars that feature prominently in public memory (1870–71, 1914–18, and 1939–45), the two countries put the past behind them and forged a new economic partnership that soon became a close relationship between the leading powers of European integration. The rewriting of history—as a space and discourse of reconciliation— eventually became a significant component of reconciliation, although it was largely ignored early on in the process, with both sides letting bygones be bygones. Historical dialogue developed only after the success of economic cooperation, thus enhancing rather than prompting reconciliation. Today Germany's and France's attention to the common past is exemplary and includes joint commemorations and coproduced school textbooks. Germany's civic commitment to atone for its past proved to be a key factor: it helped build the trust that was a necessary component of reconciliation. In time, France too embraced contrition for its own crimes, primarily vis-à-vis the Holocaust (but not regarding the legacy of colonialism, which remains a contentious political issue). The attention to education and public history that emphasized shared interests, an acknowledgment of the responsibility for past violence, and the pursuit of criminal accountability were all critical for the success of reconciliation.

France and Germany were in an ideal position because remorse could be combined with resources to pursue redress. As I have noted elsewhere (Barkan 2000), redress is always symbolic relative to the level of destruction and to the resources available to the country (such as GNP). "Symbolic," however, does not mean less important. Could the theory of economic backwardness as an advantage—which states that a country that develops later has a more rapid rate of growth (Gerschenkron 1962)—be applied to memory? The successful reconciliation between Germany and its neighbors is continuously referred to in East Asia and plays a factor in regional efforts. Will the European success be also emulated in other regions where the conflict is hotter? Or could symbolic redress precede economic integration? The French–German case also invites the questions of whether the absence of acknowledgment hindered reconciliation in northeast Asia and of why and how the lack of historical acknowledgment became a factor in regional politics, especially among Japan, China, and Korea. Did German atonement strengthen the initial economic and political contacts between Germany and France, a factor that is missing between Japan and Korea and between Japan and China, in a region where the historical memories rest heavily on the shoulders of contemporary politicians, as well as on those of the public?

There are numerous cases of extensive redress of historical wrongs in postconflict and nonconflict situations. For example, conflict between European settlers and indigenous peoples lasted for more than a hundred years and included mass violence. When redress is debated, offered, accepted, or rejected in settler societies such as Australia, New Zealand, or Canada, it is part of a democratic process, a postconflict situation that does not include the potential for renewed mass violence. In such cases, history and historical records are central to the process. Similarly, post-Communist regimes and postauthoritarian regimes engage, in the preponderance of cases, in postconflict reconciliation in the absence of current conflict. Holocaust reparation and restitution fall into this same category. In all of these cases, the memory of a conflict, often of horrific crimes that include genocide, plays a critical role, but there is little

Elazar Barkan

doubt that the conflict belongs to the past and no longer needs to be "resolved." The challenge is to offer a measure of redress to victims and their descendants and to acknowledge the nation's own responsibility for and complicity in the crimes.

In contrast to postconflict situations where historical memory has a political space relatively unencumbered by the risk of contemporary conflict, in conflict zones the opposite is true. The conflicts between Palestine and Israel and those in Cyprus, Lebanon, Kashmir, and Turkey are examples of protracted conflicts that have history at their core. One can hardly wait for the conflict to end to begin postconflict programs and peace building, yet the conflict overshadows any historical analysis. Nevertheless, it is likely that historical dialogue can take place among willing civil society stakeholders and scholars, although its contribution to reaching a solution to the conflict may be at best indirect. It is a long-term project.

There are also interesting and problematic borderline cases, such as post-conflict Northern Ireland. There is probably no other country where as many resources have been devoted to reconciliation as have been spent in Northern Ireland, including hundreds of millions of dollars by the EU. While there has been eagerness in Ireland to invest great energies in questions of criminal accountability for the violence, there has been widespread reluctance to embark on a critical historical investigation or to attempt to write a postconflict joint history. The refrain is that everyone has his or her own history, and that seems to satisfy the peace builders. To an outsider this may seem bewildering; after all, this "relativist" or "subjectivist" stance does not come from a postmodernist perspective but is rather an indication that history is considered to be too sacred, the third rail of politics. The successful Bloody Sunday commission in Northern Ireland—which took twelve years, collected testimonies from more than a thousand witnesses, cost $300 million, and produced a report of five thousand pages—will most likely be the final word on the killing in 1972. It showed that historical agreement can be reached but it did little to address any structural historical disputes.

There is great reluctance in Northern Ireland to formulate shared narratives. Perhaps too few resources have been directed at the group (macro) level of changing norms through historical dialogue. The micro-level (individual, specific cases) commissions and truth finding provide a shelter—an in-between space—but do not advance a shared interpretation of the overall national history: one that does not privilege a group or sectarian truth. Outsourcing the Bloody Sunday commission provided a measure of acknowledgment for the direct victims but allowed society to avoid any macro statements on the conflict or engagement with the Protestant or Catholic versions of history. It answered the questions about what crimes were committed and about the scope of accountability or justice but left larger questions open. Is the reluctance to engage in historical judgment a case where accountability becomes a way to avoid dialogue and the construction of a historical narrative that incorporates the competing perspectives?

Historical Dialogue

Historical dialogue refers to a nonlinear discourse with contributions from opposing sides, who are not necessarily actively engaging each other directly. Mostly it is undertaken by individuals, scholars, and civil society advocates. While outsiders contribute to the rewriting of history and good empirical historical research is not dependent on the identity of the author, in the final analysis members of the protagonists' communities have to own the historical narrative in order for it to have purchase on the public. A shift in public opinion and a reconfiguration of public and collective memory are more likely to occur when they are advocated by "insiders"—for example, when insiders endorse a scholarly critique of textbooks or museum exhibits that propagate sectarian or nationalistic views.

Historical dialogue uses various methodologies employed by diverse protagonists to examine contentious histories from critical perspectives, undermining long-held nationalistic views. The process can be formal or informal and can result in written texts as well as in narratives told in other media. It aims to reach a historical truth. Even if the theoretical formulation of truth is ambivalent, the empirical truth of contentious histories remains attractive and persuasive to the public. Historians who write empirically grounded narratives, regardless of their theoretical awareness of the epistemological limitations, aim to write the most accurate history possible. As such, it is possible to aim both to produce the best narrative and to contribute to a dialogue. The goal, therefore, in addition to that of delegitimizing historical lies, is to minimize their appeal and to offer—through openness and empathy—wider perspectives than a one-sided nationalistic view or myth could propose. Historical dialogue is most effective if it is uncompromised first and foremost as good historical work. The interpretation of the empirical evidence can be done with empathy for various issues and from different perspectives, but it must never deny or repress truth. Like all historical narratives, however, the dialogue is not the final word on the subject but is subject to further research and potential revisions.

Historical dialogue is not a marketplace where historians from opposing sides are engaged in bartering guilt and responsibility for past violence.

Contributors to historical dialogue are diverse and often do not explicitly participate in the dialogue in the sense that they are engaged in doing related but unconnected historical work. In fact, much of the work can be and is being done not under the banner of historical dialogue but rather as part of either advocacy or scholarship. For example, a historian who writes academically and critically about a conflict or its root causes may contribute to the dismantling of nationalist myths. She no doubt adds to the dialogue, though very likely she may not see herself as motivated by the possibility of doing so. At other times historical dialogue is manifested by explicit official or informal joint efforts to delineate a nonsubjective, nonpartisan history and possibly to agree upon a narrative of the past. Historical dialogue can also result when individuals from different sides in the conflict produce their own versions of history, which others then attempt to integrate into a larger contextual history.

Historical dialogue occupies a space beyond accountability and opens the possibility of engagement with conflict resolution. Historical dialogue mostly takes place as a result of the production of multifaceted historical knowledge. Historical accountability, by contrast, tends to privilege judicial or semilegal mechanisms to bring violators to justice or to acknowledge their responsibility. In most cases historical accountability's subject matter is violence from the recent past and within the lifetime of the perpetrators; its narrative is limited to the specific issue before the court or the commission and is subject to limitations of process and procedure. The goal of the court is to resolve the concrete issues before it and to decide on the question of guilt, but it is not to find a larger, macro truth. The prosecution, for example, presents the case in its most damning perspective, which is expected in a trial but detrimental to dialogue.

Another measure of accountability is directed at the responsible state and aims to have it acknowledge past crimes and pay compensation or restitution to the victims or their descendants. Again, here the goal is not reconciliation but specific material redress. While indirectly this might include admissions of guilt or responsibility, apologies, and aspects of acknowledgment that result from joint narratives, it may also involve a political power play or lead to a hardening of sectarian positions. Victims' and perpetrators' testimonies outside trials that are evoking empathy are likely to contribute to dialogue, while victims who call for revenge or perpetrators who obfuscate their roles and actions and adopt a victim's perspective can only lead to a renewal of the conflict. Truth is very much a social construct, subject to empirical evidence.

Despite these limitations, accountability overlaps with historical dialogue, as is shown by the demands for redress for slavery. Most historical research concerning slavery is in the realm of historical dialogue in that it adds knowledge about the atrocities and at times finds humane behavior among the oppressors. It thereby fosters greater openness to recognition and acknowledgment. In contrast, the discourse of reparation for slavery is comparatively ineffective, because it often fails to make the larger society more sympathetic to demands for redress.

Research methodologies in searches for accountability often rely on testimonies, oral histories, and, sometimes, adversarial trial proceedings. Contributions to historical dialogue similarly rely on extant evidence and new research but are more likely to involve critical historical research and analysis, including a close reading of archival and other documentary sources. In part this is because the latter are concerned not only with contemporary events; in part it is the result of a focus on the larger picture. That does not make one type of history a priori a better, truer history, but it does suggest that historians who employ critical history may be more aware of the problems of subjectivity and partisanship.

Another distinction between dialogue and accountability pertains to the role of the individual as opposed to that of the group. In cases of historical accountability, whether it is for a violent crime, displacement, or dispossession, the victims are viewed as specific individuals. They often are members of a class of victims, as are the perpetrators, but at the heart of the investigation is a *specific* crime. Whether the investigation takes place in court or in a TRC or even in the case of an informal testimony, the veracity of the evidence is critical. The specifics of the case determine the issues, the responsibility, the guilt, and the redress, if there is to be any. There may or may not be tension between the specific case and the structural mass violence, but the question of accountability often demands a formal process and a mechanism of adjudication. While the historical context is critical to understand the specifics, it is not sufficient to adjudicate the question of individual guilt. The inadequacy of the involvement of courts with history—as described by Richard Wilson (2011), for example— is a critical exhibit. For numerous reasons courts and truth commissions are better at documenting atrocities than at interpreting critically the macro history of a conflict, although there are examples of good histories produced as part of transitional justice mechanisms (Guatemala, Peru). This might be inserted into the record as part of an expert testimony, but it is not within the purview of the trial or the inquiry.

The tension between individual and group history is illustrated by the controversy over Rigoberta Menchú's biography (Burgos-Debray 1984; Arias 2001). Here the individual distortions were done in the service of a larger truth. The shortcomings of this approach are obvious. To be effective, micro and macro history, the specific case and the structural analysis, have to be empirically true. Illustrating the larger group truth by a false individual narrative disrespects and delegitimizes both.

Historical dialogue emphasizes placing the specific narratives and the individual cases in the larger historical context, eliciting a wider meaning with implications for the groups involved. Details are important to illuminate the macro analysis. The willingness of members of opposing groups to cooperate in telling and listening to stories pertinent to historical events in a shared framework—actively participating in a dialogue even when the sides represent very different interpretive perspectives—constitutes an active dialogue. The willingness to discuss (even if only to disagree) is a step in narrowing differences, in contrast to operating in a virtual dialogue where texts speak to each other. The sponsors of these dialogues are mostly civil society and international mediators.

At times historical dialogue is done through formal channels by historical commissions with a political goal of either furthering reconciliation or responding to demands for redress. Such commissions aim to investigate past violence as a way to acknowledge human rights abuses at the macro level and to reconcile both interstate and intrastate conflicts. Yet formal bodies are likely to emerge only in postconflict situations and have been used as such. As dealing with the past becomes more central to diplomacy, historical commissions ought to be included as a component in peace negotiations, in drawing a road map of the negotiation, and for reconciliation measures. Armenia and Turkey in their off-and-on negotiations have both raised the option of a historical commission; more than anything else, the lack of international experience with commissions as diplomatic tools has so far proved to be an insurmountable obstacle.

The diverse fora of historical dialogue include commissions that are similar to truth commissions and others that are bilateral, national, commercial, nongovernmental, informal, or academic. Some commissions work to establish a national claim, others to resolve a bilateral conflict. These commissions share an engagement with a controversial past, conduct investigations, and frequently issue reports, the substance of which reframes critical aspects of national history.

One new development is the growing number and increasingly diverse range of civil society organizations that contribute to alternative historical dialogue. They engage the past by commemorating the suffering of violence; building museums and memorials; organizing exhibits; producing movies; collecting oral histories; and organizing groups of educators, victims, and advocates. Together these contribute to a robust historical record of the conflict, more often than not from a perspective of redress. This constitutes a sea change and will in the future provide for a robust historical dialogue. These methods, however, do not provide a panacea. The same methods are used by those who advocate nationalist perspectives and myths that pose the risk of future conflict. Historical dialogue has to be understood as a field of knowledge *and* as a field of advocacy. Much like human rights advocacy, historical dialogue creates a new norm through continuous advocacy. It is about establishing the truth *and* about maintaining it. This may evolve into a growing norm of redress, and historical dialogue as a new norm in conflict resolution.

The Misuse of Historical Dialogue

The UN Human Rights Council has been struggling to overcome the legacy of its predecessor, the Commission, which was often controlled by countries like China and Libya, which recognized that human rights discourse is powerful and therefore tried to manipulate it and gain the moral high ground either by diverting attention to violations by their enemies or by reframing their own action as legitimate. Similarly, historical redress has become a powerful, rhetorically persuasive discourse, and governments try to legitimate their own position by manipulating the historical discourse by constructing self-serving historical narratives.

The Sri Lanka Lessons Learnt and Reconciliation Commission (May 2010–November 2011; see de Silva et al. 2011) was widely criticized because its investigation violated any pretense of objectivity and allowed the government to "prove" that it did not intentionally target civilians and that the number of casualties was much smaller than had previously been claimed. The history of the conflict was secondary, and the commission failed to receive international validation. International human rights groups (Amnesty International, Human Rights Watch, and International Crisis Group) refused to cooperate, as did the UN Panel of Experts on Sri Lanka. Although the historical investigation was initially recognized as critical, it was not implemented. In one of the few examples where history was explicitly mentioned—in relation to the expulsion of Muslims in the north by the Liberation Tigers of Tamil Eelam (LTTE)—the question was raised, but the Commission claimed that the matter would be addressed by a separate citizens' commission. Otherwise, the history that is referred to in passing is reverential, rather than critical.

Similarly, in Russia in 2009, a Presidential Commission of the Russian Federation to Counter Attempts to Falsify History to the Detriment of Russia's Interests was appointed in response to a struggle over history and identity, in particular in relation to Stalinism. Although ostensibly "historical," it was run by politicians, with historians constituting only a minority of the commission. President Dmitry Medvedev established the commission ostensibly "to counteract against attempts to falsify history that undermine the interests of Russia"

(Felgenhauer 2009; "Medvedev Says No to False History" 2010). He made his announcement on the eve of the military parade in Moscow to commemorate the end of World War II. The move to defend the motherland against "the falsifiers of history" was directed at, among others, Ukraine and the Baltic states but especially at internal dissenters. The Commission never became a powerful political or cultural body and had more impact through the opposition to its inception than through its work. It is an illustration of the way history is viewed by Russia as critical for its bilateral and regional relations. Furthermore, the Commission's minimal impact showed that the politics of historical writings has to engage a type of political persuasion different from naked power politics and that what is perceived as an impartial truth remains powerful and attractive.

These two examples illustrate that governments try to control the historical narrative, much as reviews of human rights are subject to political manipulations. Since scholarly approbation is a critical aspect of affirmation and international validation, international scholars and advocates have the opportunity to contribute to the discourse and to have an impact. International scholarly support for engaged nonnationalist histories is important; it gives global credence to the norm, to its veracity, as it does with human rights advocacy. In the final analysis, the effort to manipulate history stems from a desire and a need to persuade an audience, but persuasion does not work with assertions or force. While differences in historical interpretations will always remain, there is a marked difference between a plausible history and an outright falsification. The contest over what constitutes legitimate historical interpretation and what constitutes facts includes not only protagonists from all sides but also outsiders, whose influence on the debate can be significant. The international censure of Turkey over the Armenian genocide is a prominent instance in which over the years realpolitik has given way to pressure based on truth in history. Notwithstanding the impact of the Armenian diaspora, Turkey is stronger and growing more influential in the world, yet the truth about the Armenian genocide is widely accepted, and the only remaining matter of dispute is the question of whether countries are willing to act against denial or criticize Turkey for refusing to acknowledge the past. This is as clear a case as one could have of history shaping international politics and countering realpolitik.

Conclusion

History is a prime area for inciting nationalist and sectarian conflict. Because of their professional status and the reputation of impartiality that comes with the profession, historians have a relative advantage when participating in these discussions and can therefore contribute to conflict resolution and redress policies. Too often they shy away from such engagement because of their hesitation to become involved in politics. Historians ought to acknowledge, however, that constructing historical narratives is inevitably a political activity. Such an acknowledgment is difficult as it is not supported by the scholarly culture of historians, who often view their work as apolitical and refuse to do applied research. If the first step is to recognize that history is political, we can hope that a growing number of historians will frame their intervention explicitly with the aim of conflict resolution and reconciliation and not leave the field to those who use the horror of history to animate hate and nationalist ideology.

There is an evolving norm of historical redress that emulates human rights and transitional justice aspirations, and it may well begin to contribute to conflict resolution. Civil society groups are taking a leading role in this growing field; the challenge for them is not to fall into the nationalist trap. Given that the financial cost of historical work is minimal, most societies seem better off embracing historical dialogue, investigating the violent past, and redressing it. Given the failure of protection and prevention to attend to root causes of conflicts, there may well be room for historical dialogue as a new methodology of conflict resolution.

Evaluating the merits of historical dialogue during conflict is challenging if only because of a lack of experience and empirical evidence. The few cases are limited to the work of civil society primarily internally and rarely across the sectarian divide. There are even fewer bilateral efforts that take place in less formal diplomacy by social and political activists. In immediate postconflict situations, the conventional wisdom is that truth and historical redress are essential to prevent future conflict, but there is too little empirical evidence to substantiate that claim.

Faced with a historical discourse that aggravates conflict, we may need to ask not whether history plays a role in the conflict but rather how conflict resolution and peace building professionals ought to engage in historical discourse as counter measures to nationalist history. Notwithstanding how effective historical discourse may be for conflict resolution, it should be remembered that the option of ignoring the roots of violent disputes may not be available. Particularly since the 1980s and 1990s, protagonists, primarily nationalists, as well as victims (whether or not they are nationalists) underscore history as a point of political contention, refusing to let their suffering, claims, and grievances be bygone and forcing society to focus on the violent past. At times, the historical grievances are raised, manipulated by democratic leaders who campaign for votes (see Barkan and Bećirbašić's chapter in this volume). It is precisely because not all stakeholders who emphasize historical conflict are inclined to engage in it in the name of peace building that it must be taken as a challenge.

Those engaged in conflict resolution and prevention, including international organizations and state actors that operate under the mantle of the Responsibility to Protect (R2P) doctrine, would do well to expand their temporal horizon and explore new ways of dealing with the past as a tool for resolving conflicts. The challenge is to expand the aspiration for redress and accountability (as a form of redress), including the perspective of human rights activism, beyond postconflict cases, and to expand the tools of conflict resolution to include insights from historical dialogue. Whether engagement with these concerns will contribute to the prevention of future violence is impossible to say, but the goal of prevention should become one way of assessing the engagement with the past.

Historical redress goes beyond accountability and includes historical dialogue. There is no need to first resolve the conflict before addressing structural historical disputes—especially in cases of protracted conflicts and even more so in sectarian conflicts. Dealing with the past goes farther than the demands of accountability and can begin while the conflict is still ongoing, to prepare the ground for later, more formal redress. It can contribute to a better understanding, at least among the elites, and may help shift sectarian identities and hatred.

Note

1. The Carnegie Endowment sponsored a research project that paid attention to historical reconciliation but identified the historical conflicts only as a source, giving relatively thin examples of efforts at reconciliation without developing a methodology. Even so, the report stood out for its attention to the need to address historical animosity (Ivanov, Ischinger, and Nunn 2012).

11

Memory, Justice, and Postterror Futures

MARK PENDLETON

> It is justice that turns memory into a project; and it is this same project of justice that gives the form of the future and of the imperative to the duty of memory.
>
> Paul Ricoeur

Memory is a regular feature of the politics of those seeking justice. Victims of violence around the world seek justice through a variety of fora, including criminal legal proceedings and truth and reconciliation commissions, or through more informal processes of retribution or reconciliation. They also articulate memories in a range of mediated ways, such as commemorative events, life writing, memorial construction, or personal testimony. While geographically spread, these projects remain remarkably similar, issuing calls to "never forget" historical injustices and to seek out the truth of the past and promoting projects of reconciliation. Despite these transnational similarities, the ways in which individual and collective responses to past pain relate to each other and to the particular frameworks of justice that they purport to interact with remain unclear. Unresolved questions remain around how differing understandings of the past frame particular projects of justice; how national contexts shape memory projects and justice claims; and whether individual and collective justice can both be achieved. In essence I find myself wondering how the universal mnemonic imperative connects to particular, politically, culturally, and biographically distinct justice-seeking projects.

One of the key thinkers to ponder these questions in some detail is the late Paul Ricoeur, quoted earlier (2004, 88). In his discussion of what he terms "obligated memory," Ricoeur (2004, 86) warns about the "cult of memory for the sake of memory," arguing that the contemporary obsession with remembering runs the risk of obliterating both the particular future aims of justice projects and "the question of the end, the moral issue" itself. When thinking about the ways in which memory features in the politics of the victimized, it is important to consider this question of what memory is oriented toward, for it helps us understand how memory is used and can be abused. In attempting to get to the root of this problem, Ricoeur focuses on the material production of memory, on memory as something that is done, rather than something that simply is. In thinking about how this idea of memory as task (which Ricoeur connects to the Freudian notion of work of mourning) relates to the contemporary role of memory as a duty (the obligation to remember), he identifies what is missing as an "imperative element" with twin functions. Duty, for Ricoeur (2004, 88), must function both as an imposition on individual desire and as a constraint of obligation. For him, these twin features are bound up in the idea of justice—for what is justice other than a combined notion that there is something more than the individual (and his or her desires) and that this invokes a subsequent obligation that constrains action? It is the idea of justice, therefore, that turns individual memory into particular future-oriented political projects, as the epigraph that opens this chapter suggests.

In interrogating this relationship between the duty of memory and the idea of justice, Ricoeur identifies three interconnected elements. First, the idea of justice must extend beyond the self: "the duty of memory is the duty to do justice, through memories, to an other than the self" (Ricoeur 2004, 89). Second, the duty of memory relies on an indebtedness to the historical past—we are obligated to those who have gone before us for some component of what we now are, and this obligation carries over into an obligation to acknowledge "not that they are no more, but that they were" (Ricoeur 2004, 89). Finally, while moral priority belongs to victims, it is not the self as victim demanding reparation that retains moral priority but the recognition of the (potential) victim in (all) others. These three elements also help to identify the points at which memory may be either used or abused. In Ricoeur's admittedly cryptic style, this transition from use to abuse occurs through a misapplication of the idea of justice through demands raised by "impassioned memories, wounded memories, [or] against the vaster and more critical aim of history" (Ricoeur 2004, 89).

It is with this concern about the relationship between the ideal of justice and the use and potential abuse of memory that I am concerned in this chapter. I will explore this through a discussion of a particular contemporary situation in Japan, a place that, while geographically and culturally distant from the European contexts that Ricoeur wrote from, is still, as Marilyn Ivy (1995, 8) has reminded us, coincident through processes of modernity with the West. I will consider how the contemporary situation in Japan may reflect both this duty to remember (as justice) and the potential abuse of memory (as injustice). This distinction between memory in the service of justice and memory as abuse occurs, as Ricoeur suggests, through the relationship between the self and other and at the particular intersection of individual experience, collective meaning-making, and historical contextualization.

Questions of individual and collective relationships to the past have been of primary concern in the field of memory studies for some time. Maurice Halbwachs argued early in the twentieth century that social frameworks shape individual memory, pointing also to collectively shared memories not to suggest that groups can remember per se, but that individuals as group members remember instances of collective significance (1992, 48). This distinction between individual and collective memory has framed much of the field's subsequent interests and debates. In the early 1990s, Jan Assmann (2011) took up the ways in which Halbwachs described shared representations about the past through symbol and meaning to further distinguish an additional layer of cultural memory. Despite these fine gradations of individual, collective, and cultural memory, however, and the plethora of work done to explore how these gradations are materialized in various textual and performative modes and genres, the uses of memory to advance justice claims are much less clearly understood. While it is possible to point to a massive growth of interest in these areas, particularly after Barkan (2000) and as outlined in the chapters in this volume, there is still much to be grappled with in understanding the relationship between memories of victimization and the articulation of ideas of justice. Here I will focus on two interlocking case studies to try to tease out the particular mechanisms through which the duty of memory and the idea of justice intersect. I will do this through exploring how these are shaped by the emergence and expansion of (neo)liberal ideas of individualism and the politics of responsibility and by examining historical contestations around the role of the state in pursuing justice.

Memory, Justice, Violence, and Japan

This chapter explores these questions through an exploration of the sometimes contradictory politics of two prominent victims of domestic terrorism in Japan—Takahashi Shizue and Kōno Yoshiyuki. Debates over political violence, historical responsibility, and frameworks of justice were key features of political discourse in Japan over the course of the twentieth century, particularly after the Japanese war defeat and the US-led postwar occupation. The International Military Tribunal for the Far East, commonly known as the Tokyo Trials, was set up to investigate the most serious war crimes and resulted in a handful of executions and a few more convictions. The Trials remain controversial, however, having been dismissed by some as "showcase justice" and an "exercise in revenge" that also failed to bring to trial the ultimate "leader of the crime," the wartime emperor Hirohito (Dower 1999, 443–84). The question of war responsibility, as will be discussed further, continues to overshadow much of the memory politics of postwar Japan.

Debates over violence, memory, history, justice, and the state have also materialized in other ways in the years since 1945. Social movements in the 1960s prompted fierce controversy over the ethics of political violence (Kersten 2009; Marotti 2009), which only intensified as small-scale leftist groups in the late 1960s and early 1970s ramped up their violent confrontations with the Japanese state and with various other state and corporate targets internationally (Box and McCormack 2004). Much of this tension focused on the continuities between pre- and postwar state violence. Japanese feminists have also been concerned with the ethics of violence, in thinking both about Japanese responsibility for violence against women under colonialism (Mackie 2005) and about how social attitudes to violence continued to manifest in highly gendered ways (Shigematsu 2012). Alongside all of these are regular crime panics and debates over perceived crises of youth violence in contemporary Japan, which have resulted in calls for *genbatsuka*, an increase in the severity of sentences (Miyazawa 2008; Hurley 2011).

Events such as these have also prompted similar debates elsewhere. While it is important to be aware of historical and cultural specificities, the relationship between memory and justice in Japan is contested in very similar ways as elsewhere in the world, containing the potential to emerge either as state-centered retribution based on individual memories of violence or future-oriented collective responses focused on an awareness of history, a commitment to present interactions, and a desire to construct shared futures.

The violence with which I am particularly concerned in this chapter emerged over the course of a roughly six-year period from the late 1980s through 1995 as the leadership of a small religious sect named Aum Shinrikyō turned increasingly to violent tactics to maintain control of its members and to stifle dissent. At its peak, the sect, which has been rendered somewhat awkwardly as "Aum Supreme Truth" in English, had some ten thousand members in Japan and about another thirty thousand members internationally, mostly in Russia (Reader 2000, 63). Of these, about 1,100 were *shukkesha* (renunciates), who were overwhelmingly young and highly educated (Reader 2000, 96–97). By the standards of Japanese new religions, Aum was small, but because of its violent turn it wielded much greater influence than its size would suggest. Ultimately, Aum's violence spilled over into the public through the world's first confirmed nonstate use of chemical or biological weapons. In addition to the deployment of the nerve gas sarin on the Tokyo subway system in 1995, the attack with which the sect is most commonly associated, Aum was also able to synthesize other chemical weapons, including VX gas, and attempted to deploy biological agents such as botulism. That a small religious group was able to manufacture significant quantities of highly controlled substances and deploy them in modern urban settings, killing more than twenty people and injuring several thousand, is a first in the history of political violence.

These violent acts also prompted a range of memory-related activities, including the publication of a large number of victim and perpetrator narratives, participation of victims through testimony in formal legal processes, ephemeral commemorative practices, and proposals for more permanent memorial construction. These existed alongside and fed into various projects seeking justice through political and social recognition, criminal proceedings, and compensation. I have discussed some of these elsewhere (Pendleton 2009, 2011, 2014).

The violence of Aum also emerged at a time when Japan was reevaluating its collective relationship to its own troubled past, confronting a perceived national culture of forgetting in relation to the legacies of war and imperialism. The death of the wartime emperor Hirohito, in 1989, has been identified as a catalyst for this Japanese mnemonic boom (Gluck 1997), which materialized through victim testimony, particularly that of the so-called comfort women, who were victims of forced military prostitution (Mackie 2005), and then later through a series of "wars" over representations of the past that resulted in academic and popular historical revisionism (Seaton 2007, 131–50). In this period from the 1990s to the present, some major unresolved historical questions about memory, the state, and the notion of justice came to the fore in public discourse, and these questions played out alongside the particular victim politics of the two people I mentioned earlier. While the specific cases examined here may seem at first glance to be somewhat peculiar given the focus on state violence in the other chapters in this volume, it is my contention that how violence is remembered and justice is sought in contemporary Japan cannot be separated from the unresolved transition from imperial state violence and war defeat to postwar democracy. This is most apparent in the postwar battles around the legitimacy of the state's monopoly on violence, visible particularly in current

Mark Pendleton

debates on the retention of the so-called peace clause of the Japanese constitution, which renounced the right to wage war on the grounds of maintaining international peace based on justice and order. Postwar Japan is founded, at least in part, on a contested claim that connects violence to notions of justice. Before I delve more closely into how these factors interrelate, however, I will provide a short background on the two people under discussion in this chapter and their relationship to the violence of Aum Shinrikyō.

Two Victims

Takahashi Shizue is the spokesperson for the Chikatetsu Sarin Jiken Higaisha no kai (Subway Sarin Incident Victims' Association) and was the wife of a station worker who died attempting to remove packages of sarin gas from the station where he worked. This station—Kasumigaseki—serves the downtown hub of the Japanese state bureaucracy and was the primary target of Aum's March 1995 attack. In this incident, packages of sarin were roughly simultaneously punctured on five different trains across the subway system. Thirteen people were killed, several thousand were injured, and much of the city was brought to a standstill. The incident garnered significant international attention and led to the mass arrest of members of the sect, including the sect leader, Asahara Shōkō. After this incident, more than 180 Aum members were indicted on various offenses, and a total of thirteen death sentences were ultimately handed down. These sentences were finalized in 2011, although the subsequent self-reporting of a fugitive former Aum member to police in December 2011 and the arrest of the final two remaining Aum-related fugitives in June 2012 have resulted in further criminal trials.

What is less well known internationally, however, is that the Tokyo gassing was not the first time that members of Aum had deployed chemical weapons. Nine months prior to the subway gassing, the sect released sarin outside an apartment complex in the central Japanese city of Matsumoto, in Nagano prefecture, killing seven people within hours and hospitalizing more than two hundred. The complex was home to several judges who were presiding over a series of investigations into the sect, primarily relating to allegedly fraudulent land transactions.

Despite indications that Aum was responsible for the Matsumoto attack, police focused their investigations instead on a middle-aged family man, Kōno Yoshiyuki, who had a large amount of pesticide stored on his property near the apartment complex, and leaked rumors of his involvement to media outlets. Pesticide is not used in the development of sarin, but this fact did not deter the media or police in their harassment of Kōno. In addition to the false accusations by police and the media, Kōno's family was also seriously affected by the gassing, with his wife, Sumiko, slipping into a fourteen-year coma from which she never awoke. Her death, in 2008, took the death toll from the Matsumoto attack to eight. Kōno himself was hospitalized, along with his three children. Police, the media, and members of the general public continued to hound Kōno for the nine months between the Matsumoto and Tokyo gassings, after which official attention finally shifted to Aum.

In the years since 1994, Kōno has become one of the best-known public faces of Aum's victims. He has been the subject of multiple television specials and documentary and feature films, was appointed to a prefectural safety commission, and has been a regular outspoken critic of the media and the police. He has also published multiple book-length life narratives (Kōno 1998, 2001, 2008a). Takahashi Shizue, too, has become a prominent feature of mass-media reporting of crime victimization, specifically in the context of Aum. Like Kōno, Takahashi has appeared in multiple television specials and documentary films as well as editing several collections and writing her own autobiography (Takahashi 2008; see also Chikatetsu Sarin Jiken Higaisha no Kai 1998; Takahashi and Kawahara 2005).

In what follows, I focus on how these two key figures in contemporary Japanese victim activism understand memory and justice in different ways. However, Kōno and Takahashi have at various times prioritized similar goals. To take one example, both argued for a system of state-backed compensation to provide victims with financial and medical care after Aum's bankruptcy left victims with less than 40 percent of the court-ordered compensation they were owed. This compensation scheme was ultimately achieved in 2008, with unanimous parliamentary support. Despite these moments where their politics align, however, Kōno and Takahashi differ most in the way they see their own memories of victimization shaping their claims for justice.

Victim Memory, Self-Responsibility, and Criminal Justice

In addition to her involvement in the memory-related projects already mentioned, Takahashi has also been heavily involved in formal legal processes, regularly attending court hearings and advocating for greater involvement of victims of crime in court proceedings. She has also been one of the more public figures supporting capital punishment in the cases of the Aum attackers. At the time of writing, Japan had a record number of people on death row (more than 130), with the Aum attacks responsible for the single largest grouping of these prisoners. Despite an eighteen-month informal moratorium from mid-2010, Japan recommenced carrying out executions, which take place by hanging, in early 2012.

Takahashi called publicly for the death penalty in the case of Aum leader Asahara Shōkō, saying on the eve of his verdict being handed down that it was only natural that death was what she hoped for, given the nature of his crimes (Foreign Correspondents' Club of Japan 2004). In 1999, she also spoke out in support of the death sentence imposed on one of the sarin gassing perpetrators, Yokoyama Masato, who was responsible for releasing sarin on one of the Tokyo trains and accused police of brutality after his arrest. Takahashi dismissed these with the comment, "[Yokoyama] claims his mouth was cut and he bled, but when I think of my husband, I feel that I want [Yokoyama] to inhale sarin and die" (*Japan Times* 1999). She was also highly critical of perpetrators who appealed their sentences. In the case of another perpetrator, Hayashi Yasuo, whose actions resulted in the most subway casualties, she said that if he appealed his death sentence, "I will consider him to have lied when he told the court he feels sorry and wants to apologize. . . . I think he should say 'no' to his lawyers if they advise him to appeal the ruling" (*Asahi Shimbun* 2000). For Takahashi, the demand for death relates explicitly to her memories of her dead husband and the suffering he experienced at the hands of sect members. Takahashi's statements reflect an attempt to draw an equivalence between victim experience and expectations of justice—to put it simply, justice can be achieved only through a directly equivalent retributive outcome, in this case death, justified on the basis of a particular relationship to individual victim memory.

Takahashi's calls for capital punishment as retributive justice have received much airplay and are in broad alignment with popular opinion about capital punishment in Japan (Hamai and Ellis 2006). However, it is worth highlighting, as Sakagami Kaori (2004) has, that it is very often the voices of those victims who explicitly demand extreme punishment that find their way into most media reporting of crime and that this may very well influence popular support. When the media describe victim calls for the death penalty, Sakagami (2004, 74) rightly asks, "Which victims?" and "Which calls?"

In fact, Takahashi has not always supported capital punishment, opposing the death penalty in the case of a senior sect member, Hayashi Ikuo, who had assisted police in their investigations and who, to Takahashi's mind, had expressed "true remorse" about his actions (*Japan Times* 1998).[1] While prosecutors did not seek the death penalty in this case, it appears that for Takahashi the appropriateness of state killing is determined on two bases—how the perpetrator individually responded to questions about his or her personal responsibility and what effect verdicts may have on her (Takahashi) or on other victims. In a 2004 interview, she elaborated: "If I let myself drown in pain and anger and deny myself a chance to become happy, it would mean Aum had killed me along with my husband. . . . I want capital punishment for [the leader] Asahara, because the idea that he still exists somewhere would continue to upset me and draw me back into pain and anger. . . . Whether the victims maintain their hatred or forgive [the perpetrator], they need to have a reason to do so" (Matsubara 2004).

Takahashi's words reflect an ambivalence about state violence, which is also a feature of her political responses to other events such as the 9/11 attacks in the United States (Pendleton 2009). However, her politics also reflect her perception of a relationship between victim memory and the particular demands for justice that victims make, a relationship that is highly personal and individualized yet also closely related to particular models of justice. Takahashi's ideal future outcome of any justice process is related to the provision of a state-sanctioned mechanism to move beyond painful memories through a process that culminates in retribution (Pendleton 2009). This perspective on justice is by no means isolated to Takahashi; popular support for capital punishment and incarceration of convicted offenders is on the rise in Japan, against the long-term trend of more restorative models of justice, particularly for nonviolent offenses (Hamai and Ellis 2006, 173–74).

The notion of "responsibility" provides a discursive connection between Takahashi's politics and broader debates in postwar Japanese history around justice and the function of apology. These debates have occurred primarily around who was responsible for war and the effects of imperial aggression—the state, society, individuals, or some combination thereof. These debates have been clouded by the embrace of nuclear victimization after Hiroshima and Nagasaki and by the US-led occupation authorities' failure to complete their initial goals of democratic "revolution from above" and the reinstatement of war criminals into political and business leadership after the Cold War–inspired "reverse course" of 1947 (Dower 1999). Norma Field has highlighted the role that debates about apology have played in obfuscating the responsibility of the state to make material reparations for historical violence—there is a disjuncture between words and deeds. On the rare occasions when responsibility has been acknowledged, she argues, the use of terms such as "regret [*tsūseki*]" or, even more rare, "apology [*owabi*]" simply constitute the "enunciation of the word" without any recourse to any process of restitution or reparation (Field 1997, 12). Carol Gluck (2009, 88) traces a longer history of the adoption of the term "responsibility" (*sekinin*) in Japanese discourse to the emergence of "civilizing" projects in the late nineteenth century—a key function of Japan's transition to and incorporation within modernity. That the discourse of "responsibility" later emerged as a key trope in postwar Japan is for Gluck (2009, 91) a process of transformation into something "an individual must do and the obligation to bear the consequences of one's actions." This extends even further in the recent past into highly individualized notions of self-responsibility (*jiko-sekinin*), a core element of the late capitalist individualism in ascendant neoliberalist ideology (Gluck 2009, 102).

The contemporary state, in these ascendant ideological frames, becomes a tool for the enforcement of individual responsibility, rather than a historically important subject of these narratives of responsibility. Accordingly and in contrast to postwar reforms such as the constitution, which sought to limit the state's capacity to use violence as a means of seeking justice and order, justice is now framed entirely within strictures of individuality and self-responsibility, with the state constructed as impartial adjudicator and enforcer. Takahashi's calls for justice based on individualized victim memories and her demands that perpetrators accept responsibility for their actions provide two clear examples of how memory relates to responsibility and historical justice within these frames. These individualized calls for responsibility and their realization in either (perceived legitimate) words of apology or state-sanctioned retribution relate justice to a particular model of responsibility that historically emerged along with the creation of liberal subjects in Japan, was reinforced in the abandonment of progressive reforms in the immediate postwar period, and was subsequently reimagined in the contemporary ideology of neoliberalism. This model, in its reliance on the wounded and impassioned memories that Ricoeur (2004, 89) warns about, fails to extend victim memory beyond the individual. Alongside this, however, is a limited historical engagement with the development of the relationship between the state and the citizen/subject, a longstanding point of contention in Japanese political discourse. For Kōno, by contrast, this contention leads to the drawing of a very different connection between memory and justice, as I explain next.

Shared Pasts, Social Presents, and Common Futures

In the prologue to his 2008 memoir, *Inochi aru kagiri* (*As Long as There Is Life*), Kōno describes coming home from a trip to discover the trees in his garden pruned, weeds pulled out, and fallen leaves neatly swept. He recalls thinking, "Fujinaga-kun must have come by again."[2] When Kōno travels, he leaves a key out for a young man named Fujinaga Kōzo, who comes monthly to tend the garden. Fujinaga is welcome in Kōno's house and at times stays over, as he lives quite a distance away. While it may not be unusual for a middle-aged man with ongoing health problems to employ a gardener, what is unusual is that this particular gardener was partly responsible for the long coma and ultimate death of Kōno's wife. Fujinaga was a member of Aum who helped manufacture the spraying mechanism that dispersed the sarin gas near Kōno's home. He was sentenced to ten years in prison for his role and was ultimately released in March 2006 (Kōno 2008a, 4–17).

Kōno and Fujinaga first met several months after his release, when members of one of Aum's successor organizations, Aleph, paid a visit to Kōno's home around the anniversary of the Matsumoto gassing.[3] This was a regular trip made by members to pay their respects to Kōno's then comatose wife. In his book, Kōno reports observing Fujinaga during this first encounter. As was his usual practice, Kōno did not take visitors directly to where Sumiko lay, instead assembling them at the adjacent parking lot where the gas had been released. "For Fujinaga, being at that location was surely asking a lot of him," he writes (Kōno 2008a, 8). Describing Fujinaga at first sight as a serious and gentle-looking man, standing awkwardly with eyes downcast and clutching a bouquet, Kōno (2008a, 8–9) goes on to describe a shift in his physical demeanor as they moved toward the house: "Fujinaga-kun's body was frozen solid with nerves." As they passed through the house Fujinaga spoke up, saying, "I shouldn't be in a position where I can come and visit here, but I just wanted to come and bring these flowers." With that, he was unable to speak any more. On that initial visit, Fujinaga told Kōno that he had read his earlier writings, in which Kōno talked openly about his experiences and the media/police interventions in the lives of his family. After being released from prison, he contacted Aleph and requested permission to join other members in their annual visit, with the express aim of apologizing to Kōno for his actions (Kōno 2008a, 8).

After describing their initial encounter, which occurred before the death of his wife, Sumiko, Kōno writes: "For me, it is all about praying for my wife's recovery. I do not hold a single grudge against [Fujinaga] for what he did. Firstly, he has already served his prison time and therefore in societal terms he has made amends for his crimes. I wanted to hear about what had happened since he was arrested, not about what he had done [earlier]" (Kōno 2008a, 9).

In Kōno's articulation, the project of justice requires an openness to the experiences of others, along with a relationship to both the past and the future that is based on social relationships, rather than simply on individual memories of pain. For Kōno, victim memory is both indebted to those who have come before and obligated to place moral priority on others who have experienced victimization. In his articulation, this category expands much beyond the narrow confines of acceptable victimhood espoused by people like Takahashi to include Fujinaga and his fellow ex- and post-Aum acolytes.

Fujinaga, like many other Aum members, was initially arrested on an unrelated charge. In the aftermath of the belated realization that Aum Shinrikyō was responsible for the Matsumoto and Tokyo gassings, many Aum members were rounded up by police. Kōno writes that this extended as far as arresting Aum affiliates on weapons charges for using a knife and fork in a restaurant. Fujinaga, too, was initially arrested on trumped-up charges, possession of a *kongōsho* (*vajra*), a sharp-pointed instrument used in esoteric and Tibetan Buddhist practice. Later, when questioned about his role in making the gas distribution vehicle, he was asked if he knew that what he was doing might be dangerous. After responding to this question affirmatively, he was indicted and, as noted earlier, ultimately sentenced to ten years in prison. Kōno (2008a, 10–11) writes, "He got a ten-year sentence for simply following instructions from the cult and remodeling the vehicle that later just happened to be used to distribute the sarin." Addressing Fujinaga, he comments, "You didn't have much luck either, did you?"

With (bad) luck and suspicion toward the state being key points of connection between the men, Kōno introduced Fujinaga to his family and friends. He gradually became a fixture in their lives. Kōno reports that whenever Fujinaga visited before Sumiko's death, he would bring a bouquet of lilies, one of her favorite flowers. He would place them beside her bed and massage her hands and feet. On observing this, Kōno (2008a, 15–16) commented, "I wonder what he is saying to Sumiko in his heart. I cannot imagine. But if her existence helps in the creation of his new life, then that is a good thing. As he offers up his concern and encouragement to Sumiko, I am sure he in turn gets some good energy back. That is what I believe."

For Kōno, Sumiko's continued life contained within it the potential for the development of meaningful connections with others, regardless of her state of consciousness. It is this continuity of shared life that is reflected in the title of his 2008 memoir, *As Long as There Is Life*, the subject of which is ambiguous in Japanese. Is the life that Kōno refers to that of a particular person—his wife? Kōno himself? Fujinaga? Or does it refer, as I suspect, to a more generalized "life" beyond the individual? My reading of Kōno's book suggests that he is articulating an understanding of justice that is different in several key ways from the retributive model in relation to which Takahashi struggles to position herself. For Kōno, justice is related to the future precisely because of the continuity of a shared, social life that, while based inevitably on what has come before, requires, through the development of connections to others, a broadening beyond simply individual experience. In articulating this, Kōno attempts to relate his personal experiences to an ethical stance around the importance of finding a way to move beyond memories of injustice and construct ways to live with one another. This is at odds with the individualized notions of responsibility, memory, and justice articulated by Takahashi.

While the expressions of empathy and forgiveness in Kōno's relationship with Fujinaga are interesting, he does not leave these as interpersonal projects, instead attempting to broaden them into a more social frame. The key political question for Kōno is not simply how to respond to personal pain but how to transform individual experiences into projects that construct common futures. Where Takahashi initially defines victims narrowly, Kōno does so much more broadly, and this difference translates into the projects they both pursue. It is no surprise, therefore, that Kōno's thinking about the ways in which justice is framed within the law and in relation to the state also differ markedly from that of Takahashi.

Recall Takahashi's bitterness in demanding the execution of sect leaders, dismissing alleged violence by police with the recollection of her dying husband, and articulating capital punishment as a natural demand for historical justice that emerges as a result of individuals taking responsibility for their actions. By contrast, Kōno made the following statement after sect leader Asahara's death sentence was handed down: "Society has much to learn from the case and yet the trial ended without hearing any argument from Mr Asahara. No words on why the victims were killed will be heard now [that he has been sentenced to death]. I am not satisfied at all" (Kyodo News 2006).

For Kōno, the finality of capital punishment *precludes* resolution of historical injustice, precisely because he understands justice not simply as a response to individual demands. Instead, justice must also fulfil a social role of explication, education, and understanding in the construction of a common future.

Kōno has extended his critique of capital punishment in other contexts. In July 2008, for example, he gave the keynote speech at an event marking the first anniversary of the founding of OCEAN, the Japanese branch of the international organization Murder Victims' Families for Human Rights (MVFHR). OCEAN, like its parent organization, is made up of murder victims' families who oppose the death penalty, even in cases involving their family members (Ito 2007; MVFHR n.d.). Kōno started his speech with the following statement: "It is said that when a crime is committed you can easily distinguish victims and perpetrators, but in reality it is a little more complex" (Kōno 2008b). In the remainder of his speech, as in much of his other writing, Kōno is at pains to expand and complicate the notions of both victims and victimizers by placing individual experience in a social context. He describes an interaction a friend of his had with a neighborhood association chair, who said, "I hear you are friends with that Kōno guy. Having that kind of guy around here is a problem. He should get the hell out of our town" (Kōno 2008b).

This suspicion toward those seen as sympathetic to members of Aum has spilled over into vigilantism directed at former Aum members and those associated with later incarnations of the sect. In some cases, members have been driven out of towns, had their children banned from local schools, or been denied work.[4] For Kōno, this victimization is a more pervasive problem than the original crimes themselves. In a 2003 opinion article in the *Asahi* newspaper, he wrote, "As a victim of the Matsumoto sarin gas attack, I personally see no difference between the violation of human rights of Aleph followers and the way society wrongly accused me of a crime I did not commit" (Kōno 2003).

Kōno's victimization at the hands of the media and the police may have led him to this more critical stance toward the state and other social institutions. His writings reflect a greater ambivalence about the means by which justice may be achieved than are evident in those of Takahashi. His relationship with Fujinaga and his criticisms of vigilantism directed against sect members also indicate that his idea of what justice could be is more expansive. In pursuing his vision of justice, Kōno has also actively sought out opportunities to collaborate with the large number of people convicted incorrectly of crimes in Japan, such as Sugaya Toshikazu, who served seventeen years of a life sentence in prison for a crime he did not commit before DNA evidence exonerated him. The two published a book together in 2009 (Sugaya and Kōno 2009).

In addition to the different experiences that Kōno and Takahashi have had in terms of police and media attention, there is also a difference in terms of how the past is understood and related to. As discussed earlier, the relationship between memory and justice has a long historical resonance in the Japanese context, particularly in the years since the Japanese war defeat, yet this relationship is by no means entirely unidimensional. Debates over these terms have been typically constructed around "responsibility," with the additional challenge of negotiating a space for the historical experience of being both victim and perpetrator of violence. At times in postwar Japanese history, this has resulted in the abandonment of responsibility for past violence through an excessive emphasis on victimization. As Oda Makoto (1978, 157) argued in 1966, the idea that "everyone had been betrayed [and] no one had been the betrayer" created what he termed a "persecution complex," which led to a divorce of society from the state. As a result, the state was left as an abstraction, with nobody bearing individual responsibility. This ambivalent relationship between state responsibility and historical memory has been a feature of Japanese political discourse in the decades since (Orr 2001).

In Kōno's politics, we can see the continuation of a historical skepticism about the role of the state in seeking justice. This does not translate into the complete abandonment of personal responsibility, as can be seen in Kōno's acknowledgment that Fujinaga's imprisonment may be understood as a payment of a social debt. More important, it also does not equate to a rejection of the social duty to remember and, through this remembering, to constitute future-oriented political projects. In this, it differs markedly from the postwar "forgetfulness" of Japanese society that Oda points to, as well as the individualized and state-centric responses of people like Takahashi.

What we may have in Kōno's vision is the articulation of a political project akin to what Jeffrey Olick (2007, 151) has described in a different context as "a politics of regret . . . founded on an ethic of responsibility rather than on an ethic of conviction." Justice in this framework connects to a social future based on shared "knowledge and acknowledgment" rather than on "retribution for retribution's sake." Where Kōno differs from Olick, who sees this "politics of regret" as useful largely in laying down a platform of historical truth for future generations to build upon, is that the process envisaged by Kōno can occur within the ongoing life of those who suffered past pain and explicitly advocates for the prevention of future injustices. Kōno articulates the possibility of common futures based on the acknowledgment that life goes on, even in the painful present of living memory.

Memory Futures in Japan

In the two cases represented here, we see two different interactions between processes of historical remembering and projects of future-oriented justice. Takahashi Shizue represents what Miyazawa Setsuo (2008, 48) has argued is the push in Japanese justice systems toward *genbatsuka*. Miyazawa suggests that much of the impetus for this growth can be found in the corresponding growth in victims' rights movements after the subway gassing and the emergence of voices like Takahashi's into the public sphere around questions of criminal justice. He also highlights the media's use of the ambiguous term *taikan chian* (or perception of public safety/security) and the role this has played in garnering support for increased sentences and more severe punishment of those convicted of criminal offences. For Miyazawa (2008, 70), "*taikan chian* is always worsening: so, despite objective indicators of the crime situation, the public accepts *genbatsuka* based on subjective perceptions of declining security." There is a direct relationship, then, between the increasing role of victims' voices and media representations of their experiences and this trend toward increasing "penal populism," as Sakagami also pointed to earlier.

Matthias Fritsch (2005, 2–3) argues in a different context that victim "memory can easily lend itself to the oblivion, or even justification, of violence inflicted on others—in the past as well as in the present and the future"—a cogent articulation of Ricoeur's warning about the obliterating functions of the "cult of memory for the sake of memory" (Ricoeur 2004, 86). Fritsch adds that "promises of justice . . . may also lead to the justification of violent means claimed to be necessary on the way to an end that alone is seen as just." In Takahashi's politics, we can see concrete examples of how victim memory can come into the service of violent ends, on the basis of particular individualized claims for justice and their realization in state violence as the form in which these claims must be recognized.

However, this process of *genbatsuka* is not uncontested in Japan. In contrast to Takahashi, Kōno espouses a politics that draws from a very different set of experiences and discursive genealogies and relies on alternative models of the relationship among memory, justice, and the state. In this it hews much more closely to Ricoeur's framework of "obligated memory," with which I opened this chapter. In this frame, the duty of memory carries with it (through the ideal of justice) an imposition around individual desire and an obligation that functions as constraint. For Kōno, like Ricoeur, justice must be a political project that, while indebted to the past and retaining the centrality of the experience of victimization as its core moral (or ethical) drive, expands beyond the level of individual experience.

There is an important role in this politics for critical history. For Ricoeur (2004, 500), what he terms "the privilege of history" lies not just in broadening individual memory beyond the self (although this is of profound importance) but also in "correcting, criticizing, even refuting the memory of a determined community, when it folds back upon itself and encloses itself within its own sufferings to the point of rendering itself blind and deaf to the suffering of other communities." It is in this embrace of a critical historiography that Kōno's politics is most useful to a broader discussion of the relationship between memory and historical (in)justice. For, in his desire to distance himself from state-backed processes of retribution, Kōno positions himself within a history of citizen skepticism toward the Japanese state and its propensity toward violence. This skepticism has important roots that are made clear through the deployment of history as a counterbalance to an overreliance on individual memory. An awareness of the history of modern Japan can reveal the dangers of an empowered and violence-driven state infrastructure and a compliant and uncritical media, a point that Kōno, through his writing and activism, brings into a contemporary political discourse that remains heavily oriented toward individual experience.

Kōno's politics are useful, then, in providing an avenue for discussion of the historical development of liberalism, which, in Japan as elsewhere, fostered this particular political prioritization of individualism. While subsumed during the period of militarized government, the individual emerged in postwar Japan as the key frame through which politics was conducted. As liberalism has continued to morph and change in the decades since, the political dependence on individual needs and desires only accelerated and expanded. Hence we can see in contemporary Japanese discourse the combined focus, as in Takahashi's rhetoric, on self-responsibility, individualized fears around public safety and the excessive march of increased punitivism. That these same trends can be seen elsewhere is of course not surprising in a time of ascendant neo-liberalism. However, critical voices like Kōno's serve to highlight that this is a historical development that is not inevitable and that has not occurred without contestation.

Memories of victimization, then, are inevitably tied up with experiences of violence and specific historical developments, which shape the particular ways in which justice is understood and articulated. For Takahashi and Kōno, their understandings of the relationship between the individual and the social shapes their responses to the violence they were exposed to and their demands for justice. In Takahashi's case, her story is one of personal victimization. For Kōno it is broader, an institutional experience of victimization that lies beyond the individual. Takahashi's and Kōno's understandings of both the meaning of victim memory and the politics of violence therefore differ. Takahashi understands victimization as individualized experience, and this results in her desire for retribution as justice, meted out by the state through the noose. Kōno, in contrast, sees his individual experience as representative of a potentially broader victimization by the state and other institutions. This results in a critical focus on the development of interpersonal relationships as an important counterbalance to state violence—akin to Ricoeur's notion of the duty of memory beyond the self. These relationships are also placed in a broader social and historical context that enables the imagining of common futures built together. In Kōno's frame, anyone may suffer the misfortune that befell both him and Fujinaga. However, a reliance on the historically questionable state for resolution of this is inadequate for his conceptualization of justice. Kōno is suggesting, therefore, that the only workable project of justice is one that keeps a historical memory of the past alive, while individuals seek to work together in the present to construct a shared future. In this imagined future constructed on both the

Mark Pendleton

duty to remember and the idea(l) of justice, further victimization, whether by individuals or by the state, becomes, if not impossible, at least less inevitable.

Conclusion

In the context of this volume, oriented as it is toward future directions in thinking about the relationship between historical justice and memory, the stories presented in this chapter may on first reading appear unusual, focused as they are on nonstate violence and varied political responses to such violence. However, as with Patrizia Violi's description of Spain, postwar Japan can be read as what she terms "a paradigmatic case of a never-ending transition," where the emergence of democratic processes did not neatly coincide with a "culture of transition." Places like post-Franco Spain and post-militarist Japan continue to struggle with the ongoing legacies of conflict, resulting in highly differentiated understandings of what is to be remembered and therefore what constitutes justice. These are fundamentally unresolved differences that continue to mark and shape how both historical memory and historical justice are understood in these contexts. Barkan and Bećirbašić point to similar problems in Bosnia and Herzegovina and the other former Yugoslav states, problems that are enhanced by the maintenance of divisions on the basis of perceived ethnic identification, and suggest a need to distinguish between the basic rights of victims and the broader construction of public memory, maintained by independent bodies. Yet the examples of Spain and Japan show the difficulties in doing this when history itself cannot be agreed upon. On what basis can independent bodies draw their authority? In all of these cases, understandings of history, memory, and justice continue to constitute points of division well past the moments of conflict. These enduring divisions are themselves often the starting points for retaliation and further victimization, particularly when incorporated within national(ist) processes of identity formation and consolidation. It is clear that how communities and individuals understand and relate to past conflicts has fundamental and material implications in the present.

Through the case studies presented in this chapter and in the volume overall, we have seen that (historical) justice, or that which Ricoeur (2004, 88) says "turns memory into a project, and . . . gives the form of the future," while universal in ambition, remains culturally and historically contingent. Understanding what "justice" means in its specific applications to various memory projects and in the individual cases through which these projects are articulated is an important starting point for imagining what the ends of historical justice may be. Present truths emerge from both individual experiences and shared historical circumstances, the meanings of which are constructed collectively in the present and all too often in seemingly intractable opposition to each other. While Ricoeur (2004, 500) is not wrong to argue that history provides a means through which memory can be corrected, criticized, and refuted when it closes itself off to the sufferings of others, a path forward can be found only through the opening up of dialogue within and between such communities of memory. As Tessa Morris-Suzuki (2005, 27–28) argues, there is perhaps a need to move on from debates about the facts of history and instead to focus on how people create meaning about the past and how these shared memories come to inform the present. For Morris-Suzuki this requires an openness to others that is implicit in Ricoeur's notion of a memory beyond the self. This openness, she argues, is reliant not on authoritative historical truths but on an "historical truthfulness . . . a kind of ongoing dialogue, through which we listen to an expanding repertoire of voices from the past, tell and retell the stories that we have heard, and so define and redefine our position in the present" (Morris-Suzuki 2005, 27–28). From this position of accepting difference but committing to truthful dialogue about past injustices and their resonances in the present, we may begin to develop a shared commitment to one another and, through this, restore the belief that the future is something that can collectively be made.

Notes

1. Hayashi Ikuo was a medical doctor who released sarin on the subway and has also accepted responsibility for several other crimes, including administering drugs, which caused the death of Kariya Kiyoshi, at his court trials and in his 2001 memoir (Hayashi 2001, 566–75). He was the only subway attacker to be sentenced to life imprisonment. See also Reader (2000, 24).

2. "Kun" is a common diminutive often attached to younger male names. In addition to its connotation of an age difference, it also contains an element of familiarity and affection.

3. After the arrest of the guru Asahara and the subsequent bankruptcy of Aum, the sect underwent a number of changes, renaming itself Aleph in 2000. A former spokesperson, Jōyū Fumihiro, led a splinter from Aleph in 2007, which named itself Hikari no wa (The Circle of Light). Both groups remain under intensive police surveillance.

4. In a 2001 documentary, the independent filmmaker Mori Tatsuya explores this phenomenon in great detail, featuring scenes in which Kōno meets with ex-Aum members and representatives of one of the sect's successor organizations, Aleph (Mori Tatsuya, dir., *A2*, Japan, 2001). There are also multiple books published from the perspective of these citizens' groups, such as Kondō (2000).

Bibliography

Abdel-Nour, Farid. 2003. "National Responsibility." *Political Theory* 31: 693–719.

Abraham, Nicolas, and Maria Torok. 1986. *The Wolf Man's Magic Wand: A Cryptonomy*. Minneapolis: University of Minnesota Press.

Adorno, T. W. (1959) 1986. "What Does Coming to Terms with the Past Mean?" In *Bitburg in Moral and Political Perspective*, edited by Geoffrey Hartman, 114–29. Bloomington: Indiana University Press.

Agence France-Presse. 2010. "Srebrenica Massacre 'Not Genocide.'" 13 July. http://news.smh.com.au/breaking-news-world/srebrenica-massacre-not-genocide-20100713-1083q.html.

Aguilar, Paloma. 2001. "Justice, Politics and Memory in the Spanish Transition." In *The Politics of Memory: Transitional Justice in Democratizing Societies*, edited by Alexandra Barahona De Brito, Carmen González-Enríquez, and Paloma Aguilar, 92–118. Oxford: Oxford University Press.

———. 2002. *Memory and Amnesia: The Role of the Spanish Civil War in the Transition to Democracy*. Translated by Mark Oakley. New York: Berghahn.

———. 2008. *Políticas de la memoria y memoria de la política*. Madrid: Alianza.

———. 2009. "Transitional or Post-transitional Justice? Recent Developments in the Spanish Case." *South European Society and Politics* 13, no. 4: 417–33.

Aguilar, Paloma, and Carsten Humlebæk. 2002. "Collective Memory and National Identity in the Spanish Democracy: The Legacies of Francoism and the Civil War." *History and Memory* 14, nos. 1–2: 121–65.

Alexander, Jeffrey C. 2004. "Toward a Theory of Cultural Trauma." In *Cultural Trauma and Collective Identity*, edited by J. Alexander et al., 1–30. Berkeley: University of California Press.

Alonso, Gregorio, and Diego Muro, eds. 2011. *The Politics and Memory of Democratic Transition: The Spanish Model*. New York: Routledge.

Alter, Karin. 2012. "The New Terrain of International Law: Courts, Politics, Rights." Lecture, American Academy in Berlin, 12 May. http://www.americanacademy.de/home/media/videos/new-terrain-international-law-courts-politics-rights.

Andersen, Astrid Nonbo. 2013. "'We Have Reconquered the Islands': Figurations in Public Memories of Slavery and Colonialism in Denmark 1948–2012." *Journal of Politics, Culture, and Society* 26, no. 1: 57–76.

Anderson, David. 2005. *Histories of the Hanged: The Dirty War in Kenya and the End of Empire.* London: Weidenfeld and Nicholson.

Anderson, Elizabeth. 1993. *Value in Ethics and Economics.* Cambridge, Mass.: Harvard University Press.

Ángel Marfull, M. 2008. Interview with Emilio Silva. Público.es, 27 December. http://www.publico.es/espana/186446/la-ley-de-memoria-ha-servido-para-muy-poco.

Anwander, Norbert. 2005. "Contributing and Benefiting: Two Grounds for Duties to the Victims of Injustice." *Ethics and International Affairs* 19: 39–45.

Apel, Dora. 2002. *Memory Effects: The Holocaust and the Art of Secondary Witnessing.* New Brunswick, N.J.: Rutgers University Press.

Arendt, Hannah. 1958. *The Origins of Totalitarianism.* Cleveland: World Publishing Company.

———. (1958) 1998. *The Human Condition.* Chicago: University of Chicago Press.

———. (1963) 2006. *Eichmann in Jerusalem: A Report on the Banality of Evil.* New York: Penguin.

Arias, Arturo, ed. 2001. *The Rigoberta Menchú Controversy.* Minneapolis: University of Minnesota Press.

Arnautović, Marija. 2012. "Dodik i politicko manipulisanje Srebrenicom." Radio Slobodna Evropa, 2 February. http://www.slobodnaevropa.org/content/dodik_i_politicko_manipulisanje_srebrenicom/24471733.html.

Arriaza, Laura J., and Naomi Roht-Arriaza. 2010. "Weaving a Braid of Histories: Local Post-Armed Conflict Initiatives in Guatemala." In *Localizing Transitional Justice: Interventions and Priorities after Mass Violence,* edited by Rosalind Shaw and Lars Waldorf, 205–27. Stanford: Stanford University Press.

Arthur, Paige. 2009. "How 'Transitions' Reshaped Human Rights: A Conceptual History of Transitional Justice." *Human Rights Quarterly* 31, no. 2: 321–54.

Asahi Shimbun. 2000. "Aum Victims' Kin Express Anger." 30 June.

Assmann, Aleida. 2009. "From Collective Violence to a Common Future: Four Models for Dealing with a Traumatic Past." In *Justice and Memory—Confronting Traumatic Pasts: An International Comparison,* edited by Ruth Wodak and Gertraud Auer Borea, 31–48. Wien: Passagen Verlag.

Assmann, Aleida, and Ute Frevert. 1999. *Geschichtsvergessenheit, Geschichtsversessenheit: Vom Umgang mit deutschen Vergangenheiten nach 1945.* Stuttgart: Deutsche Verlags-Anstalt.

Assmann, Jan. 2011. *Cultural Memory and Early Civilization: Writing, Remembrance, and Political Imagination.* Cambridge: Cambridge University Press.

Associated Press. 2004. "Bosnian Serbs Issue Apology for Massacre." 11 November. http://www.bosnia.org.uk/bosrep/report_format.cfm?articleid=1147&reportid=166.

———. 2013. "Bosnia's Ethnic Rivals Join Forces to Protest Government." 11 June. http://www.foxnews.com/world/2013/06/11/bosnia-ethnic-rivals-join-forces-in-anti-government-protests-being-called-baby/.

Auswärtiges Amt (Federal Republic of Germany). 2014. "Entschädigung für NS-Unrecht." 11 November. http://www.auswaertiges-amt.de/DE/Aussenpolitik/InternatRecht/Entschaedigung_node.html.

B92. 2008. "Dodik's Statements Stir New Controversy." 12 December. http://www.b92.net/eng/news/region-article.php?yyyy=2008&mm=12&dd=12&nav_id=55686.

———. 2010. "Bosnia Impossible State." 29 September. http://www.b92.net/eng/news/region-article.php?mm=9&dd=29&yyyy=2010.

Baier, Annette. 1985. *Postures of the Mind: Essays on Mind and Morals.* London: Methuen.

Baines, Erin K. 2009. "Complex Political Perpetrators: Reflections on Dominic Ongwen." *Journal of Modern African Studies* 47, no. 2: 163–91.

Bakiner, Onur. 2011. "Coming to Terms with the Past: Power, Memory and Legitimacy in Truth Commissions." PhD diss., Yale University.

Balkan Insight. 2008. "Acquitted Bosniak Gets Hero's Welcome." 4 July. http://www.balkaninsight.com/en/article/acquitted-bosniak-gets-hero-s-welcome.

———. 2009. "Dodik Says Had Moral Reasons to Welcome Plavsic." 28 October. http://www.balkaninsight.com/en/article/dodik-says-had-moral-reasons-to-welcome-plavsic.

———. 2011. "Sarajevo Shuns Recognition of Bosniak War Crimes." 23 December. http://www.balkaninsight.com/en/article/sarajevo-shuns-recognition-of-bosniak-war-crimes.

Barkan, Elazar. 2000. *Guilt of Nations: Restitution and Negotiating Historical Injustices.* Baltimore: Johns Hopkins University Press.

———. 2009. "Introduction: Historians and Historical Reconciliation." *American Historical Review* 114, no. 4: 899–913.

Bass, Gary. 2000. *Stay the Hand of Vengeance.* Princeton, N.J.: Princeton University Press.

Bastedo, Kip. 2009. "Transitional 'Truths': Dealing with the Past in Bosnia & Herzegovina." *Perspectives on Global Issues* 3, no. 2.

BBC Monitoring International Reports. 2008. "Bosnian Muslim Leader Announces Departure from War 'Victim Philosophy.'" 24 December.

BBC News. 2005. "Kenya Wants UK 'Atrocity' Apology." 4 March. http://news.bbc.co.uk/2/hi/africa/4318277.stm.

———. 2011. "Is Britain to Blame for Many of the World's Problems?" 7 April. http://www.bbc.co.uk/news/magazine-12992540.

Bećirbašić, Belma. 2011. *Tijelo, zenskost i moc: Upisivanja patrijarhalnog diskursa u tijelo.* Zagreb: Synopsis.

Benhabib, Seyla. 2002. *The Claims of Culture.* Princeton, N.J.: Princeton University Press.

Benjamin, Walter. 1968. *Illuminations: Essays and Reflections.* Edited by Hannah Arendt. Translated by Harry Zohn. New York: Schocken Books.

Berg, Manfred. 2009. "Historical Continuity and Counterfactual History in the Debate over Reparations for Slavery." In *Historical Justice in International Perspective:*

How Societies Are Trying to Right the Wrongs of the Past, edited by Manfred Berg and Bernd Schaefer, 69–91. Washington, D.C.: German Historical Institute.

Berg, Manfred, and Bernd Schaefer. 2009. "Introduction." In *Historical Justice in International Perspective: How Societies Are Trying to Right the Wrongs of the Past*, edited by Manfred Berg and Bernd Schaefer, 1–17. Washington, D.C.: German Historical Institute.

Bernecker, Walther L. 2009. "Dealing with the Past in Spain: Between Amnesia and Collective Memory." In *Justice and Memory—Confronting Traumatic Pasts: An International Comparison*, edited by Ruth Wodak and Gertraud Auer Borea, 123–46. Wien: Passagen Verlag.

Bertelsmann Stiftung. 2012. "BTI 2012—Bosnia and Herzegovina Country Report." Bertelsmann Stiftung, Gütersloh. http://www.bti-project.org/fileadmin/Inhalte/reports/2012/pdf/BTI%202012%20Bosnia%20and%20Herzegovina.pdf.

Bickford, Louis. 1999. "The Archival Imperative: Human Rights and Historical Memory in Latin America's Southern Cone." *Human Rights Quarterly* 21, no. 4: 1097–1122.

———. 2007. "Unofficial Truth Projects." *Human Rights Quarterly* 29, no. 4: 994–1035.

Bilbija, Ksenija. 2005. "Story Is History Is Story." In *The Art of Truth-telling about Authoritarian Rule*, edited by Ksenija Bilbija, Jo Ellen Fair, Cynthia E. Milton, and Leigh A. Payne, 112–17. Madison: University of Wisconsin Press.

Bilbija, Ksenija, Jo Ellen Fair, Cynthia E. Milton, and Leigh A. Payne, eds. 2005. *The Art of Truth-telling about Authoritarian Rule*. Madison: University of Wisconsin Press.

Bilten Srebrenica. 2006. "Medjunarodna zajednica mora ukinuti Republiku Srpsku." *Bilten Srebrenica* 37: 10–11.

Blackburn, Simon. 2001. "Group Minds and Expressive Harm." *Maryland Law Review* 60, no. 3: 467–91.

Blake, Michael. 2002. "Distributive Justice, State Coercion, and Autonomy." *Philosophy and Public Affairs* 30, no. 3: 257–96.

Blustein, Jeffrey. 2008. *The Moral Demands of Memory*. New York: Cambridge University Press.

———. 2012. "Human Rights and the Internationalization of Memory." *Journal of Social Philosophy* 43, no. 1: 19–32.

———. 2014. *Forgiveness and Remembrance: Remembering Wrongdoing in Personal and Public Life*. New York: Oxford University Press.

Bojić, Milijana. 2010. "Kandićeva radi na nestanku RS." *Press Dnevne Novine*, 31 August. http://www.zarekom.org/press/Kandiceva-radi-na-nestanku-RS-Press-31_08_2010_.en.html.

Booth, James W. 2001. "The Unforgotten: Memories of Justice." *American Political Science Review* 95, no. 4: 777–91.

———. 2006. *Communities of Memory: On Witness, Identity, and Justice*. Ithaca, N.Y.: Cornell University Press.

———. 2011. "'From This Far Place': On Justice and Absence." *American Political Science Review* 105, no. 4: 750–64.

Borer, Tristan Anne, ed. 2006. *Telling the Truths: Truth Telling and Peace Building in Post-Conflict Societies.* Notre Dame, Ind.: University of Notre Dame Press.

Borneman, John. 2002. "On Money and the Memory of Loss." *Etnográfica* 6, no. 2: 281–302.

———. 2011. *Political Crime and the Memory of Loss.* Bloomington: Indiana University Press.

Box, Meredith, and Gavin McCormack. 2004. "Terror in Japan." *Critical Asian Studies* 36, no. 1: 91–112.

Boxill, Bernard R. 1972. "The Morality of Reparation." *Social Theory and Practice* 2, no. 1: 113–23.

———. 2003. "A Lockean Argument for Black Reparations." *Journal of Ethics* 7, no 1: 63–91.

Božović, Luka. 2011. "Rekom—jedna ljudska ideja, a ne pokušaj vaskrsenja Jugoslavije." *Nova Srpska Politička Misao*, 3 July.

Brahm, Eric. 2006. "Truth and Consequences: The Impact of Truth Commissions in Transitional Societies." PhD diss., University of Colorado at Boulder.

Braithwaite, John. 2011. "Partial Truth and Reconciliation in the *Longue Durée.*" *Contemporary Social Science* 6, no. 1: 129–46.

Bratman, Michael. 2014. *Shared Agency: A Planning Theory of Acting Together.* Oxford: Oxford University Press.

"Brazil Approves Jewish Studies Agreement with Israel." 2012. *Martyrdom and Resistance* 30, no. 3: 13.

Brendon, Piers. 2007. "A Moral Audit of the British Empire." *History Today* 57: 44–47.

Brett, Sebastian, Louis Bickford, Liz Sevcenko, and Marcela Rios. 2007. "Memorialization and Democracy: State Policy and Civic Action." New York: International Center for Transitional Justice. http://ictj.org/sites/default/files/ICTJ-Global-Memorialization-Democracy-2007-English_o.pdf.

Brooks, Roy L. 1999. *When Sorry Isn't Enough: The Controversy over Apologies for Human Injustice.* New York: New York University Press.

———. 2004. *Atonement and Forgiveness: A New Model for Black Reparations.* Berkeley: University of California Press.

Brudholm, Thomas. 2008. *Resentment's Virtue: Jean Amery and the Refusal to Forgive.* Philadelphia: Temple University Press.

Buñuel, Luis. 1983. *My Last Sigh.* Translated by Abigail Israel. New York: Knopf.

Burgos-Debray, Elizabeth, ed. 1984. *I, Rigoberta Menchú: An Indian Woman in Guatemala.* Translated by Ann Wright. London: Verso.

Bußler, Werner. 2013. "Neues Mahnmal gegen das Vergessen." *Frankenpost*, 16 April. http://www.frankenpost.de/lokal/muenchberg/mhtz/Neues-Mahnmal-gegen-das-Vergessen;art2441,2500153.

Butt, Daniel. 2006. "Nations, Overlapping Generations and Historic Injustice." *American Philosophical Quarterly* 43, no. 4: 357–67.

———. 2007. "On Benefiting from Injustice." *Canadian Journal of Philosophy* 37, no. 1: 129–52.

———. 2009a. *Rectifying International Injustice: Principles of Compensation and Restitution between Nations*. Oxford: Oxford University Press.

———. 2009b. "Victors' Justice? Historic Injustice and the Legitimacy of International Law." In *Legitimacy, Justice and Public International Law*, edited by Lukas H. Meyer, 163–85. Cambridge: Cambridge University Press.

———. 2013a. "Colonialism and Postcolonialism." In *International Encyclopedia of Ethics*, edited by Hugh LaFolette, 892–98. Oxford: Wiley-Blackwell.

———. 2013b. "Inheriting Rights to Reparation: Compensatory Justice and the Passage of Time." *Ethical Perspectives* 20, no. 2: 245–69.

Caine, Philip. 2008. "The International Criminal Tribunal for the Former Yugoslavia: Planners and Instigators or Foot Soldiers?" *International Journal of Police Science and Management* 11, no. 3: 345–57.

Camo, Hamdo. 2009. "Ko podržava Republiku Srpsku, podržava genocid." *Bilten Srebrenica* 43. http://bosnjaci.net/prilog.php?pid=25784.

Caney, Simon. 2002. "Survey Article: Cosmopolitanism and the Law of Peoples." *Journal of Political Philosophy* 10: 95–123.

Capital News. 2013. "It's Not Over as 8,000 More Seek Mau Mau Cash." 8 June. http://www.capitalfm.co.ke/news/2013/06/its-not-over-as-8000-more-seek-mau-mau-cash/.

Caruth, Cathy. 1996. *Unclaimed Experience: Trauma, Narrative, and History*. Baltimore: Johns Hopkins University Press.

Casanova, Julián, ed. 2002. *Morir, matar, sobrevivir: La violencia en la dictadura de Franco*. Barcelona: Crítica.

Čekić, Smail. 2009. "Research of Genocide Victims, with a Special Emphasis on Bosnia and Herzegovina." Translated by Branka Ramadanović. Institute for the Research of Crimes against Humanity and International Law, University of Sarajevo. http://www.institut-genocid.unsa.ba/pdf/zrtve_engleski.pdf.

Cenarro, Ángela. 2002. "Memory beyond the Public Sphere: The Francoist Repression Remembered in Aragon." *History and Memory* 14, nos. 1–2: 165–88.

Chakma, Suhas. 2003. "The Issue of Compensation for Colonialism and Slavery at the World Conference Against Racism." In *Human Rights in Development Yearbook 2001: Reparations: Redressing Past Wrongs*, edited by George Ulrich and Louise Krabbe Boserup, 57–71. The Hague: Kluwer Law International.

Chapman, Audrey R., and Patrick Ball. 2001. "The Truth of Truth Commissions: Comparative Lessons from Haiti, South Africa, and Guatemala." *Human Rights Quarterly* 23, no. 1: 1–43.

Chapman, Audrey R., and Hugo van der Merwe. 2008. *Truth and Reconciliation in South Africa: Did the TRC Deliver?* Philadelphia: University of Pennsylvania Press.

Chêne, Marie. 2009. "Corruption and Anti-Corruption in Bosnia and Herzegovina." Transparency International, 29 November. http://www.u4.no/helpdesk/helpdesk/query.cfm?id=221.

Chikatetsu Sarin Jiken Higaisha no Kai, ed. 1998. *Soredemo ikite iku: Chikatetsu sarin jiken higaisha shukishū*. Tokyo: Sanmāku.

Clark, Helen. 2002. "Address to Chinese New Year Celebrations." 12 February. http://www.beehive.govt.nz/speech/address-chinese-new-year-celebrations.

Clark, Phil. 2010. *The Gacaca Courts, Post-Genocide Justice and Reconciliation in Rwanda: Justice without Lawyers*. Cambridge: Cambridge University Press.

Clavero, Bartolomé. 2008. *Genocide or Ethnocide 1933–2007*. Milan: Giuffrè Editore.

Coalition for RECOM. 2011. "The Statute: Proposal." 26 March. http://www.zarekom.org/uploads/documents/2011/04/i_836/f_28/f_1865_en.pdf.

Cohen, Jean. 2008. "Rethinking Human Rights, Democracy, and Sovereignty in the Age of Globalization." *Political Theory* 36, no. 4: 578–606.

———. 2012. *Globalization and Sovereignty: Rethinking Legality, Legitimacy, and Constitutionalism*. New York: Cambridge University Press.

Cohen, Stanley. 2001. *States of Denial: Knowing about Atrocities and Suffering*. Cambridge: Polity Press.

Cole, Elizabeth, ed. 2007. *Teaching the Violent Past*. Lanham, Md.: Rowman and Littlefield.

Coleman, Jules L. 1992. *Risks and Wrongs*. Cambridge: Cambridge University Press.

Collste, Göran. 2010. "'. . . Restoring the Dignity of the Victims': Is Global Rectificatory Justice Feasible?" *Ethics and Global Politics* 3, no. 2: 85–99.

Colo, Edita, Suzana Bozic, and Goran Bubalo, eds. 2011. "Analiza potreba i baza kontakata udruzenja logorasa, porodica nestalih, poginulih, oboljelih od PTSP-a i RVI-a u Bosni i Hercegovini." Catholic Relief Service and USAID, August.

Colonomos, Ariel, and Andrea Armstrong. 2006. "German Reparations to the Jews after World War II: A Turning Point in the History of Reparations." In *The Handbook of Reparations*, edited by Pablo de Greiff, 390–419. New York: Oxford University Press.

Commission for Investigation of the Events in and around Srebrenica between 10th and 19th July 1995 (Commission). 2004. "The Events in and around Srebrenica between 10th and 19th July 1995." Banja Luka: Republika Srpska Government. http://trial-ch.org/fileadmin/user_upload/documents/trialwatch/Srebrenica_Report2004.pdf.

Commonwealth of Australia. 1997. *Bringing Them Home: Report of the National Inquiry into the Separation of Aboriginal and Torres Strait Islander Children from Their Families*. Canberra: Human Rights and Equal Opportunity Commission.

Conference on Security and Co-operation in Europe. 1975. "Final Act." http://www.osce.org/mc/39501?download=true.

Coombes, Annie E. 2003. *Visual Culture and Public Memory in a Democratic South Africa*. Durham, N.C.: Duke University Press.

Cove, John J. 1995. *What the Bones Say: Tasmanian Aborigines, Science and Domination*. Ottawa: Carleton University Press.

Cowen, Tyler. 2006. "How Far Back Should We Go? Why Restitution Should Be Small." In *Retribution and Reparation in the Transition to Democracy*, edited by Jon Elster, 17–32. New York: Cambridge University Press.

Croatian Democratic Union. 2010. "Obilježena 19. obljetnica utemeljenja Hrvatske zajednice Herceg-Bosne." Press release, 18 November. http://www.hdzbih.org

/vijesti/793-obiljezena-19-obljetnica-utemeljenja-hrvatske-zajednice-herceg-bosne
.html.

Cunningham, Michael. 1999. "Saying Sorry: The Politics of Apology." *Political Quarterly* 70, no. 3: 285–93.

———. 2008. "It Wasn't Us and We Didn't Benefit: The Discourse of Opposition to an Apology by Britain for Its Role in the Slave Trade." *Political Quarterly* 79, no. 2: 252–59.

Dani. 2000. "The Exclusive Truth about the Crimes of Caco." 1 June. Translated by Balkan Peace. www.balkanpeace.org/index.php?index=article&articleid=10321.

———. 2002. "Caco je i heroj i zlocinac." 1 March. http://www.bhdani.com/arhiva /246/intervju.shtml.

de Greiff, Pablo. 2006. "Justice and Reparations." In *The Handbook of Reparations*, edited by Pablo de Greiff and International Center for Transitional Justice, 451–77. New York: Oxford University Press.

———. 2012. "Theorizing Transitional Justice." In *Transitional Justice*, edited by Melissa S. Williams, Rosemary Nagy, and Jon Elster, 31–77. New York: New York University Press.

de Greiff, Pablo, and International Center for Transitional Justice. 2006. *The Handbook of Reparations.* New York: Oxford University Press.

Derrida, Jacques. 2006. *Spectres of Marx: The State of the Debt, the Work of Mourning and the New International.* New York: Routledge.

de Silva, Chitta Ranjan, et al. 2011. "Report of the Commission of Inquiry on Lessons Learnt and Reconciliation." 15 November. http://www.priu.gov.lk/news_update /Current_Affairs/ca201112/FINAL%20LLRC%20REPORT.pdf.

Diner, Dan. 1995. *Kreisläufe: Nationalsozialismus und Gedächtnis.* Berlin: Berlin-Verlag.

Dnevni Avaz. 2012. "Lutka za zlocinacke lazi." 2 April.

Douglas, Lawrence. 2001. *The Memory of Judgment: Making Law and History in the Trials of the Holocaust.* New Haven, Conn.: Yale University Press.

Dowell, Katy. 2013. "Ndiku Mutua & Ors v Foreign and Commonwealth Office." *The Lawyer*, 7 January. http://www.thelawyer.com/ndiku-mutua-and-ors-v-foreign-and-commonwealth-office/1016287.article.

Dower, John W. 1999. *Embracing Defeat: Japan in the Aftermath of World War II.* London: Penguin.

Dudden, Alexis. 2008. *Troubled Apologies among Japan, Korea and the United States.* New York: Columbia University Press.

Dudziak, Mary L. 2002. *Cold War Civil Rights: Race and the Image of American Democracy.* Princeton, N.J.: Princeton University Press.

Durkheim, Émile. 1973. "Individualism and the Intellectuals." In *Emile Durkheim on Morality and Society*, edited by Robert Bellah, 43–57. Chicago: University of Chicago Press.

Elkins, Caroline. 2005. *Imperial Reckoning: The Untold Story of Britain's Gulag in Kenya.* New York: Henry Holt.

Fabre, Cécile. 2007. *Justice in a Changing World.* Cambridge: Polity.

Fackler, Martin, and Choe Sang-Hun. 2007. "Japanese Researchers Rebut Premier's Denials on Sex Slavery." *New York Times*, 18 April.

Falk, Richard. 2006. "Reparation, International Law, and Global Justice: A New Frontier." In *The Handbook of Reparations*, edited by Pablo de Greiff, 478–503. New York: Oxford University Press.

Feinberg, Joel. 1980. "The Rights of Animals and Unborn Generations." In *Rights, Justice, and the Bounds of Liberty: Essays in Social Philosophy*, 159–84. Princeton, N.J.: Princeton University Press.

———. 1992. *Freedom and Fulfilment: Philosophical Essays*. Princeton, N.J.: Princeton University Press.

Felgenhauer, Pavel. 2009. "Medvedev Forms a Commission to Protect Russian History." *Eurasia Daily Monitor* 6, no. 98 (21 May). http://www.jamestown.org/single/?no_cache=1&tx_ttnews[tt_news]=35018.

Ferguson, Niall. 2002. *Empire: The Rise and Demise of the British World Order and the Lessons for Global Power*. London: Allen Lane.

Ferrándiz, Francisco. 2006. "The Return of Civil War Ghosts: The Ethnography of Exhumations in Contemporary Spain." *Anthropology Today* 22, no. 3: 7–12.

———. 2008. "Cries and Whispers: Exhuming and Narrating Defeat in Spain Today." *Journal of Spanish Cultural Studies* 9, no. 2: 177–92.

Ferro, Marc. 1997. *Colonization: A Global History*. Translated by K. D. Prithipaul. London: Routledge.

Feyrer, James, and Bruce Sacerdote. 2009. "Colonialism and Modern Income: Islands as Natural Experiments." *Review of Economics and Statistics* 91: 245–26.

Field, Norma. 1997. "War and Apology: Japan, Asia, the Fiftieth, and After." *positions: east asia cultures critique* 5, no. 1: 1–49.

Fishkin, James S. 1991. "Justice between Generations: Compensation, Identity, and Group Membership." In *Compensatory Justice*, edited by John W. Chapman, 85–96. New York: New York University Press.

Foreign Correspondents' Club of Japan. 2004. "Press Conference with Egawa Shōko and Takahashi Shizue." Audio recording, 26 February.

François, Etienne, and Hagen Schulze, eds. 2001. *Deutsche Erinnerungsorte*. 3 vols. Munich: Beck.

Freeman, Mark. 2006. *Truth Commissions and Procedural Fairness*. Cambridge: Cambridge University Press.

Freeman, Mark, and Priscilla B. Hayner. 2003. "Truth-Telling." In *Reconciliation after Violent Conflict: A Handbook*, edited by David Bloomfield, 122–39. Stockholm: International Institute for Democracy and Electoral Assistance.

Fricker, Miranda. 2007. *Epistemic Injustice: Power and the Ethics of Knowing*. New York: Oxford University Press.

Fritsch, Matthias. 2005. *The Promise of Memory: History and Politics in Marx, Benjamin, and Derrida*. Albany: SUNY Press.

Fullinwider, Robert. 1975. "Preferential Hiring and Compensation." *Social Theory and Practice* 3, no. 3: 307–20.

Galtung, Johan. 1996. *Peace by Peaceful Means: Peace and Conflict, Development and Civilization*. Oslo: PRIO.

Garland, David. 2001. *The Culture of Control: Crime and Social Order in Contemporary Society*. Chicago: University of Chicago Press.

Gerschenkron, Alexander. 1962. *Economic Backwardness in Historical Perspective: A Book of Essays*. Cambridge, Mass.: Belknap Press.

Gibson, James L. 2004. *Overcoming Apartheid: Can Truth Reconcile a Divided Nation?* New York: Russell Sage Foundation.

Gilbert, Margaret. 2002. "Collective Guilt and Collective Guilt Feelings." *Journal of Ethics* 6, no. 2: 115–43.

Glenn Gray, J. 1998. *The Warriors: Reflections on Men in Battle*. Lincoln: University of Nebraska Press.

Gluck, Carol. 1997. "The 'End' of the Postwar: Japan at the Turn of the Millennium." *Public Culture* 10, no. 1: 1–23.

———. 2007. "Operations of Memory: 'Comfort Women' and the World." In *Ruptured Histories: War, Memories, and the Post-Cold War in Asia*, edited by Sheila Miyoshi Jager and Rana Mitter, 47–77. Cambridge, Mass.: Harvard University Press.

———. 2009. "*Sekinin*/Responsibility in Modern Japan." In *Words in Motion: Toward a Global Lexicon*, edited by Carol Gluck and Anna Lowenhaupt Tsing, 83–106. Durham, N.C.: Duke University Press.

Golob, Stephanie R. 2008. "Volver: The Return of/to Transitional Justice Politics in Spain." *Journal of Spanish Cultural Studies* 9, no. 2: 127–41.

———. 2011. "Left Behind: Spain's Socialist Party (PSOE) and Its 'Historical Memory' Agenda." Paper presented at the Sixth General Conference of the European Consortium for Political Research (ECPR). University of Iceland, 25–27 August.

Goodin, R. 1987. "Exploiting a Situation and Exploiting a Person." In *Modern Theories of Exploitation*, edited by A. Reeve, 166–200. London: Sage.

Gordon, Avery F. (1997) 2008. *Ghostly Matters: Haunting and the Sociological Imagination*. 2nd ed. Minneapolis: University of Minnesota Press.

Gordon, Robert W. 1996. "Undoing Historical Injustice." In *Justice and Injustice in Law and Legal Theory*, edited by Austin Sarat and Thomas R. Kearns, 35–75. Ann Arbor: University of Michigan Press.

Gosseries, Axel. 2004. "Historical Emissions and Free-riding." *Ethical Perspectives* 11, no. 1: 38–62.

Grandin, Greg. 2005. "The Instruction of Great Catastrophe: Truth Commissions, National History, and State Formation in Argentina, Chile, and Guatemala." *American Historical Review* 110, no. 1: 46–67.

Gray, David C. 2010. "Extraordinary Justice." *Alabama Law Review* 62: 55–109.

Greimas, Algirdas Julien, and Joseph Courtés. 1979. *Sémiotique: Dictionnaire raisonné de la théorie du langage*. Paris: Hachette.

Grimm, Dieter. 2009. *Souveränität: Herkunft und Zukunft eines Schlüsselbegriffs*. Berlin: Berlin University Press.

Gunson, Phil. 2013. "Jorge Rafaél Videla Obituary." *The Guardian*, 18 May. http://www.guardian.co.uk/world/2013/may/17/jorge-rafael-videla.

Habermas, Jürgen. 1999. "Kants Idee des ewigen Friedens." In *Die Einbeziehung des Anderen*, edited by Jürgen Habermas, 192–236. Frankfurt am Main: Suhrkamp.

———. 2009. "Zur Legitimation durch Menschenrechte." In *Philosophische Texte*, vol. 4, 298–312. Frankfurt am Main: Suhrkamp.

Halbwachs, Maurice. 1925. *Les cadres sociaux de la mémoire*. Paris: Alcan.

———. 1992. *On Collective Memory*. Translated and edited by Lewis Coser. Chicago: University of Chicago Press.

Hallam, Elizabeth, and Jenny Hockey. 2001. *Death, Memory, and Material Culture*. Oxford: Berg.

Hamai, Koichi, and Thomas Ellis. 2006. "Crime and Criminal Justice in Modern Japan: From Re-integrative Shaming to Popular Punitivism." *International Journal of the Sociology of Law* 34, no. 3: 157–78.

Hamber, Brandon. 2009. *Transforming Societies after Political Violence*. Dordrecht: Springer.

Hayakawa, K., and K. Kawamura. 2005. *Watashi ni totte Oumu to wa nan datta no ka*. Tokyo: Poplar.

Hayashi, I. 2001. *Oumu to Watashi*. Tokyo: Bungei Shunjûsha.

Hayner, Priscilla B. 2011. *Unspeakable Truths: Transitional Justice and the Challenge of Truth Commissions*. 2nd ed. New York: Routledge.

Hazan, Pierre. 2010. *Judging War, Judging History: Behind Truth and Reconciliation*. Stanford: Stanford University Press.

Henley, John. 2005. "French Angry at Law to Teach Glory of Colonialism." *The Guardian*, 15 April. http://www.guardian.co.uk/world/2005/apr/15/highereducation.artsandhumanities.

Herman, Judith. 1992. *Trauma and Recovery: The Aftermath of Violence—from Domestic Abuse to Political Terror*. New York: Basic Books.

Herzfeld, Michael. 1982. *Ours Once More: Folklore, Ideology, and the Making of Modern Greece*. Austin: University of Texas Press.

Hirsch, Marianne. 1997. *Family Frames: Photography, Narrative and Postmemory*. Cambridge, Mass.: Harvard University Press.

———. 2012. *The Generation of Postmemory: Writing and Visual Culture after the Holocaust*. New York: Columbia University Press.

Hjelmslev, Louis. 1954. "La stratification du langage." *Word* 10: 163–88.

Hoare, Attila Marko. 2008. "From Nuremberg to the International Criminal Tribunal for the former Yugoslavia." *Globus*, 12 December. http://www.bosnia.org.uk/news/news_body.cfm?newsid=2530.

Hobsbawm, Eric. 1994. *The Age of Extremes: A History of the World, 1914–1991*. New York: Vintage.

Hochschild, Arlie Russell. 2012. *The Outsourced Self: Intimate Life in Market Times*. New York: Metropolitan Books.

Hongo, J. 2008."Sarin Killer's Death Penalty Is Finalized." *Japan Times*, 16 February.

Honneth, Axel. 1995. *The Struggle for Recognition: The Moral Grammar of Social Conflicts*. Cambridge, Mass.: Polity Press.

Horkheimer, Max, and Theodor W. Adorno. 1972. *Dialectic of Enlightenment*. Translated by John Cumming. London: Allen Lane.

House of Commons (United Kingdom). 2013. "Mau Mau Claims (Settlement)." Hansard, 6 June, 1692–99. http://www.publications.parliament.uk/pa/cm201314 /cmhansrd/chan13.pdf.

Human Rights House. 2005. "Vice President Demands British Apology over Mau Mau." 3 March. http://humanrightshouse.org/noop/page.php?p=Articles/6424 .html&d=1.

Humlebæk, Carsten. 2011. "The 'Pacto de Olvido.'" In *The Politics and Memory of Democratic Transition: The Spanish Model*, edited by Gregorio Alonso and Diego Muro, 183–98. New York: Routledge.

Humphrey, Michael. 2003. "From Victim to Victimhood: Truth Commissions and Trials as Rituals of Political Transition and Individual Healing." *Australian Journal of Anthropology* 14, no. 2: 171–87.

Hurley, Adrienne Carey. 2011. *Revolutionary Suicide and Other Desperate Measures: Narratives of Youth and Violence from Japan and the United States*. Durham, N.C.: Duke University Press.

Huyssen, Andreas. 2003. *Present Pasts: Urban Palimpsests and the Politics of Memory*. Stanford: Stanford University Press.

———. 2005. "Resistance to Memory: The Uses and Abuses of Public Forgetting." In *Globalizing Critical Theory*, edited by Max Pensky, 165–84. Lanham, Md.: Rowman and Littlefield.

———. 2009. "Transnationale Verwertungen von Holocaust und Kolonialismus." In *VerWertungen von Vergangenheit*, edited by Elisabeth Wagner and Burkhardt Wolf, 30–51. Berlin: Vorwerk 8.

———. 2011. "International Human Rights and the Politics of Memory: Limits and Challenges." *Criticism* 53, no. 4: 607–24.

Iida, Keisuke. 2004. "Human Rights and Sexual Abuse: The Impact of International Human Rights Law on Japan." *Human Rights Quarterly* 26, no. 2: 428–53.

Inic, Slobodan. 1996. "Biljana Plavsic: Geneticist in the Service of a Great Crime." *Helsinska povelja*, November. http://www.barnsdle.demon.co.uk/bosnia/plavsic.html.

International Commission on Intervention and State Sovereignty. 2001. "The Responsibility to Protect." December. http://responsibilitytoprotect.org/ICISS%20Report .pdf.

International Criminal Tribunal for the Former Yugoslavia (ICTY). 2013. "Six Senior Herceg-Bosna Officials Convicted." Press release, 29 May. http://www.icty.org/sid /11324.

International Institute for Middle East and Balkan Studies (IFIMES). 2010. "Who Is Manipulating the Civilian War Victims?" 27 October. http://www.ifimes.org/en /researches/who-is-manipulating-the-civilian-war-victims/.

Irwin-Zarecka, Iwona. 1994. *Frames of Remembrance: The Dynamics of Collective Memory*. Piscataway, N.J.: Transaction.

Isa Intel. 2011. "Republika Srpska Vows to Hold Referendum on War Crimes Coopera-tion." 15 April. http://www.isaintel.com/2011/04/15/bosnia-republika-srpska-vows-to-hold-referendum-on-war-crimes-cooperation-how-will-the-international-community-respond.

Islamska Zajednica u Bosni i Hercegovini. 2011. "The First Report on Islamophobia, Discrimination and Intolerance on the Territory of the Islamic Community in BH (2004–2011)." April. http://www.rijaset.ba/images/stories/Za-download/The%20First%20Report%20on%20Islamophobia%20-%202004-2010.pdf.

———. 2012. "Hutba reisu-l-uleme u džamiji u Hadžićima." 10 February. http://www.rijaset.ba/index.php?option=com_content&view=article&id=13768:hutba-reisu-l-uleme-u-dzamiji-u-hadzicima&catid=203:mina-vijesti-kat&Itemid=459.

Istrazivacko-dokumentacioni Centar. 2010. "Bosanski Atlas ratnih zlocina—brosura." 22 February.

Ito, M. 2007. "Victim-Criminal Dialogue Can Be Cathartic." *Japan Times*, 12 June.

Ivanov, Igor, Wolfgang Ischinger, and Sam Nunn. 2012. "EASI—Euro-Atlantic Secu-rity Initiative: Toward a Euro-Atlantic Security Community: Final Report." Feb-ruary. Carnegie Endowment for International Peace. http://carnegieendowment.org/2012/02/03/toward-euro-atlantic-security-community/9d3j.

Ivy, Marilyn. 1995. *Discourses of the Vanishing: Modernity, Phantasm, Japan*. Chicago: University of Chicago Press.

Japan Times. 1998. "Aum Doctor Gets Life Sentence for Subway Attack." 26 May.

———. 1999. "Aum Cultist Given Death Sentence for Part in Subway Attack." 30 September.

———. 2003. "Death Penalty Is Upheld for Aum's Sarin Attack." 20 May.

Jaspin, Elliott. 2007. *Buried in the Bitter Waters: The Hidden History of Racial Cleansing in America*. New York: Basic Books.

Jelin, Elizabeth. (2002) 2003. *State Repression and the Labors of Memory*. Translated by J. Rein and M. Godoy-Anativia. Minneapolis: University of Minnesota Press.

Jerez-Farrán, Carlos, and Samuel Amago, eds. 2010. *Unearthing Franco's Legacy: Mass Graves and the Recovery of Historical Memory in Spain*. Notre Dame, Ind.: Univer-sity of Notre Dame Press.

Jewish Claims Conference. 2013. "Claims Conference Reaches $1 Billion Agreement with German Government for Survivor Homecare." 28 May. http://www.claimscon.org/2013/05/negotiations/.

———. n.d. "Article 2 Fund." http://www.claimscon.org/what-we-do/compensation/background/article2/.

John Paul II. 2001. "Apology for the Sack of Constantinople (2001)." Facts on File, 4 May. http://www.fofweb.com/History/MainPrintPage.asp?iPin=SIWH0189&DataType=WorldHistory&WinType=Free.

Juliá, Santos. 1999. *Victimas de la guerra civil*. Madrid: Ed.Temas de Hoy.

———. 2006. "Bajo el imperio de la memoria." *Revista de Occidente*, nos. 302–3: 7–20.

Kaplan, Brett Ashley. 2011. *Landscapes of Holocaust Postmemory*. New York: Routledge.

Kassow, Samuel D. 2008. *Who Will Write Our History? Rediscovering a Hidden Archive from the Warsaw Ghetto*. London: Penguin.

Kersten, Rikki. 2009. "The Intellectual Culture of Postwar Japan and the 1968–1969 University of Tokyo Struggles: Repositioning the Self in Postwar Thought." *Social Science Japan Journal* 12, no. 2: 227–45.

Kihuria, Njonjo. 2014. "Construction of Mau Mau Memorial Takes off." *The Star* (Nairobi), 1 August. http://www.the-star.co.ke/news/article-181769/construction-mau-mau-memorial-takes.

Kondō, Y. 2000. *Satsujin shūkyo 'Oumu' to no tatakai: 'Oumu Shinrikyō' higaisha no kai ionen no kiroku*. Nagoya: Fūbaisha.

Kōno, Y. 1998. *Tsuma yo! Waga'ai to kibō to tatakai no hibi*. Tokyo: Ushio shuppansha.

———. 2001. *'Giwaku' wa hareyō tomo: Matsumoto Sarin Jiken no hannin to sareta watashi*. Tokyo: Bungeishunjūsha.

———. 2003. "We Have No Right to Banish Ex-Aum Followers." *Asahi Shimbun*, 6 February.

———. 2008a. *Inochi aru kagiri: Matsumoto sarin jiken wo koete koete*. Tokyo: Daisanbunmeisha.

———. 2008b. "Higaisha to kagaisha ga deau koto no imi." Speech to First Anniversary of the Establishment of Ocean. 26 July. http://www.ocean-ocean.jp/text/2008text/080726.html.

Krog, Antjie. 1999. *Country of My Skull*. New York: Three Rivers Press.

Kupchan, Charles. 2012. *No One's World: The West, the Rising Rest, and the Coming Global Turn*. New York: Oxford University Press.

Kwak, Jun-Hyeok, and Melissa Nobles, eds. 2013. *Inherited Responsibility and Historical Reconciliation in East Asia*. New York: Routledge.

Kyodo News. 2006. "AUM-Related Victims, Others React to Asahara's Death Sentence." 15 September.

Labanyi, Jo. 2000. "History and Hauntology; or, What Does One Do with the Ghosts of the Past? Reflections on Spanish Film and Fiction of the Post-Franco Period." In *Disremembering the Dictatorship: The Politics of Memory in the Spanish Transition to Democracy*, edited by Juan Ramon Resina, 65–82. Amsterdam: Rodopi.

Ladson-Billings, Gladys. 2007. "Pushing Past the Achievement Gap: An Essay on the Language of Deficit." *Journal of Negro Education* 76, no. 3: 316–23.

Landes, David S. 1998. *The Wealth and Poverty of Nations: Why Some Are So Rich and Some So Poor*. New York: W. W. Norton.

Lange, Matthew, James Mahoney, and Matthias vom Hau. 2006. "Colonialism and Development: A Comparative Analysis of Spanish and British Colonies." *American Journal of Sociology* 111, no. 5: 1412–62.

Laplante, Lisa J., and Kimberly S. Theidon. 2007. "Truth with Consequences: Justice and Reparations in Post-Truth Commission Peru." *Human Rights Quarterly* 29, no. 1: 228–50.

Larsen, Neil. 2000. "Imperialism, Colonialism, Postcolonialism." In *A Companion to Postcolonial Studies*, edited by Henry Schwarz and Sangeeta Ray, 23–52. Oxford: Blackwell.

Lemkin, Raphael. 1944. *Axis Rule in Occupied Europe*. Washington, D.C.: Carnegie Endowment for International Peace.

Levy, Daniel, and Natan Sznaider. 2006. *Holocaust Memory in the Global Age*. Philadelphia: Temple University Press.

———. 2010. *Memory and Human Rights*. University Park: Pennsylvania State University Press.

Lind, Jennifer M. 2008. *Sorry States: Apologies in International Politics*. Ithaca, N.Y.: Cornell University Press.

Link, Perry. 2009. "China's Charter 2008." Translated by Perry Link. *New York Review of Books*, 15 January. http://www.nybooks.com/articles/archives/2009/jan/15/chinas-charter-08/.

Logar, Tea. 2010. "Exploitation as Wrongful Use: Beyond Taking Advantage of Vulnerabilities." *Acta Analytica* 25: 329–46.

Lotman, Yuri M. 1990. *Universe of the Mind: A Semiotic Theory of Culture*. Translated by Ann Shukman. Bloomington: Indiana University Press.

———. 2005. "On the Semiosphere." Translated by Wilma Clark. *Signs Systems Studies* 33, no. 1: 205–29.

———. 2009. *Culture and Explosion*. Translated by Wilma Clark. Berlin: Mouton de Gruyter.

Lovrenović, Ivan. 2009. "Kojim smjerom, Hrvati?" *BH Dani*, 6 February.

Lyons, David. 1977. "The New Indian Claims and Original Rights to Land." *Social Theory and Practice* 4, no. 3: 249–72.

Macintyre, Stuart, and Anna Clark. 2004. *The History Wars*. Melbourne: Melbourne University Press.

Mackie, Vera. 2005. "In Search of Innocence: Feminist Historians Debate the Legacy of Wartime Japan." *Australian Feminist Studies* 20, no. 47: 207–17.

Mahoney, Chris. 2012. "Victor's Justice: What's Wrong with Warlord Charles Taylor's Conviction." *The Atlantic*, 30 April. http://www.theatlantic.com/international/archive/2012/04/victors-justice-whats-wrong-with-warlord-charles-taylors-conviction/256522/.

Malamud-Goti, Jaime E., and Lucas Sebastian Grosman. 2006. "Reparations and Civil Litigation: Compensation for Human Rights Violations in Transitional Democracies." In *The Handbook of Reparations*, edited by Pablo de Greiff, 539–59. New York: Oxford University Press.

Mamdani, Mahmood. 2002. "Amnesty or Impunity? A Preliminary Critique of the Report of the Truth and Reconciliation Commission of South Africa (TRC)." *Diacritics* 32, nos. 3–4: 33–59.

Mann, Michael. 1986. *The Sources of Social Power*. Volume 1, *A History of Power from the Beginning to AD 1760*. Cambridge: Cambridge University Press.

———. 1993. *The Sources of Social Power*. Volume 2, *The Rise of Classes and Nation-States 1760–1914*. Cambridge: Cambridge University Press.

Margalit, Avishai. 2002. *The Ethics of Memory*. Cambridge, Mass.: Harvard University Press.

Marotti, William. 2009. "Japan 1968: The Performance of Violence and the Theater of Protest." *American Historical Review* 114, no. 1: 97–135.

Matsubara, Hiroshi. 2004. "Cult's Reign of Terror Left the Victimized with Unhealing Scars." *Japan Times*, 26 February.

Matsumoto, S. 2010. *Watashi wa naze Asahara Shôkô no musume ni umareteshimatta no ka.* Tokyo: Tokuma Shoten.

Maynard, Kimberly A. 1999. *Healing Communities in Conflict: International Assistance in Complex Emergencies.* New York: Columbia University Press.

McCarthy, Thomas. 2002. "*Vergangenheitsbewältigung* in the USA: On the Politics of the Memory of Slavery." *Political Theory* 30, no. 5: 623–48.

———. 2004. "Coming to Terms with Our Past, Part II." *Political Theory* 32: 750–72.

McGregor, Katharine E. 2012. "Time, Memory and Historical Justice: An Introduction." *Time and Society* 21, no. 1: 5–20.

"Medvedev Says No to False History." 2010. *Russia Today*, 7 April. http://rt.com/politics /medvedev-says-no-to-false-history/.

Meier, Christian. 2010. *Das Gebot zu vergessen und die Unabweisbarkeit des Erinnerns: Vom öffentlichen Umgang mit schlimmer Vergangenheit.* Munich: Siedler.

Meister, Robert. 2010. *After Evil: A Politics of Human Rights.* New York: Columbia University Press.

Mendeloff, David. 2004. "Truth-Seeking, Truth-Telling, and Postconflict Peacebuilding: Curb the Enthusiasm?" *International Studies Review* 6, no. 3: 355–80.

Méndez, Juan E. 1997. "Derecho a la verdad frente a las graves violaciones a los derechos humanos." In *La aplicación de los tratados sobre derechos humanos por los tribunales locales*, edited by Martin Abregú and Christian Courtis, 517–40. Buenos Aires: Del Puerto-CELS.

———. 1997a. "Accountability for Past Abuses." *Human Rights Quarterly* 19, no. 2: 255–82.

———. 2006. "The Human Right to Truth: Lessons Learned from Latin American Experiences with Truth Telling." In *Telling the Truths: Truth Telling and Peace Building in Post-Conflict Societies*, edited by Tristan Anne Borer, 115–50. Notre Dame, Ind.: University of Notre Dame Press.

Meyer, Lukas H. 2005. *Historische Gerechtigkeit.* Berlin: Walter de Gruyter.

Miller, David. 2004. "Holding Nations Responsible." *Ethics* 114, no. 2: 240–68.

———. 2007. *National Responsibility and Global Justice.* Oxford: Oxford University Press.

Miller, Jon, and Rahul Kumar, eds. 2007. *Reparations: Interdisciplinary Inquiries.* Oxford: Oxford University Press.

Mills, Charles. 1997. *The Racial Contract.* Ithaca, N.Y.: Cornell University Press.

Mills, Nicolaus. 2001. "The New Culture of Apology." *Dissent* 48, no. 4: 113–16.

Minow, Martha. 1998. *Between Vengeance and Forgiveness: Facing History after Genocide and Mass Violence.* Boston: Beacon Press.

———. 2000. "The Hope for Healing: What Can Truth Commissions Do?" In *Truth v. Justice: The Morality of Truth Commissions*, edited by Robert I. Rotberg and Dennis Thompson, 235–60. Princeton, N.J.: Princeton University Press.

Miyazawa, Setsuo. 2008. "The Politics of Increasing Punitiveness and the Rising Populism in Japanese Criminal Justice Policy." *Punishment and Society* 10, no. 1: 47–77.

Mori, Tatsuiya, dir. 2001. *A2.* Japan.

Morris-Suzuki, Tessa. 2005. *The Past within Us: Media, Memory, History.* London: Verso.

———. 2009. "The Forgotten Japanese in North Korea: Beyond the Politics of Abduction." *Japan Focus: The Asia-Pacific Journal* 43. http://japanfocus.org/-Tessa-Morris_Suzuki/3241.

Mouawad, Jad. 2009. "Shell to Pay $15.5 Million to Settle Nigerian Case." *New York Times*, 8 June.

Moyn, Samuel. 2010. *The Last Utopia: Human Rights in History.* Cambridge, Mass.: Harvard University Press.

Murakami, Haruki. 2000. *Underground: The Tokyo Gas Attack and the Japanese Psyche.* Translated by Alfred Birnbaum and Philip Gabriel. New York: Harvill Press.

Murder Victims' Families for Human Rights (MVFHR). n.d. *For Victims, against the Death Penalty* (blog). Accessed 22 April 2010. http://www.mvfhr.org/.

Murphy, Jeffrie G. 1988. "Forgiveness and Resentment." In *Forgiveness and Mercy*, edited by Jeffrie G. Murphy and Jean Hampton, 14–34. New York: Cambridge University Press.

Nagel, Thomas. 2005. "The Problem of Global Justice." *Philosophy and Public Affairs* 33, no. 2: 113–47.

Naqvi, Yasmin. 2006. "The Right to the Truth in International Law: Fact or Fiction?" *International Review of the Red Cross* 88, no. 862: 245–73.

Neumann, Klaus. 2000. *Shifting Memories: The Nazi Past in the New Germany.* Ann Arbor: University of Michigan Press.

———. 2011. "Asylum Seekers, Willy Wong, and the Uses of History: From 2010 to 1962, and Back." *Australian Historical Studies* 42, no. 1: 126–39.

Newsinger, John. 2006. *The Blood Never Dried: A People's History of the British Empire.* London: Bookmarks.

Ngugi, Brian. 2013. "Mau Mau's Sh2.6b May Not Wipe Tears." *The People* (Nairobi), 7 June.

Nickel, James. 1975. "Preferential Policies in Hiring and Admissions: A Jurisprudential Approach." *Columbia Law Review* 75, no. 3: 534–58.

Nobles, Melissa. 2008. *The Politics of Official Apologies.* Cambridge: Cambridge University Press.

Nora, Pierre, ed. 1984–92. *Les lieux de mémoire.* 7 vols. Paris: Gallimard.

Novick, Peter. 1999. *The Holocaust in American Life.* Boston: Houghton Mifflin.

Nozick, Robert. 1974. *Anarchy, State, and Utopia.* New York: Basic Books.

Nuhanović, Hasan. 2010. "Tranzicijska pravda, sta je to?" *Bilten Srebrenica* 13, no. 47: 2–4.

Oda, Makoto. 1978. "The Ethics of Peace." In *Authority and the Individual in Japan: Citizen Protest in Historical Perspective*, edited by J. Victor Koschmann, 154–70. Tokyo: University of Tokyo Press.

Office of the High Representative (OHR). 2010. "RS Government Special Session a Distasteful Attempt to Question Genocide." 20 April. http://www.ohr.int/print /?content_id=44835.

Olaniyan, Tejumola. 2000. "Africa: Varied Colonial Legacies." In *A Companion to Postcolonial Studies*, edited by Henry Schwarz and Sangeeta Ray, 269–81. Oxford: Blackwell.

Olick, Jeffrey. 2007. *The Politics of Regret: On Collective Memory and Historical Responsibility*. London: Routledge.

Olick, Jeffrey K., and Brenda Coughlin. 2003. "The Politics of Regret: Analytical Frames." In *Politics and the Past: On Repairing Historical Injustices*, edited by John Torpey, 37–62. Lanham, Md.: Rowman and Littlefield.

Olsen, Tricia D., Leigh A. Payne, and Andrew G. Reiter. 2010. *Transitional Justice in Balance: Comparing Processes, Weighing Efficacy*. Washington, D.C.: United States Institute of Peace Press.

Onishi, Norimitsu. 2007. "Japan Court Rules against Sex Slaves and Laborers." *New York Times*, 28 April.

Orbus. 2008. "Tihic protiv uspomene na bosnjacku zrtvu." 26 December. http:// www.orbus.be/aktua/2008/aktua2458.htm.

Orr, James J. 2001. *The Victim as Hero: Ideologies of Peace and National Identity in Postwar Japan*. Honolulu: University of Hawai'i Press.

Oslobodjenje. 2012. "Glad That Lagumdzija Joined BiH Demolition." 3 September. http://www.oslobodjenje.ba/daily-news/glad-that-lagumdzija-joined-bih-demolition.

Osterhammel, Jürgen. 1997. *Colonialism: A Theoretical Overview*. Translated by Shelley L. Frisch. Princeton, N.J.: Marcus Wiener.

Page, Edward. 2012. "Give It up for Climate Change: A Defence of the Beneficiary Pays Principle." *International Theory* 4, no. 2: 300–330.

Pasternak, Avia. 2011. "The Collective Responsibility of Democratic Publics." *Canadian Journal of Philosophy* 41, no. 1: 99–124.

Paxton, Robert. 2014. "Jews: How Vichy Made It Worse." *New York Review of Books*, 6 March.

Pendleton, Mark. 2009. "Mourning as Global Politics: Embodied Grief and Activism in Post-Aum Tokyo." *Asian Studies Review* 33, no. 3: 333–49.

———. 2011. "Subway to Street: Spaces of Traumatic Memory, Counter-Memory and Recovery in Post-Aum Tokyo." *Japanese Studies* 31, no. 3: 359–71.

———. 2014. "Theme Parks and Station Plaques: Memory, Forgetting and Tourism in Post-Aum Japan." In *Death Tourism: Disaster Sites as Recreational Landscape*, edited by Brigitte Sion, 75–94. London: Seagull Books.

Pogge, Thomas. 2002. *World Poverty and Human Rights*. Cambridge, Mass.: Polity.

Prost, Antoine, and Jay Winter. 2011. *René Cassin et les droits de l'homme: Le projet d'une génération*. Paris: Fayard.

Rabinbach, Anson. 2009. *Begriffe aus dem Kalten Krieg: Totalitarismus, Antifaschismus, Genozid*. Jena: Wallstein Verlag.

Ramulić, Edin. 2011. "Zablude o Rekom-u." *Mirovne novosti*, no. 1 (February): 11–14. http://www.carbkbih.org/images/stories/mvijesti/mirovne_novosti_1_2011.pdf.

Ranzato, Gabriele. 2008. "Riparare l'irreparabile: La memoria della guerra civile nella Spagna democratica." *Spagna contemporanea* 17, no. 33: 3–13.

Rawls, John. 1971. *A Theory of Justice*. Cambridge, Mass.: Harvard University Press.

———. 1999. *The Law of Peoples*. Cambridge, Mass.: Harvard University Press.

Reader, Ian. 2000. *Religious Violence in Contemporary Japan: The Case of Aum Shinrikyō*. Honolulu: University of Hawai'i Press.

Renshaw, Layla. 2011. *Exhuming Loss: Memory, Materiality and Mass Graves of the Spanish Civil War*. Walnut Creek, Calif.: Left Coast Press.

Republic of Srpska Government. 2012. "Prime Minister Dzombic at Solemn Academy upon Veterans Day of First Serbian Uprising." Press release, 5 February. http://www.vladars.net/eng/vlada/prime_minister/media/news/Pages/Prime_Minister_Dzombic_at_Solemn_Academy_upon_Veterans_Day_of_First_Serbian_Uprising.aspx.

Reshetov, Iu A. 1990. "The Temporal Operation of Norms on Criminal Responsibility." In *The Nuremberg Trial and International Law*, edited by G. Ginsburg and V. N. Kudriavtsev, 111–17. Dordrecht: Martinus Nijhoff.

Reuters. 2011. "Bosnian Wartime General Freed by Austrian Court." 29 July. http://www.trust.org/item/?map=bosnian-wartime-general-freed-by-austrian-court.

———. 2012. "EU Says Bosnian Serbs Seek to Undermine Peace Deal." 13 November. http://www.reuters.com/article/2012/11/13/us-bosnia-un-idUSBRE8AC13F20121113.

Ricoeur, Paul. 2004. *Memory, History, Forgetting*. Translated by Kathleen Blamey and David Pellauer. Chicago: University of Chicago Press.

Robinson, Randall. 2000. *The Debt: What America Owes to Blacks*. New York: Penguin Putnam.

Roht-Arriaza, Naomi. 1999. "The Need for Moral Reconstruction in the Wake of Past Human Rights Violations: An Interview with José Zalaquett." In *Human Rights in Political Transitions: Gettysburg to Bosnia*, edited by Carla Hesse and Robert Post, 195–213. New York: Zone Books.

———. 2004. "Reparations in the Aftermath of Repression and Mass Violence." In *My Neighbor, My Enemy: Justice and Community in the Aftermath of Mass Atrocity*, edited by Eric Stover and Harvey M. Weinstein, 121–39. Cambridge: Cambridge University Press.

Rotberg, Robert I. and Dennis Thompson, eds. 2000. *Truth v. Justice: The Morality of Truth Commissions*. Princeton, N.J.: Princeton University Press.

Rothberg, Michael. 2009. *Multidirectional Memory: Remembering the Holocaust in the Age of Decolonization*. Stanford: Stanford University Press.

Rousso, Henry. 1991. *The Vichy Syndrome: History and Memory in France since 1944*. Translated by A. Goldhammer. Cambridge, Mass.: Harvard University Press.

Rubio Marín, Ruth. 2006. *What Happened to the Women? Gender and Reparations for Human Rights Violations*. New York: Social Science Research Council.

Rymhs, Deena. 2006. "Appropriating Guilt: Reconciliation in the Aboriginal Canadian Context." *English Studies in Canada* 32, no. 1: 105–23.

Sakagami, K. 2004. "'Higaisha' no koe o kiku to iu koto: Shikei ni kansuru 'katari' o megutte." *Gendai shisō* 32, no. 3: 72–83.

Sand, Jordan. 1999. "Historians and Public Memory in Japan: The 'Comfort Women' Controversy: Introduction." *History and Memory* 11, no. 2: 117–26.

Sarkin, Jeremy. 2009. *Colonial Genocide and Reparations Claims in the 21st Century: The Socio-Legal Context of Claims under International Law by the Herero against Germany for Genocide in Namibia, 1904–1908.* Westport, Conn.: Praeger.

Sarlo, Beatriz. 2005. *Tiempo pasado: Cultura de la memoria y giro subjetivo.* Buenos Aires: Siglo Veintiuno Editores.

Satz, Debra. 2007. "Countering the Wrongs of the Past: The Role of Compensation." In *Reparations: Interdisciplinary Inquiries,* edited by Jon Miller and Rahul Kumar, 176–92. Oxford: Oxford University Press.

Savelsberg, James J., and Ryan D. King. 2007. "Law and Collective Memory." *Annual Review of Law and Social Science* 3: 189–211.

Sayare, Scott. 2012. "France Reflects on Its Role in Wartime Fate of Jews." *New York Times,* 28 July.

Sayare, Scott, and Sebnem Arsu. 2012. "Genocide Bill Angers Turks as It Passes in France." *New York Times,* 23 January.

Scanlon, T. M. 1998. *What We Owe to Each Other.* Cambridge, Mass.: Harvard University Press.

Schaap, Andrew. 2004. "Political Reconciliation through a Struggle for Recognition?" *Social Legal Studies* 13, no. 4: 523–40.

Seaton, Philip. 2007. *Japan's Contested War Memories: The "Memory Rifts" in Historical Consciousness of World War II.* London: Routledge.

Sen, Amartya. 2009. *The Idea of Justice.* Cambridge, Mass.: Harvard University Press.

Sepinwall, Amy J. 2006. "Responsibility for Historical Injustices: Reconceiving the Case for Reparations." *Journal of Law and Politics* 22, no. 3: 183–229.

Shaw, Rosalind. 2005. "Rethinking Truth and Reconciliation Commissions: Lessons from Sierra Leone." United States Institute of Peace Special Report 130. http://www.usip.org/publications/rethinking-truth-and-reconciliation-commissions-lessons-sierra-leone.

Shaw, Martin. 2007. "The International Court of Justice: Serbia, Bosnia, and Genocide." Open Democracy, February 28. http://www.opendemocracy.net/globaliza tion-institutions_government/icj_bosnia_serbia_4392.jsp.

Sher, George. 1981. "Ancient Wrongs and Modern Rights." *Philosophy and Public Affairs* 10, no. 1: 3–17.

———. 2005. "Transgenerational Compensation." *Philosophy and Public Affairs* 33, no. 2: 181–200.

Shigematsu, Setsu. 2012. *Scream from the Shadows: The Women's Liberation Movement in Japan.* Minneapolis: University of Minnesota Press.

Shriver, Donald W. 2005. *Honest Patriots: Loving a Country Enough to Remember Its Misdeeds*. New York: Oxford University Press.

Sikkink, Kathryn. 2011. *The Justice Cascade: How Human Rights Prosecutions Are Changing World Politics*. New York: W. W. Norton.

Silas, Susan. 2012. "Helmbrechts Walk." http://www.helmbrechtswalk.com/index .html.

Silva, Emilio. 2005. *Las fosas de Franco: Crónica de un desagravio*. Madrid: Temas de Hoy.

———. 2008. "Entrevista con Emilio Silva." *Journal of Spanish Cultural Studies* 9, no. 2: 143–55.

Silva, Emilio, Pancho Salvador, Asunción Esteban, and Javier Castán, eds. 2004. *La memoria de los olvidados: Un debate sobre el silencio de la repression franquista*. Valladolid: Ambito.

Simpson, Graeme, Edin Hodžić, and Louis Bickford. 2011. "'Looking Back, Looking Forward': Promoting Dialogue through Truth-Seeking in Bosnia and Herzegovina." United Nations Development Program. http://www.undp.ba/upload /publications/Looking%20back,%20looking%20forward.pdf.

Snyder, Jack, and Leslie Vinjamuri. 2003. "Trials and Errors: Principle and Pragmatism in Strategies of International Justice." *International Security* 28, no. 3: 5–44.

Snyder, Timothy. 2003. *The Reconstruction of Nations: Poland, Ukraine, Lithuania, Belarus, 1569–1999*. New Haven, Conn.: Yale University Press.

Sokoloff, Kenneth L., and Stanley L. Engerman. 2000. "History Lessons: Institutions, Factor Endowments, and Paths of Development in the New World." *Journal of Economic Perspectives* 14, no. 3: 217–32.

Soyinka, Wole. 2000. "Memory, Truth and Healing." In *The Politics of Memory: Truth, Healing, and Social Justice*, edited by Ifi Amadiume, 21–37. London: Zed Books.

Spinner-Halev, Jeff. 2012. *Enduring Injustice*. Cambridge: Cambridge University Press.

Stan, Lavinia, and Nadya Nedelsky, eds. 2013. *Encyclopedia of Transitional Justice*. 3 vols. Cambridge: Cambridge University Press.

Stern, Steve J. 2004. *Remembering Pinochet's Chile: On the Eve of London, 1998*. Durham, N.C.: Duke University Press.

———. 2006. *Battling for Hearts and Minds: Memory Struggles in Pinochet's Chile, 1973–1988*. Durham, N.C.: Duke University Press.

———. 2010. *Reckoning with Pinochet: The Memory Question in Democratic Chile, 1989–2006*. Durham, N.C.: Duke University Press.

Sugaya, Toshikazu, and Kōno Yoshiyuki. 2009. *Ashikaga jiken, Matsumoto sarin jiken*. Tokyo: TO Books.

Takahashi, H. 1996. *Oumu kara no kikan*. Tokyo: Sōshisha.

Takahashi, S. 2008. *Koko ni iru koto: Chikatetsu sarin jiken no izoku toshite*. Tokyo: Iwanami shoten.

Takahashi, S., and M. Kawahara. 2005. *"Hanzai higaisha" ga hōdō o kaeru*. Tokyo: Iwanami Shoten.

Tan, Kok-Chor. 2007. "Colonialism, Reparations, and Global Justice." In *Reparations: Interdisciplinary Inquiries*, edited by Jon Miller and Rahul Kumar, 280–306. Oxford: Oxford University Press.

Taylor, Charles. 1994. *Multiculturalism and the Politics of Recognition*. Princeton, N.J.: Princeton University Press.

Teitel, Ruti G. 2000. *Transitional Justice*. New York: Oxford University Press.

———. 2011. *Humanity's Law*. Oxford: Oxford University Press.

Thompson, Janna. 2002. *Taking Responsibility for the Past: Reparation and Historical Justice*. Oxford: Polity Press.

———. 2009. "Apology, Historical Obligations and the Ethics of Memory." *Memory Studies* 2, no. 2: 195–210.

———. 2012. "Is Political Apology a Sorry Affair?" *Social and Legal Studies* 21, no. 2: 1–11.

Thomson, Judith Jarvis. 1986. *Rights, Restitution and Risk: Essays in Moral Theory*. Cambridge, Mass.: Harvard University Press.

Tocqueville, Alexis de. 2000. *Democracy in America*. Edited and translated by Harvey D. Mansfield and Delba Winthrop. Chicago: University of Chicago Press.

Tolbert, David. 2013. "Can International Justice Foster Reconciliation?" Al Jazeera, 10 April. http://www.aljazeera.com/indepth/opinion/2013/04/20134107435444190.html.

Torpey, John. 2006. *Making Whole What Has Been Smashed: On Reparations Politics*. Cambridge, Mass.: Harvard University Press.

———. 2009. "An Avalanche of History: The Collapse of the Future and the Rise of Reparations Politics." In *Historical Justice in International Perspective: How Societies Are Trying to Right the Wrongs of the Past*, edited by Manfred Berg and Bernd Schaefer, 21–38. Washington, D.C.: German Historical Institute.

Truth and Reconciliation Commission of Canada. 2012. Interim Report. Winnipeg, Manitoba. http://www.myrobust.com/websites/trcinstitution/File/Interim%20report%20English%20electronic.pdf.

Tsosie, Rebecca. 2007. "Acknowledging the Past to Heal the Future: The Role of Reparations for Native Nations." In *Reparations: Interdisciplinary Inquiries*, edited by Jon Miller and Rahul Kumar, 43–68. Oxford: Oxford University Press.

Tucker, Aviezer. 2006. "Rough Justice: Rectification in Post-authoritarian and Post-totalitarian Regimes." In *Retribution and Reparation in the Transition to Democracy*, edited by Jon Elster, 276–98. New York: Cambridge University Press.

Turner, Christian. 2014. "Launch of the Mau Mau Memorial in Kenya." Speech, 22 May. https://www.gov.uk/government/speeches/launch-of-the-mau-mau-memorial-in-kenya.

Tyre, Stephen. 2008. "France and Its Colonies: Historiography." In *A Historical Companion to Postcolonial Literatures: Continental Europe and Its Empires*, edited by Prem Poddar, Rajeev Shridhar Patke, and Lars Jensen, 152–57. Edinburgh: Edinburgh University Press.

Ugrešić, Dubravka. 1998. *The Culture of Lies: Antipolitical Essays.* University Park: Pennsylvania State University Press.

United Nations. 1997. "Question of the Impunity of Perpetrators of Human Rights Violations (Civil and Political), Revised Final Report Prepared by Mr. Joinet Pursuant to Sub-Commission Decision 1996/119." UN Doc. E/CN.4/Sub.2/1997/20/Rev. 1, 2 October.

———. 2001. "Declaration of the World Conference against Racism, Racial Discrimination, Xenophobia and Related Intolerance." http://www.un.org/WCAR/durban.pdf.

———. 2005. "Impunity: Report of the Independent Expert to Update the Set of Principles to Combat Impunity, Diane Orentlicher, Addendum, Updated Set of Principles for the Protection and Promotion of Human Rights through Action to Combat Impunity." UN Doc. E/CN.4/2005/102/Add. 1, 8 February.

———. 2006a. "Study on the Right to the Truth: Report of the Office of the United Nations High Commissioner for Human Rights." UN Doc. E/CN.4/2006/91, 8 February.

———. 2006b. "Basic Principles and Guidelines on the Right to a Remedy and Reparation for Victims of Gross Violations of International Human Rights Law and Serious Violations of International Humanitarian Law." UN Doc. A/RES/60/147, 21 March.

———. 2007. "Right to the Truth: Report of the Office of the Higher Commissioner for Human Rights." UN Doc. A/HRC/5/7, 7 June 2007.

———. 2009. "Right to the Truth: Report of the Office of the High Commissioner for Human Rights." UN Doc. A/HRC/12/19, 21 August 2009.

———. 2013. "Report of the Special Rapporteur on the Promotion of Truth, Justice, Reparation and Guarantees of Non-recurrence." UN Doc. A/HRC/24/42, 28 August.

van Boven, Theo. 2005. "Basic Principles and Guidelines on the Right to a Remedy and Reparation for Victims of Gross Violations of International Human Rights Law and Serious Violations of International Humanitarian Law." United Nations Audiovisual Library of International Law. 16 December. http://legal.un.org/avl/ha/ga_60-147/ga_60-147.html.

Verdeja, Ernesto. 2009. *Unchopping a Tree: Reconciliation in the Aftermath of Political Violence.* Philadelphia: Temple University Press.

Verdery, Katherine. 1999. *The Political Lives of Dead Bodies: Reburial and Postsocialist Change.* New York: Columbia University Press.

Vernon, Richard. 2003. "Against Restitution." *Political Studies* 51, no.3: 542–57.

———. 2012. *Historical Redress: Must We Pay for the Past?* London: Continuum.

Vesti Online. 2011. "U Srebrenici genocid i nad 3.265 Srba." 3 September. www.vesti-online.com/Dijaspora/drzava/Australija/Vesti/161763/U-Srebrenici-genocid-i-nad-3256-Srba.

———. 2012. "Dodik: BiH je neodrziva tvorevina." 27 April. www.vesti-online.com/Vesti/Ex-YU/220886/Dodik-BiH-je-neodrziva-tvorevina.

Vincent, Mary. 2010. "Breaking the Silence? Memory and Oblivion since the Spanish Civil War." In *Shadows of War: A Social History of Silence in the Twentieth Century*, edited by Efrat Ben-Ze'ev, Ruth Ginio, and Jay Winter, 47–67. Cambridge: Cambridge University Press.

Violi, Patrizia. 2012. "Trauma Site Museums and Politics of Memory: Tuol Sleng, Villa Grimaldi and the Bologna Ustica Museum." *Theory, Culture and Society* 29, no. 1: 36–75.

Vukušić, Iva. 2008. "Aldin Arnautović: 'Bh. društvu treba suočavanje s istinom'." MediaCentar_Online, 8 March. http://www.media.ba/bs/ratni-zlocini/aldin-arnautovic-bh-drustvu-treba-suocavanje-s-istinom.

Waldron, Jeremy. 1992. "Superseding Historic Injustice." *Ethics* 103, no. 1: 4–28.

Walker, Margaret Urban. 2006a. "The Cycle of Violence." *Journal of Human Rights* 5, no. 1: 81–105.

———. 2006b. *Moral Repair: Reconstructing Moral Relations after Wrongdoing*. New York: Cambridge University Press.

———. 2006c. "Restorative Justice and Reparations." *Journal of Social Philosophy* 37, no. 3: 377–95.

———. 2007. *Moral Understandings: A Feminist Study in Ethics*. 2nd ed. New York: Oxford University Press.

———. 2010. "Truth Telling as Reparations." *Metaphilosophy* 41, no. 4: 525–45.

———. 2013. "The Expressive Burden of Reparations: Putting Meaning into Money, Words, and Things." In *Justice, Responsibility and Reconciliation in the Wake of Conflict*, edited by Alice McLachlan and Allen Speight, 205–25. Dordrecht: Springer.

———. 2014. "Moral Vulnerability and the Task of Reparations." In *Vulnerability: New Essays in Ethics and Feminist Philosophy*, edited by Catriona Mackenzie, Susan Dodds, and Wendy Rogers, 110–33. New York: Oxford University Press.

———. 2015. "Troubles with Truth Commissions: Putting the Moral Aims of Truth Commissions to the Fore." In *The Performance of Memory as Transitional Justice*, edited by S. Elizabeth Bird and Fraser Ottanelli, 7–21. Antwerp: Intersentia.

Weiss, Peter. 2012. "Should Corporations Have More Leeway to Kill Than People Do?" *New York Times*, 24 February.

Wenar, Leif. 2006. "Reparations for the Future." *Journal of Social Philosophy* 37, no. 3: 396–405.

Wertheimer, A. 1996. *Exploitation*. Princeton, N.J.: Princeton University Press.

Wiebelhaus-Brahm, Eric. 2010. *Truth Commissions and Transitional Societies*. New York: Routledge.

Wieviorka, Annette. 2006. *The Era of the Witness*. Translated by Jared Stark. Ithaca, N.Y.: Cornell University Press.

Wilkins, Burleigh. 2002. "Joint Commitments." *Journal of Ethics* 6, no. 2: 145–55.

Wilson, Richard Ashby. 2011. *Writing History in International Criminal Trials*. Cambridge: Cambridge University Press.

Winter, Stephen. 2006. "Uncertain Justice: History and Reparations." *Journal of Social Philosophy* 37, no. 2: 377–95.

Woocher, Lawrence. 2009. "Preventing Violent Conflict: Assessing Progress, Meeting Challenges." Special Report no. 231. United States Institute for Peace, September. http://www.usip.org/files/resources/preventing_violent_conflict.pdf.

Workman, Tim. 2010. "The Government of the Republic of Serbia v. Ejup Ganic." Judgment, City of Westminster Magistrates' Court, 27 July.

Wyman, Katrina Miriam. 2008. "Is There a Moral Justification for Redressing Historical Injustices?" *Vanderbilt Law Review* 61, no. 1: 127–96.

Young, James E. 1993. *The Texture of Memory: Holocaust Memorials and Meaning.* New Haven, Conn.: Yale University Press.

Young, Robert. 2001. *Postcolonialism: An Historical Introduction.* Blackwell: Oxford.

Ypi, Lea. 2013. "What's Wrong with Colonialism." *Philosophy and Public Affairs* 41, no. 2: 158–91.

Ypi, Lea, Robert E. Goodin, and Christian Barry. 2009. "Associative Duties, Global Justice, and the Colonies." *Philosophy and Public Affairs* 37, no. 2: 103–35.

Contributors

Onur Bakiner is an assistant professor of political science at Seattle University. His research and teaching interests include transitional justice, human rights, and judicial politics, particularly in Latin America and the Middle East. Currently he is working on a research project examining judicial actors during prolonged internal conflict in Colombia and Turkey. His past research investigates the role truth commissions play in contemporary societies. For this research he conducted interviews with political decision-makers, NGO activists, intellectuals, and victims of political violence and their relatives in Chile and Peru. His articles have been published in the *International Journal of Transitional Justice*, *Nationalities Papers*, and *Memory Studies*.

Elazar Barkan is a professor of international and public affairs and the director of the Human Rights Concentration at Columbia's School of International and Public Affairs and the Institute for the Study of Human Rights at Columbia University. His research interests focus on human rights and on the role of history in contemporary society and politics and the response to gross historical crimes and injustices. His books include *Choreographies of Shared Sacred Sites: Religion, Politics, and Conflict Resolution* (2014, edited with Karen Barkey); *No Return, No Refuge: Rites and Rights in Minority Repatriation* (2011, with Howard Adelman); *The Guilt of Nations: Restitution and Negotiating Historical Injustices* (2000); *Claiming the Stones/Naming the Bones: Cultural Property and the Negotiation of National and Ethnic Identity* (2003, edited with Ronald Bush); and *Taking Wrongs Seriously: Apologies and Reconciliation* (2006, edited with Alexander Karn).

Belma Bećirbašić is a researcher, journalist, writer, and activist from Sarajevo, Bosnia and Herzegovina. Spanning over ten years, her investigative work has received awards, including the Amnesty International Human Rights Journalism Award (2003) for a report on children born to survivors of sexual violence during the war in Bosnia. She was a recipient of a Fulbright Visiting Scholarship at Columbia University (2011/12). Her work, merging in-depth research with reporting practices and feminist critical analysis, centers around the postwar exploitation of traumatic legacy, production of conflicting ethnic memories, and victimhood narratives—some of which are discussed in her book *Tijelo, zenskost i moc: Upisivanja patrijarhalnog diskursa u tijelo* (Body, femininity and power: Inscribing patriarchal discourse in post-conflict) (2011). At present, she works with the Kvinna till Kvinna Foundation, which supports women's rights and participation in conflict zones.

Jeffrey Blustein is the Arthur Zitrin Professor of Bioethics and a professor of philosophy at City College of the City University of New York. His primary research interests are bioethics and the ethics of memory. He has published two books on the latter subject, *The Moral Demands of Memory* (2008), selected as a Choice Outstanding Academic Title for 2008, and *Forgiveness and Remembrance: Remembering Wrongdoing in Personal and Public Life* (2014).

Daniel Butt is an associate professor of political theory in the Department of Politics and International Relations at the University of Oxford, and Fellow and Tutor in Political Theory at Balliol College, Oxford. He is a course director for Oxford's MPhil in political theory, and a member of the Centre for the Study of Social Justice. He has published widely on questions of international justice and historic wrongdoing, and is the author of *Rectifying International Injustice: Principles of Compensation and Restitution Between Nations* (2009).

Andreas Huyssen is the Villard Professor of German and Comparative Literature at Columbia University and one of the founding editors of *New German Critique*. He has published on German literature from the eighteenth to the twentieth centuries, international modernism in literature and the visual arts, postmodernism and mass culture, urban imaginaries, and memory politics in transnational contexts. His works have been translated into many languages worldwide. His most recent book is *Miniature Metropolis: Literature in an Age of Photography and Film* (2015).

Klaus Neumann is a trained historian who has published books and articles on subjects as diverse as history-making in Papua New Guinea, World War II civilian internment, Australian immigration policy, and the Nazi past in postwar Germany. His most recent book is *Across the Seas: Australia's Response to Refugees: A History* (2015). His current work is concerned with historical justice, contemporary and historical refugee and asylum seeker regimes, and the politics of compassion. He works as a research professor at the Swinburne Institute for Social Research, Swinburne University of Technology, in Melbourne.

Mark Pendleton is a cultural and social historian and a lecturer in Japanese studies in the School of East Asian Studies at the University of Sheffield. His research is focused on the relationship between past, present, and future in East Asia and beyond. He has published articles in a range of academic journals including the EastAsiaNet

Award-winning "Subway to Street: Spaces of Traumatic Memory, Counter-memory and Recovery in post-Aum Tokyo" (*Japanese Studies*, 2011). His recent publications also include chapters in the edited collections *Routledge Handbook of Sexuality Studies in East Asia* and *Death Tourism: Disaster Sites as Recreational Landscape* (both 2014).

Janna Thompson is a philosopher who has published books and articles on historical justice, global justice, and intergenerational justice, including *Taking Responsibility for the Past: Reparation and Historical Injustice* (2002) and *Intergenerational Justice: Rights and Responsibilities in an Intergenerational Polity* (2009). Her current research is on collective responsibility. She is a professorial fellow in the Department of Politics and Philosophy at La Trobe University in Melbourne, Australia.

John Torpey is a professor of sociology and history at the Graduate Center, City University of New York, and director of its Ralph Bunche Institute for International Studies. He is the author or editor of eight books, including *Old Europe, New Europe, Core Europe: Transatlantic Relations after the Iraq War* (2005, edited with Daniel Levy and Max Pensky; Japanese and Chinese translations); *Making Whole What Has Been Smashed: On Reparations Politics* (2006; Japanese translation forthcoming); *The Post-Secular in Question* (2012, coedited with Philip S. Gorski, David Kyuman Kim, and Jonathan van Antwerpen); and, with Christian Joppke, *Legal Integration of Islam: A Transatlantic Comparison* (2013). His current work addresses the origins of world religions, changes in the nature of warfare in the contemporary world, and the nature of progress in human society since 1750.

Patrizia Violi is a professor of semiotics at the University of Bologna, Department of Communication, and coordinator of the PhD program in semiotics. She is the director of TRAME, Interdisciplinary Centre for the Study of Memory and Cultural Traumas (www.trame.unibo.it), at the University of Bologna. Her main areas of research include text analysis, language and gender, and semantic theory, on which theme she has published numerous articles and books, among others, *Meaning and Experience* (2001). She is currently working on cultural semiotics and traumatic memory, and in particular on memorials and memory museums. Among her most recent publications are *Paesaggi della memoria: Il trauma, lo spazio, la storia* (2014) and a chapter in *Gender and Conflict* (2014, edited by G. Frerks, A. Ypeij, and R. König).

Margaret Urban Walker is the Donald J. Schuenke Chair in Philosophy at Marquette University. She researches across disciplinary boundaries to ground philosophical approaches to issues of justice in the wake of violence and oppression and to the ethics and moral psychology of responses to grave wrongs. She is working on a book on reparations that features the essential role of hope.

Index

Critical Human Rights